What Your Colleagues Are Saying . . .

This thought-provoking and very practical book will be welcomed by all educators who are striving to provide a more equitable curriculum for students. As Gottlieb and Castro suggest, this endeavor requires classroom teachers to think critically about the language they use with students, and develop the knowledge and skills to provide students with explicit and well-planned support for the development of academic language. *Language Power* will assist educators in making these endeavors a reality.

—Pauline Gibbons
Author of *Scaffolding Language, Scaffolding Learning,* Second Edition
and Associate Professor, University of New South Wales
Sydney, Australia

As educators strive for equitable, collaborative classrooms inclusive of all students in an uncertain educational and political landscape, Gottlieb and Castro focus on students who may find themselves marginalized or otherwise left out due to their developing grasp of academic language. This timely book provides educators with accessible, research-based tools for students to learn the power of language. . . . I'm definitely integrating Gottlieb and Castro's framework into my future professional development!

—Diane Staehr Fenner, President
SupportEd, Washington, DC

Language Power is helpful not only for teachers who want to adapt materials for English language learners, but also for all teachers, no matter what content area, who want to move their students beyond the comprehension level. It breaks down the notion of academic language to four key uses—discuss, argue, recount, and explain—identifies the language associated with those uses, and offers practical examples for classroom instruction. . . . We're very proud at BrainPOP® to provide content for the examples used in this valuable resource for teachers.

—Bev Fine, Editorial and Outreach Director
BrainPOP® ESL, New York, NY

(Continued)

(Continued)

For the first time, Drs. Gottlieb and Castro move beyond a theoretical description of the critical role of academic language to describe key uses, tools, and strategies that facilitate the instruction and acquisition of academic language across content areas and relevant assessment resources to capture students' performance level. This is a powerful resource.

—David Nieto, Executive Director
BUENO Center for Multicultural Education
University of Colorado Boulder, School of Education
Boulder, CO

Language Power is a compelling resource for educators in 21st century schools. Through skillful use of the inquiry cycle and practical tools for application, Gottlieb and Castro empower teachers to support learners in multilingual and multisemiotic classrooms. Understanding key uses of academic language helps teachers unlock opportunities for their multilingual students. With a commitment to social justice and integration of technology, *Language Power* challenges teachers with a forward-thinking perspective on how we can serve multilingual students who must navigate today's globally interconnected learning environments.

—Jon Nordmeyer, International Programs Director
WIDA at University of Wisconsin-Madison, Madison, WI

Language Power

Key Uses for
Accessing Content

Margo Gottlieb

Mariana Castro

Foreword by Pauline Gibbons

CORWIN
A SAGE Publishing Company

FOR INFORMATION:

Corwin

A SAGE Company

2455 Teller Road

Thousand Oaks, California 91320

(800) 233-9936

www.corwin.com

SAGE Publications Ltd.

1 Oliver's Yard

55 City Road

London EC1Y 1SP

United Kingdom

SAGE Publications India Pvt. Ltd.

B 1/I 1 Mohan Cooperative Industrial Area

Mathura Road, New Delhi 110 044

India

SAGE Publications Asia-Pacific Pte. Ltd.

3 Church Street

#10-04 Samsung Hub

Singapore 049483

Program Director: Dan Alpert

Senior Associate Editor: Kimberly Greenberg

Editorial Assistant: Katie Crilley

Production Editor: Melanie Birdsall

Copy Editor: Jared Leighton

Typesetter: C&M Digitals (P) Ltd.

Proofreader: Caryne Brown

Indexer: Molly Hall

Cover Designer: Gail Buschman

Marketing Manager: Maura Sullivan

Printed in the United States of America

ISBN 978-1-5063-7551-9

This book is printed on acid-free paper.

17 18 19 20 21 10 9 8 7 6 5 4 3 2 1

Contents

Note From the Publisher: The authors have provided video and web content throughout the book that is available to you through QR (quick response) codes. To read a QR code, you must have a smartphone or tablet with a camera. We recommend that you download a QR code reader app that is made specifically for your phone or tablet brand.

List of Resources

Foreword

Margo Gottlieb and Mariana Castro have chosen some challenging and inspirational words to begin the final chapter of this thoughtful, carefully designed, and practical book. Drawing the reader's attention to some of the major challenges for teachers, they include these words from the work of Barnett Berry (2016):

> It is time for America's young people—all of them, not just a privileged few—to take part in deeper learning. And it is time for policymakers and practitioners to create the system of teacher leadership for them to do so.

Few educators would disagree with these words. Ongoing research has shown that students from *all* backgrounds are more engaged in learning, and achieve at higher levels, when they have opportunities to participate in a cognitively challenging curriculum and the kind of "deeper learning" to which Berry refers.

School success therefore also depends largely on a student's ability to control disciplinary and subject-specific language, and to participate in the higher-level thinking that this language makes possible.

The development of academic language is of particular relevance to students who are English language learners (ELLs). While most ELLs quickly develop the "everyday" language used in informal contexts, such as the language used between peers in the playground, this kind of informal language is very different from the academic language needed for learning across the curriculum in school. Without specific and targeted language support in *all* subjects, ELLs may not develop the tools for subject learning, and so are unable to participate fully in school. This is also true for many other students, (including those who speak nonstandard varieties of English, or those who, in the words of Berry, are not the "privileged few"). Indeed, for almost all students, subject-specific discourses represent less familiar ways of using language.

Ultimately, therefore, if learners are not to be disadvantaged in their long-term learning, and are to have the time and opportunity to learn the subject-specific discourses of school, all subject learning needs to be integrated with the teaching of academic language, along with the recognition by all teachers that they are teachers of language, not simply of subject "content." Without this focus on language, schools cannot provide education that leads to equitable outcomes.

The challenge for teachers and school leaders, therefore, is how to plan a curriculum that integrates subject learning with related academic language, and how to provide the appropriate language support that will enable all students to develop the essential academic and subject-based language for learning across the curriculum. Margo Gottlieb and Mariana Castro have taken up that challenge in this book. *Language Power* focuses on the key uses of academic language, demonstrates how these uses can be integrated, assessed, and implemented, and suggests ways to involve and collaborate with the broader school community. The book is aimed primarily at practitioners and educators in the field and provides not only theoretical frameworks for teachers, teacher leaders, and other professionals to think about their own professional work, but also a wealth of practical ideas, teacher tools, and language-centered resources for use in the classroom. These resources are based on the assumption that all language development involves a continuing process of meaning making; that academic language is best learned in the context of actually using it for authentic purposes across the curriculum; and that teachers themselves need time and support for their own professional learning. These are important messages not only for classroom-based teachers but also for teacher leaders and administrators.

Language Power urges teachers and other professional educators to "reenvision" teaching and, through a better understanding of the role that academic language plays in learning and school assessment, to see it as more than the teaching of subject content. Using interactive activities to stimulate in-depth conversations between teachers, the authors suggest a process for reflecting on teaching in new ways. Central to this reflection is a conceptual tool they refer to as *DARE (discuss, argue, recount, and explain)*. DARE is used in many contexts throughout the book, and through these reflections teachers are able to not only increase their own understanding of the nature of academic language but also understand how this tool can be used with their students in all areas of the curriculum.

This thought-provoking and very practical book will be welcomed by all educators who are striving to provide a more equitable curriculum for students. As the book suggests, this endeavor requires classroom teachers to think critically about the language they use with students, and develop the knowledge and skills to provide students with explicit and well-planned support for the development of academic language. *Language Power* will assist educators in making these endeavors a reality.

—Pauline Gibbons
Author of *Scaffolding Language, Scaffolding Learning*, Second Edition
and Associate Professor, University of New South Wales, Sydney, Australia

REFERENCE

Berry, B. (2016). *Teacher leadership and deeper learning for all students.* Center for Teaching Quality. Retrieved from http://www.teachingquality.org/deeperlearning.

About This Book

Language Power: Key Uses for Accessing Content is a book for teachers and school leaders seeking to provide students equitable access to content and language practices throughout the school day. Most important, in preparing our students for college, career, community, and acquisiton of 21st century classroom skills, we emphasize collaboration, multimodalities, critical thinking, and problem solving. A common thread among these skills is the role that language plays in their development and execution. As a matter of fact, language plays an essential role in *all* learning, and for this reason, we focus the book on language—more specifically, academic language use.

THE PURPOSES FOR THE BOOK

Academic language has caught the attention of the educational community because of its positive link to academic success (Friedberg, Mitchell, & Brooke, 2016). There is a substantial body of literature on academic language, from theoretical frameworks (Bailey & Butler, 2007; Cummins, 1981; Gottlieb, 2003; Scarcella, 2003; Zacarian, 2012), to research reviews (Anstrom et al., 2010; de Oliveira, 2013; Snow & Uccelli, 2009) to instructional approaches (Chamot & O'Malley, 1994; Echevarria, Vogt, & Short, 2017). Recently, academic language has been recognized in standards, for content, including college and career readiness standards (de Oliveira, 2016), language development standards (WIDA, 2012), and both sets of standards (Gottlieb & Ernst-Slavit, 2014a). Additionally, we have witnessed the grounding of academic language curriculum design as enacted in standards-referenced classrooms (Gottlieb & Ernst-Slavit, 2013, 2014b; Zwiers, 2014).

Given the growing body of literature on academic language, we wished to create an easy-to-read guide that consolidates the complexities of language learning into practical ideas from a range of perspectives. With that backdrop in mind, we wrote this book around three main purposes:

1. To highlight the critical role of academic language use in a variety of contexts tied to teaching and learning

2. To present a conceptual tool—DARE—to facilitate students' and teachers' academic language use within and across the disciplines or content areas

3. To offer educators language-centered resources to add to their instructional and assessment repertoires

It is our intent to ensure that every teacher has an understanding of the importance of academic language use in their craft, no matter who their students are and what their discipline is. We feel confident that this goal can be accomplished, as we have distilled the literature, combed instructional materials, analyzed standards, and had deep conversations with our colleagues over multiple years. These experiences have been integral to the creation of teacher tools related to academic language use, including Can Do Descriptors, Key Uses Edition, and los descriptores Podemos (see multiple entries of WIDA at the end of this section).

ORGANIZATION OF THE BOOK

The overall organizational scheme for the book is illustrated in the figure "Reenvisioning Teaching and Learning Through Key Uses of Academic Language" at the close of this section. It reflects the centrality of key uses of academic language (in the middle). Its outreach, in the form of a semantic web, shows the varying components of school life that are influenced by academic language use; in each chapter, we elaborate their multiple perspectives.

Additionally, each chapter is arranged around phases of an inquiry cycle: *ask, explore, apply, reflect,* and *take action.* There is a central question that is posed in the *ask* section, examined in *explore,* and then *applied* to four different perspectives. In *reflect,* we summarize the main message of the chapter and then invite you, the reader, to *take action.* We share with you the central questions and each chapter synopsis so that you have a sense of what to expect.

Chapter 1: What is the nature of key uses of academic language? What is the language associated with each key use? In this introductory chapter, we investigate the construct of academic language and provide a rationale for *discuss, argue, recount,* and *explain* (DARE)—key uses of academic language. Subsequently, we identify the language features associated with each key use and offer example language-centered instructional tasks and resources geared to different grade levels. In doing so, we set the tone for easing teachers into the practice of thinking about academic language use when engaging in teaching complex academic concepts, sharing their thoughts with students, and exchanging their ideas with colleagues and school leaders.

Chapter 2: How do we plan for the integration of key uses of academic language in our practice? What are some helpful tools? Having established a firm foundation for the efficacy of key uses of academic language and their utility with stakeholders, from students to educational leaders, we turn our attention to identifying DARE in standards. Subsequently, we suggest ways for inserting key uses of academic language into disciplinary practices and ultimately integrating DARE into curriculum. Additionally, we draw from the community to ensure that students are able to make connections among their languages, cultures, and daily lives to learning in school.

Chapter 3: How might we assess key uses of academic language in our content classrooms? Planning, collecting, analyzing, and reporting data gathered from various forms of assessment is synonymous with schooling. But to what extent have teachers considered the impact of language on student performance? In this chapter, we illustrate how authentic classroom assessment can be shaped by key uses of academic language that serve as the basis for defining what students can do. We pay special attention to student-centered assessment that stems from disciplinary practices. Much of the chapter is devoted to investigating how to identify, measure, and document DARE in the major content areas: language arts, mathematics, science, and social studies.

Chapter 4: What are some viable ways of embedding key uses of academic language into classroom life so that learning is equitable for all students? Implementation of key uses of academic language involves the careful selection of a variety of instructional materials and the scaffolding of instruction so that it is personalized for and accessible to all students. In that way, students can maximize their opportunities to participate in learning experiences and achieve grade-level content. More important, however, is giving students choice and voice throughout the school day. By providing stimulating options that motivate students, teachers encourage student engagement in school and beyond. Additionally, students are led to become metalinguistically and metacognitively aware of their academic language use and its interaction with their thinking processes, with the ultimate goal of becoming agents of and responsible for their own learning.

Chapter 5: How can key uses of academic language be stimuli for cementing relationships among stakeholders so that students can maximize their learning? The stakeholder group most impacted by key uses of academic language is students; therefore, we speak to how students can be active participants in determining their educational destiny by taking responsibility for their own learning and becoming valued contributors to a community of learners. We also recognize families as critical stakeholders who can initiate academic language use at home and strengthen key uses of academic language introduced in school. We show how families can become aware of the importance of academic language development, whether in English or another language. Then, we acknowledge teachers whose leadership and advocacy help students become more attuned to communicating with intent. Finally, we address school leaders who must also be the conveyers of key uses of academic language and ensure that they are integral to school life.

FEATURES OF THE BOOK

There is a full complement of features to lead educators to better understand, reflect, and communicate with others the power of language. *Take the DARE* is a feature that challenges the reader, teacher teams, or professional learning communities, along with school leaders, to reenvision teaching and learning through a language lens. It encourages these stakeholders to take time to extend their thinking on a particular issue or apply ideas related to DARE to their own settings. Questions are suited for stimulating educators to think about taking next steps for incorporating key uses of academic language into their own work.

Figures are illustrative or extensions of information presented in the text. As teachers and teacher educators ourselves, we are aware of the ongoing search for classroom tools. We hope that these are both stimulating and useful, as we converted many of them into resources.

Resources are educator tools designed for students, classrooms, and schools; they are intended to be stimuli for many stakeholders, including teachers, teacher teams, professional learning communities, and school leaders to ponder, plan, and practice. These charts, graphs, and activity sheets are presented in a chapter with exemplars. They are duplicated as blank forms at the close of each chapter for personal use or to share with other educators, students, and families. They are noted in the manuscript by the icon you see of two persons putting together two puzzle pieces.

Source: BrainPOP®, https://www.brainpop.com

To read a QR code, you must have a smartphone or tablet with a camera. We recommend that you download a QR code reader app that is made specifically for your phone or tablet brand.

The *QR codes* that are embedded in the pages throughout the book take you directly to the BrainPOP® website where you are able to utilize the cited source. We hope that you take advantage of these free materials, including movies, text, graphic organizers, activities, concept maps, and games. We have used these materials as a jump start for thinking about and illustrating academic language use in classrooms.

The *references* that relate to the four perspectives are presented at the close of each chapter and include cited references as well as seminal work in the field we suggest for further reading. We feel that the close proximity of references to the topic at hand increases the awareness of the literature base from which we draw and reinforces our ideas. References also serve as resources unto themselves for those of you who wish to probe more deeply into specific content.

HOW TO USE THIS BOOK

Language Power is geared to stimulating in-depth conversations among educators in K–8 settings that lead to mutually agreed-upon goals for teaching and learning. It is written to foster collaboration, first and foremost, among teachers who wish to delve into refocusing curriculum, assessment, and instruction around academic language use. Our intent is to reach out to classroom teachers, content specialists, and special education teachers to ask them to think deeply about how to represent language learning more equitably within content learning for their students, with special attention to English language learners (ELLs), ELLs with disabilities, and students who speak other varieties of English (other English learners). In the same spirit, we also encourage partnerships between language specialists and content experts, whether teachers, coaches, or other instructional leaders.

School leaders who embody the mission and vision of their building are invited to see how academic language works in tandem with content throughout their schools. Building a school climate that is inclusive of the linguistic and cultural assets of its student body

Reenvisioning Teaching and Learning Through Key Uses of Academic Language

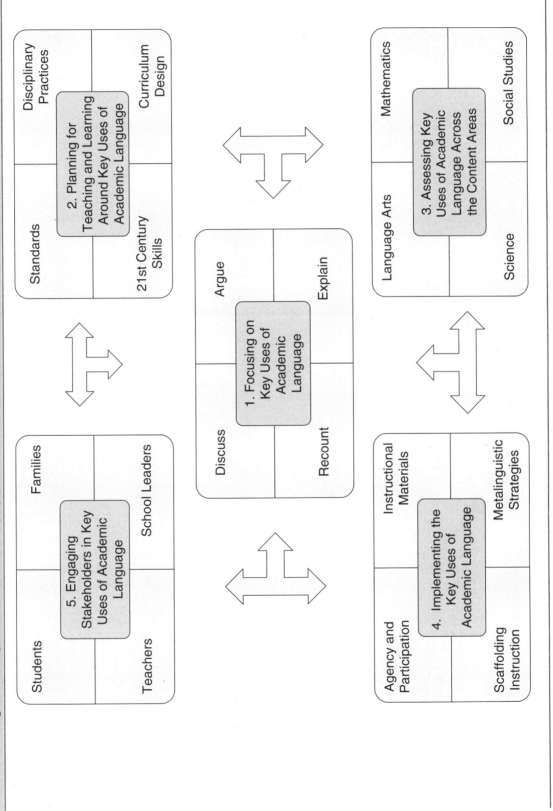

will be embraced by the community and the students themselves. There are resources dedicated to envisioning academic language use that are applicable to standards, curriculum design, and assessment that can readily be implemented at a school level.

As teachers and teacher educators who have tried our utmost to instill confidence in our students by building their academic language through content, we hope we have shared our passion and our can-do spirit throughout this book. We believe that all teachers need opportunities to be introspective and think deeply about how they use language to best promote their students' academic achievement to ensure their success in school.

We ask you to refer to the figure "Reenvisioning Teaching and Learning Through Key Uses of Academic Language" often, as it serves as an overview of the book. The focus on key uses of academic language highlights its positioning in relation to the multiple perspectives we address in planning, assessing, and implementing teaching and learning experiences, as well as the active role of stakeholders in the process. Language is a powerful tool for reasoning, communicating, being, and doing; we hope you join us in furthering academic language use in school.

References and Further Reading

Anstrom, K., DiCerbo, P., Butler, F., Katz, A., Millet, J., & Rivera, C. (2010). *A review of the literature on academic English: Implications for K–12 English language learners.* Arlington, VA: George Washington University Center for Equity and Excellence in Education.

Bailey, A. L., & Butler, F. A. (2007). A conceptual framework of academic English language for broad application to education. In A. L. Bailey (Ed.), *The language demands of school: Putting academic language to the test* (pp. 68–102). New Haven, CT: Yale University Press.

Chamot, A. U., & O'Malley, J. M. (1994). *The CALLA handbook: Implementing the cognitive academic language learning approach.* Boston, MA: Addison Wesley.

Cummins, J. (1981). The cross-lingual dimensions of language proficiency: Implications for bilingual education and the optimal age issue. *TESOL Quarterly, 14,* 175–185.

de Oliveira, L. C. (2013). Academic language in the social studies for English learners. In M. B. Arias & C. J. Faltis (Eds.), *Academic language in second language learning* (pp. 149–170). Charlotte, NC: Information Age Publishing.

de Oliveira, L. C. (Ed.). (2014/2015). *The Common Core State Standards and English language learners.* Alexandria, VA: TESOL Press.

de Oliveria, L. C. (Ed.). (2016). *Common Core State Standards for literacy in history/social studies, science, and technical subjects for English language learners.* Alexandria, VA: TESOL Press.

Echevarria, J., Vogt, M. E., & Short, D. J. (2017). *Making content comprehensible for English learners: The SIOP model* (5th ed.). Boston, MA: Allyn & Bacon.

Freeman, Y. S., & Freeman, D. E. (2009). *Academic language for English language learners and struggling readers: How to help students succeed across the content areas.* Portsmouth, NH: Heinemann.

Friedberg, C., Mitchell, A., & Brooke, E. (2016). *Understanding academic language and its connection to school success.* Retrieved from http://www.lexialearning.com/sites/default/files/resources/Whitepaper_Understanding_Academic_Language.pdf

Gottlieb, M. (2003). *Large-scale assessment of English language learners: Addressing educational accountability in K–12 settings.* Alexandria, VA: Teachers of English to Speakers of Other Languages.

Gottlieb, M., & Ernst-Slavit, G. (2013). (Eds.). *Academic language in diverse classrooms: Promoting content and language learning. Mathematics, Grades K–2, 3–5, 6–8.* Thousand Oaks, CA: Corwin.

Gottlieb, M., & Ernst-Slavit, G. (2014a). *Academic language in diverse classrooms: Definitions and contexts.* Thousand Oaks, CA: Corwin.

Gottlieb, M., & Ernst-Slavit, G. (2014b). (Eds.). *Academic language in diverse classrooms: Promoting content and language learning. English language arts, Grades K–2, 3–5, 6–8.* Thousand Oaks, CA: Corwin.

Scarcella, R. (2003). *Academic English: A conceptual framework.* Irvine: University of California Linguistic Minority Research Institute.

Snow, C. E., & Uccelli, P. (2009). The challenge of academic language. In D. R. Olson & N. Torrance (Eds.), *The Cambridge handbook of literacy* (pp. 112–133). Cambridge, UK: Cambridge University Press.

WIDA. (2012). *Amplification of the English language development standards, Kindergarten–grade 12.* Madison: Board of Regents of the University of Wisconsin System.

WIDA. (2016a). *Can do descriptors: Key uses edition. Grades K, 1, 2–3, 4–5, 6–8, and 9–12.* Madison: Board of Regents of the University of Wisconsin System.

WIDA. (2016b). *Los descriptores PODEMOS. Kinder, 1, 2–3, 4–5, 6–8, 9–12 grados.* Madison: Board of Regents of the University of Wisconsin System.

WIDA. (2016c). *WIDA early years can do booklet.* Madison: Board of Regents of the University of Wisconsin System.

Zacarian, D. (2012). *Mastering academic language: A framework for supporting academic achievement.* Thousand Oaks, CA: Corwin.

Zwiers, J. (2014). *Building academic language: Meeting Common Core Standards across disciplines, Grades 5–12* (2nd ed.). San Francisco, CA: Jossey-Bass.

About the Authors

Margo Gottlieb, PhD, is cofounder and lead developer for WIDA at the Wisconsin Center for Education Research, University of Wisconsin–Madison, having also served as director of assessment and evaluation for the Illinois Resource Center. She has contributed to the crafting of language proficiency and development standards for American Samoa, Guam, TESOL, and WIDA and has designed assessments, curricular frameworks, and instructional assessment systems for language learners. Her professional experiences span from being an inner-city language teacher to working with thousands of educators across states, school districts, publishing companies, governments, universities, and educational organizations.

Highlights of Margo's career include being a Fulbright Senior Specialist in Chile and being appointed to the U.S. Department of Education's Inaugural National Technical Advisory Council. In 2016, Margo was honored by TESOL International Association's 50 at 50 "as an individual who has made a significant contribution to the TESOL profession within the past 50 years." She has had opportunities to travel extensively and has presented in American Samoa, Argentina, Brazil, Canada, Chile, China, the Commonwealth of the Northern Mariana Islands, Denmark, Finland, Guam, Italy, Jakarta, Mexico, Panama, Singapore, South Korea, Taiwan, United Arab Emirates, and the United Kingdom, as well as close to home across the United States.

Margo's publications include over 70 articles, technical reports, monographs, chapters, and encyclopedia entries. Additionally, this past decade, she has authored, coauthored, and coedited 11 books: *Assessing English Language Learners: Bridges to Educational Equity* (2nd ed., 2016), *Academic Language in Diverse Classrooms: Definitions and Contexts* (with G. Ernst-Slavit, 2014), a foundational book for the series *Promoting Content and Language Learning* (a compendium of three mathematics and three English language arts volumes coedited with G. Ernst-Slavit, 2014, 2013), *Common Language Assessment for English Learners* (2012), *Paper to Practice: Using the TESOL's English Language Proficiency Standards in PreK–12 Classrooms* (with A. Katz & G. Ernst-Slavit, 2009), and *Assessment and Accountability in Language Education Programs: A Guide for Administrators and Teachers* (with D. Nguyen, 2007).

Mariana Castro, PhD, is director of standards for WIDA at the Wisconsin Center for Education Research, University of Wisconsin–Madison, where she has also served as director of academic language and literacy initiatives and director of teaching and learning. Mariana is, foremost, an educator, having taught science, ESL courses, and bilingual classes in K–12 systems. As an educator, she also led professional development for ESL and bilingual educators at her district. Mariana has also taught undergraduate and graduate courses at UW–Whitewater and Edgewood College in Madison, Wisconsin, where she lives with her husband, Andy, and three children, Amy, Andrés, and Diego. During her career as an educator, she worked with multilingual students, students with significant cognitive disabilities, and students with limited or interrupted formal education and collaborated with educators and administrators, in and out of the classroom. It was this work that provided the foundation and inspiration for her career.

Over the last 10 years, Mariana has worked with in-service teachers and administrators across the U.S. and abroad on building capacity related to instruction and programming, with a focus on language development. She has also presented at national conferences, including TESOL, Learning Forward, NABE, La Cosecha, ASCD, AERA, and AAAL, and at many regional and local conferences across the country. Internationally, she has worked with educators in Mexico, Dubai, Thailand, and Argentina in designing spaces for meaningful participation and multilingual development for language learners.

Mariana's service to the field includes serving as an expert in policy and theory-to-practice panels related to the education of English learners, being an active member of the Second Language Research Special Interest Group at the American Educational Research Association, and serving as a reviewer for the *South African Journal of Education* and the *TESOL Journal*. She participated in the development of the Framework for English Language Proficiency Development Standards corresponding to the Common Core State Standards and the Next Generation Science Standards and in the development of a variety of standards, including WIDA English Language Development Standards, K–12; WIDA Spanish Language Development Standards, K–12; and WIDA Early Language Development Standards for children 2.5 through 5.5 years old, in English and Spanish. She has also led the development of multiple publications derivative of the aforementioned standards. Mariana has also served as principal investigator for a variety of grants and research related to early language development, English language development, Spanish language development, data literacy, and family engagement. Mariana's research interests also include translanguaging and social justice in education.

Mariana's publications include a coedited volume, *Common Core, Bilingual and English Language Learners: A Resource for Educators* (with G. Valdés and K. Menken), *Formative Language Assessment for English Learners: A Four-Step Process* (with R. MacDonald, T. Boals, H. G. Cook, T. Lundberg, & P. A. White), a chapter in *Intersectionality and Urban Education: Identities, Policies, Spaces, and Power* (with L. Mancilla & T. Boals), and articles in *Language Magazine*, *Soleado*, and the *WIDA Focus Bulletin* series.

Acknowledgments

It is always interesting to see how simple ideas blossom into manuscripts and how manuscripts become realized in books. If it wasn't for the confidence that Corwin places in its authors, it couldn't have been able to position itself as such a stronghold in the educational field and a voice of advocacy for the teaching force. We applaud its ongoing commitment to seeking new ideas and inspiration for bettering education opportunities for students and educators.

Dan Alpert, program director of equity and professional learning, embodies this trust. He is a true champion of equity, and we can't thank him enough for believing in this project and in us. With the support of Maura Sullivan, marketing manager, this dynamic duo has a clear vision of how to conceptualize and communicate the importance of promoting educational change through the power of language. We also cannot forget Kimberly Greenberg, senior associate editor, who, in the team spirit, is always willing to help in any way.

Other important Corwin folks have contributed to bringing our book to fruition. Katie Crilley, editorial assistant, is a detail person who has meticulously combed the manuscript to ensure that it complies with publishing guidelines. Marketing plays an important role in informing the educational community of the upcoming addition to the field, and Kimberly Schmidt, marketing associate, has worked feverishly to help publicize our book. Gail Buschman has taken our ideas for the cover and converted them to represent the strength of language power. Lastly, we extend our gratitude to Melanie Birdsall, senior project editor, Books Production, who has led the way to converting a manuscript into a book and to Jared Leighton, our copy editor, who helped us polish our text, figures, and resources to ready them for you.

There are two organizations to whom we are greatly indebted. The first, BrainPOP®, has generously offered its myriad resources to assist us in concretizing how key uses of academic language can be operationalized through multimodal, content-based materials. Beverly Fine, as editorial and outreach director of BrainPOP ESL™, clearly sees the value of connecting language and content. She has been an advocate on our behalf and has supported us in securing the digital materials we proudly display that you, the reader, can digitally access. Last but not least, WIDA, our home away from home, has given us the latitude and confidence to take a spark of an idea, explore it in depth with colleagues and experts, grapple with how to represent it, and share its product with educators. With encouragement and collaboration of many wonderful WIDAites in Madison, Wisconsin, across the country, and around the globe, our dreams have become reality. For this and more, we are eternally grateful for WIDA, the many friendships it has personally spurred, and its dedication to equitable education for language learners worldwide.

We dedicate this book to our children—Graham, Amy, Andrés, and Diego—and to all children around the world who have the power to realize the potential of language.

Dedicamos nuestro libro a nuestros hijos y a los niños alrededor del mundo quienes poseen el poder de realizar el potencial del lenguaje.

Preface

The basic purpose of school is achieved through communication.

—Courtney Cazden (2001)

If communication is the vehicle for school achievement, how can we change the educational mindset so that every educator sees language as a tool for attaining this goal? That's what we have set out to accomplish in this book: to present a conceptual tool that is centered on overarching purposes for academic language use. It may appear simplistic, but we and our colleagues have spent an extraordinary amount of time trying to distill the complexities of language learning into a manageable set of key uses. So read the passage below on nutritional guidelines, from the FYI section of BrainPOP®'s "Nutrition" topic, and try to identify what they might be.

> The U.S. Department of Agriculture (USDA) has been giving out nutritional guidelines since the early 1900s. Its first standardized recommendations came in 1956, when it introduced the Basic Four Food Groups: grains; fruits and vegetables; dairy products; and a catchall protein category.
>
> In 1992, the USDA decided to display its nutrition guidelines in the form of a pyramid. The shape of the original pyramid, which had six food groups instead of four, was ideal for showing the proportions of servings needed from each group to create a balanced diet. For instance, grains, which we need most, were at the base, while sweets and fats, which we should only occasionally snack on, were at the top.
>
> Over the years, however, many nutritionists and doctors claimed that the food guide had a number of flaws. Eventually, as part of an overall campaign to get people to make healthier food choices, the USDA decided to revise and update the pyramid—and in 2005, the new and improved "MyPyramid" was unveiled.
>
> The horizontal wedges of the original pyramid were replaced with vertical slices of various colors and thicknesses. Each represented the recommended number of daily servings from six different food groups: grains, vegetables, fruits, milk, meat and beans, and oils. To remind people about the importance of exercise, a staircase was added to the left side of the pyramid, with a stick figure climbing the steps to good health.

But MyPyramid was also criticized for being too abstract—people didn't know what group each colored wedge stood for. So the MyPlate logo was introduced in 2011, and officially unveiled by First Lady Michelle Obama.

"We realized we needed something that made sense not just in classrooms or laboratories, but at dinner tables and school cafeterias. We needed something useful, something simple," Mrs. Obama said. Many nutritionists agreed, noting that people tend to eat off of plates, not pyramids!

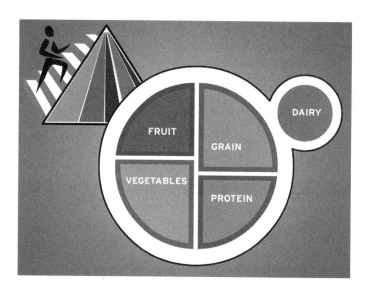

Source: BrainPOP®, https://www.brainpop.com/health/nutrition/nutrition/fyi/#tab=0

Source: BrainPOP®, https://www.brainpop.com/health/nutrition/nutrition/fyi

We have come to the conclusion that four key uses of academic language give teachers and students tremendous insight into how oral and written text is organized to express specific intents. And so we share them with you, realizing that authentic text is not neatly organized around one key use or another but, in fact, may be perceived as having multiple purposes. Here is an interpretation of that BrainPOP® passage on nutritional guidelines around four key uses of academic language (DARE), the conceptual tool used in this book:

Discuss the pros and cons of the various images that represent nutritional guidelines.

Argue for the nutritional guidelines that you believe are most effective.

Recount the history of nutritional guidelines in the U.S.

Explain how and why nutritional guidelines are helpful.

Take the DARE

One of the themes woven throughout the book is that students' exposure to multimodality, especially ELLs, ELLs with disabilities, and other language learners, helps increase their opportunities for meaning making. BrainPOP® included the visual on page 2 with the text on nutritional guidelines. How does it enhance the overall meaning? How might it be beneficial to your students? What can you do to increase students' comprehension through visualization? Why are visuals important for students who might be challenged by text written in English, by print, or both?

Academic language use provides students access to the content learned in school, and it is the vehicle for their meaningful participation during teaching and learning. Language is also the medium through which students share what they know and demonstrate what they have learned. It is not enough for students, however, to just know the language or know about the language. Students need to understand how language is used in academic contexts and the expectations for its use throughout the school day.

THE INQUIRY CYCLE

In this book, we use the inquiry cycle as an organizing scheme to provide a structure for each chapter. We choose this five-phase inquiry cycle, shown in Figure P.1, as we wish teachers to probe deeply into compelling issues that stimulate conversation by (1) *asking* about academic language use, (2) *exploring* it more in depth, (3) *applying* it to their classrooms, (4) *reflecting* on its utility, and (5) *taking action* to ensure that it has meaningful and lasting impact. Additionally, we feel that implementing the inquiry cycle prompts collaboration among teachers who are constantly seeking to improve their practices. The power of collaborative inquiry, especially in a professional learning community, has proven to be transformative, evoking real change in schools and classrooms (Donohoo & Velasco, 2016).

FIGURE P.1 Applying the Inquiry Cycle as the Organizational Frame for the Book

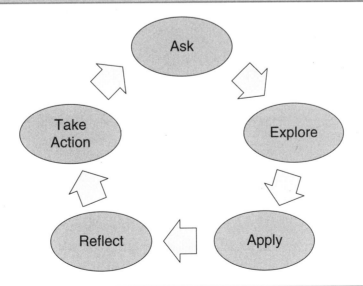

We also would like to highlight the essential role of inquiry in the generation of new knowledge. As we identify questions or learn new concepts, we need time to explore ideas related to them and time to apply that new knowledge. A critical part of the inquiry cycle is to provide space to reflect on those new ideas and on how we might integrate them into our practice. With that in mind, for each new idea presented throughout the book, we provide additional references for those who wish to dive in deeper on any concept presented and examples to see it applied to instruction and assessment. We also offer challenges throughout each chapter to invite you to take action on your new knowledge along with questions for reflection. Finally, we offer myriad resources, which include templates of activities and tools ready for you to use.

The following is a detailed description with an exemplar of how each section of our chapters unfolds within a specific phase of the inquiry cycle based on perspectives of academic language use.

ASK

We begin each chapter by posing a question related to key uses of academic language. As an example, for this prelude, we ask the question, *Why focus on academic language use?* We explore each chapter's question from four perspectives that are presented in a diagram in the "Ask" section, such as the one shown in Figure P.2. Here, we highlight four perspectives in the quadrant—(1) teaching and learning theory, (2) academic achievement, (3) educational equity, and (4) global interconnectedness—to offer a rationale for focusing on academic language use.

FIGURE P.2 A Rationale for Focusing on Academic Language Use

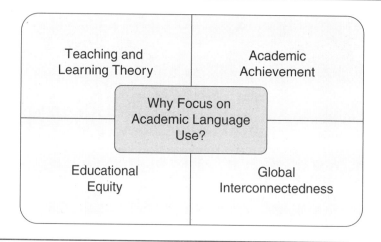

We conclude this section with a list of chapter objectives, as we invite educators to *take the DARE* (*discuss, argue, recount,* and *explain*) to guide conversations around the central question. For this set of perspectives offered in the quadrant, we DARE teachers, school leaders, and teacher educators to do the following:

Discuss the literature and research bases on the role of language in teaching and learning.

Argue for the importance of mastery of academic language in academic achievement.

Recount the function of academic language as an agent of educational equity.

Explain how academic language can serve as a home–school connector.

EXPLORE

This section addresses the overarching question and each perspective stated in the "Ask" section. It also invites the reader to implement the ideas and concepts discussed. In this prelude, we illustrate how each perspective contributes to the rationale for increased intentional academic language use in elementary school classrooms.

TEACHING AND LEARNING THEORY

For a long time, language has been recognized as a vehicle for learning (Dewey, 1916; Vygotsky, 1934/1962). The ways in which language is used by students, teachers, and families have an impact on how children learn. Some researchers, for example, have attributed how well students do in school to the particular language patterns used by the social groups to which they belong (Bernstein, 1970; Brice-Heath, 1983). These studies highlight the unique ways in which language is used in school and the need to socialize children into those ways so that they can be successful. In spite of the existing research on the critical role that language plays in school, language development has not been fully integrated into the learning taking place in our classrooms.

Many of our current teaching approaches come from sociocultural theory, which sees learning as a social activity. This theory proposes that learning happens through social interaction, with assistance from teachers and peers who are more knowledgeable, and as they engage in culturally meaningful tasks (Vygotsky, 1978). In this social and interactive perspective, language plays a central role; it is a tool for negotiating meaning, for problem solving, and for making sense of the world, individually and with others. Language is not seen as an abstract system of linguistic forms or an individual form of activity, but instead, it is a continuous generative process that is learned through dialogue (Bakhtin, 1986). This dialogue takes place within particular social contexts and cultures that impact the ways in which people use languages (Martin, Christie, & Rothery, 1994).

For example, the ways one uses language when writing an e-mail, when filling out an application, or when producing a book report are very different. Because of the many contexts, thinking about goals or purposes for language use without a framework can become overwhelming. Key uses of academic language afford us the opportunity to focus and organize teaching and learning in a more manageable manner and, at the same time, to better and more purposefully integrate language and content instruction.

In sum, learning theory highlights the important role of language for students to be able to access and achieve content-related ideas and concepts. Further, since learning is social in nature and not an individual endeavor, language provides opportunities for students to engage meaningfully with others in learning activities. A focus on key uses of academic language ensures that all students possess the means to be able to internalize and share what they learn in school.

Take the DARE

Throughout the book, we challenge you to *take the DARE* by posing questions, providing activities, and offering resources for you to reflect on in each section. Whether you are reading this book on your own or with colleagues, each activity is aimed at helping you identify ways to focus on academic language use in your practice.

As an example, in this section, we ask you to engage in deep reflection about language by answering the following questions:

1. How do you define academic language use?

2. What is your teaching and learning philosophy? Does it include academic language use? If so, how? If not, how might you include it?

3. What common beliefs about academic language development do you share with colleagues?

4. What role do you believe academic language use has in teaching and learning?

5. How do you include discussions about language use in your classroom or promote them in your school?

ACADEMIC ACHIEVEMENT

In the previous section, we explored what theory has to say about the role of academic language in learning; in this section, we focus on identifying the impact language has on academic achievement. We define academic achievement as students' success in meeting short- or long-term goals in education in relation to their performance outcomes and challenging state academic standards. In this continuing era of assessment and accountability, educators need to be able to show evidence of academic achievement of all of their students.

Recently, research has emerged that connects academic language to academic achievement (Bailey, 2007; Francis, M. Rivera, Lesaux, Kieffer, & H. Rivera, 2006; Heppt, Henschel, & Haag, 2016; Schleppegrell, 2004). This research points to the fact that students who master the use of academic language are more successful in accessing the knowledge and information in textbooks, academic resources, and assessments (Francis et al., 2006). While students may be able to accrue knowledge without the use of academic language, as information becomes more complex, so too does language. Therefore, students who have not had experiences with using academic language have a more challenging time engaging with content in school than children who have had exposure to its use early on.

The scope of academic language is not limited to discipline-specific vocabulary but also includes grammatical forms and ways of organizing oral and written information in academic-specific ways. These conventions have been established and look differently from one discipline to another. For example, the language of sequencing the steps in solving a mathematical story problem is quite distinct from the language of sequencing the events in a biography. It becomes apparent that students use language in many different ways throughout the day. Most important, however, academic language encompasses disciplinary discourse, and key uses of academic language assist in leveraging how oral and written text is organized and communicated.

While we have known about the critical role of language in learning and in academic achievement, we often presume students already have the language needed to engage in learning or that they will acquire it through their environment or exposure. While this may be true for some language development and some of the students, an intentional focus on language use ensures that of all students are included in teaching and learning. More specifically, an intentional focus on language provides more equitable opportunities for students to interact with academic discourse and assures that all students have the tools to participate meaningfully in activities designed to mediate learning.

Remember that for ELLs and ELLs with disabilities, academic language use is not necessarily confined to English but, in fact, should be inclusive of their home language(s) as well. These students have extensive linguistic and cultural repertoires that are resources to tap in expanding their thinking, knowing, and doing. So when we speak of academic language use, we are not language specific; we wish to acknowledge and encourage the potential transferability of thoughts and actions between languages.

Take the DARE

Here are some ideas to begin thinking about academic language use in your classroom:

- Identify the various ways in which language is used in texts.
- Observe how students use language(s) during group work or presentations.
- Record yourself, and reflect on your own use of language in your classroom.
- Review student work with a focus on their use of language.
- Recognize how many opportunities your students have during class to use language with each other in meaningful ways.
- Document student language in your classroom environment (e.g., word, phrase, or concept walls; posters; charts; and bulletin boards).

EDUCATIONAL EQUITY

As we mention throughout this prelude, there are countless ways of using language. The fact that many children come to our schools from minority backgrounds—racial, cultural, social, and linguistic—often means that they may have had different experiences and perspectives (Gutiérrez, 2007; Tate & Rousseau, 2007). With these experiences come different assets and strengths that students bring to school; however, these positive qualities and talents often become invisible when students walk in the door. Taking on the mission for educational equity means finding ways to make students' resources visible, relevant, and connected to teaching and learning in meaningful ways (Rigby & Tredway, 2015; U.S. Department of Education, 2013).

In brief, educators' direct access to academic language development is an avenue that contributes to educational equity. Key uses of academic language facilitates educators' and students' recognition, use, and expansion of linguistic resources. We DARE—*discuss*, *argue*, *recount*, and *explain*—teachers and school leaders to focus on the value of language, along with content for each discipline.

Take the DARE

Some resources or activities that take place in schools facilitate students' academic language learning. Identify which of the following occurs in your school, and *discuss* with colleagues:

- ☐ Teams of educators identify the presence of academic language in your state's academic content standards.
  - ○ How has it been made known to all teachers?
  - ○ How are these language demands distributed across units of instruction throughout a school year to ensure their coverage?
- ☐ Grade-level or instructional teams state language goals, language targets, or objectives for their units of instruction.
  - ○ How are these communicated to students and families?
  - ○ How are students involved in determining specific language objectives?
- ☐ Educators design activities that provide opportunities for students to develop their oral and written language during instruction.
  - ○ How are these lesson-based activities related to the larger language goals and/or language targets for units of instruction?
  - ○ How do these activities help determine whether a language goal and/or target has been met?
- ☐ Assessments contain language that is grade-level relevant yet accessible to students.
  - ○ How do assessments elicit language from students?
  - ○ How are students expected to use language in assessment?

- ☐ Educators monitor students' language development, especially for ELLs and ELLs with disabilities.
  - ○ How are language data recorded or shared among educators?
  - ○ How is language development reported to families?
- ☐ Educators analyze the relationship between students' language development and their academic achievement with careful attention to ELLs and ELLs with disabilities.
  - ○ How are language data analyzed and interpreted?
  - ○ How do language data impact content area instruction?

Whether you complete this DARE on your own or as part of a team, identification of language use is only the beginning. An extension activity would include determining plausible next steps, coupled with existing resources.

GLOBAL INTERCONNECTEDNESS

Reexamining the quadrant at the beginning of this prelude, we approach the last perspective for advancing our rationale for academic language use. For it is through global interdependence that we see our students of the 21st century absorbed in a fast-paced, ever-changing world. Being immersed in a global society means we are constantly being bombarded with new information—not only from our immediate surroundings but within a nanosecond of clicking a button on our technology-enabled devices, we are connected with the world. As teachers and school leaders in this international community, it is our responsibility to ensure that its newest members are prepared to participate, contribute, and thrive in our interconnected society.

Globalization of schooling entails focusing our efforts on elucidating and respecting wide-ranging perspectives as the intermingling of different languages, cultures, and religions becomes accepted practice in our diverse classrooms. To do so, we have to expand our dialogue, reflection, and creative engagement in intercultural and multicultural education and rely on its global networks as a vehicle for promoting global interconnectedness (Grant & Brueck, 2011).

Not only do our students access the worldview instantaneously, as meaning makers, they make sense of their world in multisemiotic ways by integrating language and images. So in our book, while we acknowledge the primacy of print in literacy development, we move beyond this traditional way of communicating to embrace media, visual design, and fine arts as integral to a multimodal literacy system.

Additionally, we believe that many of the 21st century skills are requisite to connecting with others around the world. The World Economic Forum has a comprehensive view of 21st century skills, categorically placing them within lifelong learning into three groups: (1) foundational literacies—cultural and civic literacy, financial literacy, scientific literacy, numeracy, and information (digital) literacy; (2) competencies—collaboration, communication, creativity, and critical thinking; and (3) character qualities—leadership, adaptability, curiosity, social and cultural awareness, perseverance, and initiative (Soffel, 2016). It is their contention and ours that many of the 21st century competencies and qualities are developed through social and emotional learning, which has to be combined with multiliteracy development to best equip students to succeed in the world they live.

APPLY

This section offers guidance in implementing DARE by including examples of tools educators may wish to use. These templates, presented in figures and resources, are neither exhaustive nor rigid. In other words, we suggest that you incorporate them into your existing resources, that you add to them, or that you modify them to make them applicable to your context. In our experience, teachers adopt or adapt tools that are easy to use in planning students' learning experiences or enacting those experiences during assessment and instruction. So our advice is to remember that as you modify these templates, avoid making tools that become too complicated.

As an example, Figure P.3 provides a rationale for encouraging academic conversations among students that has been drawn from five distinct areas of learning (per Zwiers & Crawford, 2011). Many the themes presented here are recurring throughout the book. It is paired with Resource P.1, which, in this case, replicates the figure and asks you to select the statements that best fit what you do in school to promote student learning.

REFLECT

This section summarizes ideas presented on each perspective. We discuss how teachers can *take the DARE* to benefit students, especially those who have been historically underserved, namely English language learners, ELLs with disabilities, and speakers of other varieties of English.

Because academic language affords students opportunities to access college and career readiness standards, content, and practices, it is vital that students who have been historically underserved—ELLs, students with interrupted formal education, students with diverse socioeconomic status, and students with disabilities, among others—experience, develop, and use academic language. Throughout the book, we offer ways to be more inclusive of students in integrating language into the planning and designing of curriculum, assessment, and instruction.

Spotlighting academic language in the classroom can be influential in promoting students' academic achievement; however, it is more powerful as a focus at the school level. Systemic approaches to enhancing academic language for all students provides the most effective impact on their academic achievement. To accomplish this, it is

FIGURE P.3 Reasons for Promoting Academic Conversations in School

ACADEMIC CONVERSATIONS AMONG STUDENTS				
1. REINFORCE LANGUAGE AND LITERACY DEVELOPMENT BY ...	2. ENHANCE COGNITIVE ENGAGEMENT BY ...	3. PROMOTE CONTENT AREA ACHIEVEMENT BY ...	4. HAVE SOCIAL AND CULTURAL BENEFITS BY ...	5. TAP PSYCHOLOGICAL AND SOCIAL EMOTIONAL NEEDS BY ...
• Encouraging academic language use • Increasing vocabulary in authentic contexts • Connecting experiences to literacy skills • Building oral language and communication skills	• Focusing on higher-order thinking • Promoting different perspectives and empathy • Advancing creativity • Fostering skills for negotiating meaning and staying on topic	• Building conceptual understanding • Cultivating connections among disciplines • Helping students coconstruct understanding • Helping teachers and students assess learning	• Strengthening relationships and trust • Building an academic learning environment • Making activities more culturally sensitive and relevant • Fostering equity	• Developing inner dialogue and self-talk • Fostering engagement and motivation • Boosting confidence • Cultivating choice, ownership, and control over thinking • Raising academic identity • Advancing self-discovery • Enabling student voice and empowerment

Source: Adapted from Gottlieb and Ernst-Slavit (2014, p. 17).

important for every educator in the school or system to have a common definition and understanding of academic language. Learning and working together promotes collaboration among educators and, most important, provides consistency for students across classes and grade levels. It is here that the role of administrators becomes critical in creating structures and opportunities for educators to come together and plan around academic language use.

Take the DARE

Use the questions from the following table to find out about or document the language use of your students who receive support services. Share the data you gather with other educators who work with these students.

STUDENTS IDENTIFIED WITH LEARNING DISABILITIES, INCLUDING ELLS	STUDENTS WHO SPEAK OTHER VARIETIES OF ENGLISH, INCLUDING STANDARD ENGLISH LEARNERS (OTHER LANGUAGE LEARNERS)	STUDENTS IDENTIFIED AS ELLS
• What is the student's preferred mode to communicate? • How does the student express himself or herself? • Does the student experience difficulty with receptive language (e.g., listening and/or reading)? • Does the student experience difficulty with expressive language (e.g., speaking and/or writing)? • Does the student have language goals as part of his or her individualized education program (IEP)? • What are some of his or her strengths in the use of language or in communicating with others?	• How does the student use language at school with peers and adults? • How does the student use language when learning new ideas or concepts? • How does the student use language to describe or share what he or she knows? • What are the strengths of the student's language use? • Does the student know and use a language other than English? If so, which one?	• What language(s) does the student speak or understand? • How does the student use his or her languages? With whom? For what purposes? Under what circumstances? • Which language(s) does the student understand orally? In written form? • What language(s) does the student speak? Write? • What was the language(s) used in his or her previous schooling? • Has the student participated in a language support program (i.e., Title I, Title III, or special education)? • What are some of the student's language goals?

TAKE ACTION

This last section puts forward questions and suggests activities that, we hope, move the ideas in each chapter into action. It aims to provide inspiration in the work of teachers and school leaders to *take the DARE* and begin discussions with others at school.

As educators begin to think about academic language use, here are some ideas and questions to ponder or *discuss* with others.

1. Gather demographic data on your students, including school history, academic achievement, and other languages spoken at home. After reviewing the data, exchange information with colleagues in answering the following questions:

a. What assets and challenges do our students bring with them?

b. What linguistic and cultural resources do they possess?

c. How can we connect the language required of college and career readiness standards to students' experiences with language?

2. How is academic language use present throughout our school—in hallways, classrooms, and common areas? How can we make it more visible? How can we elicit students to help us?

3. What is your own experience in learning academic language in English or an additional language? What were some of your challenges, and how did you overcome them? What were some advantages of language learning, and how did you leverage them to make yourself understood by others?

4. What are some existing structures or resources that can support a focus on academic language use at your school? How can you make academic language learning a whole-school effort? What might you need? How can you get it?

Our goal with this book is to begin conversations in spaces where they may not exist and to move the conversation forward for educators who may already be thinking about academic language use and its impact on academic achievement. With this in mind, we touch on some important themes throughout the book to help you, the reader, make connections to other initiatives in your schools or to identify points of entry for discussions around language. These themes include

- 21st century schools and classrooms

- Linguistic and cultural sustainability

- Increased attention and acknowledgment of students and families as decision makers in education

In order to make academic language use and the themes of our book more tangible and powerful, we have included a range of materials, tools, and resources in each chapter. Each resource within a chapter is partially completed to suggest how you might wish to approach it; there is a corresponding blank template of each resource at the close of each chapter for your personal use. We thank our friends at BrainPOP® (www.brainpop.com) for sharing their wealth of resources to help us bring key uses of academic language to life.

RESOURCE P.1 Reasons for Promoting Academic Conversations in School

Individually or in teacher teams, brainstorm how you might strategically increase the quantity and quality of academic conversations in your classroom. You are welcome to borrow ideas from Figure P.3 and suggest others on your own. Refer to this resource throughout the year to evaluate the extent you are reaching the whole student.

Teacher or Teacher Team: _____ Date: _____

ACADEMIC CONVERSATIONS AMONG STUDENTS				
1. REINFORCE LANGUAGE AND LITERACY DEVELOPMENT BY . . .	2. ENHANCE COGNITIVE ENGAGEMENT BY . . .	3. PROMOTE CONTENT AREA ACHIEVEMENT BY . . .	4. HAVE SOCIAL AND CULTURAL BENEFITS BY . . .	5. TAP PSYCHOLOGICAL AND SOCIAL EMOTIONAL NEEDS BY . . .

References and Further Reading

Bailey, A. L. (2007). (Ed.). *The language demands of school: Putting academic English to the test*. New Haven, CT: Yale University Press.

Bakhtin, M. (1986). The problem of speech genres (V. McGee, Trans.). In C. Emerson & M. Holquist (Eds.), *Speech genres and other late essays* (pp. 60–102). Austin: University of Texas Press.

Bernstein, B. (1970). Education cannot compensate for society. *New Society, 15*(387), 344–347.

Brice-Heath, S. (1983). *Way with words: Language, life and work in communities and classrooms*. New York, NY: Cambridge University Press.

Cazden, C. B. (2001). *Classroom discourse: The language of learning and teaching* (2nd ed.). Portsmouth, NH: Heinemann.

Dewey, J. (1916). *Democracy and education: An introduction to the philosophy of education*. New York, NY: Macmillan.

Donohoo, J., & Velasco, M. (2016). *The transformative power of collaborative inquiry: Realizing change in schools and classrooms*. Thousand Oaks, CA: Corwin.

Ferguson, R. F. (2007). *Toward excellence with equity: An emerging vision for closing the achievement gap*. Cambridge, MA: Harvard University Press.

Francis, D. J., Rivera, M., Lesaux, N., Kieffer, M., & Rivera, H. (2006). *Practical guidelines for the education of English language learners: Research-based recommendations for instruction and academic interventions*. Portsmouth, NH: RMC Research Corporation, Center on Instruction. Retrieved from http://centeroninstruction.org/files/ELL1-Interventions.pdf

Gottlieb, M., & Ersnt-Slavit, G. (2014). *Academic language in diverse classrooms: Promoting content and language learning: Definitions and contexts*. Thousand Oaks, CA: Corwin.

Grant, C. A., & Brueck, S. (2011). A global invitation: Toward the expansion of dialogue, reflection and creative engagement for intercultural and multicultural education. In C. A. Grant & A. Portera (Eds.), *Intercultural and multicultural education: Enhancing global interconnectedness* (pp. 3–11). New York, NY: Routledge.

Gutiérrez, R. (2007). (Re)defining equity: The importance of a critical perspective. In N. S. Nasir & P. Cobb (Eds.), *Improving access to mathematics: Diversity and equity in the classroom* (pp. 37–50). New York, NY: Teachers College Press.

Heppt, B., Henschel, S., & Haag, N. (2016). Everyday and academic language comprehension: Investigating their relationships with school success and challenges for language minority learners. *Learning and Individual Differences, 47*, 244–251.

Martin, J. R., Christie, F., & Rothery, J. (1994). Social processes in education: A reply to Sawyer and Watson (and others). In B. Stierer & J. Maybin (Eds.), *Language, literacy and learning in educational practice* (pp. 232–247). Clevedon, UK: Multilingual Matters.

Rigby, J., & Tredway, L. (2015). Actions matter: How school leaders enact equity principles. In M. Khalifa, N. W. Arnold, A. F. Osanloo, & C. M. Grant (Eds.). *Handbook of urban educational leadership* (pp. 329–348). Lanham, MD: Rowman & Littlefield.

Schleppegrell, M. J. (2001). Linguistic features of the language of schooling. *Linguistics and Education, 12*(4), 431–459.

Schleppegrell, M. J. (2004). *The language of school: A functional linguistics perspective*. Mahwah, NJ: Lawrence Erlbaum Associates.

Skria, L., & Scheurich, J. J. (2004). (Eds.). *Educational equity and accountability: Paradigms, policies, and politics*. London, UK: Routledge.

Soffel, J. (2016, March 10). What are the 21st-century skills every student needs? [Web log post]. Retrieved from https://www.weforum.org/agenda/2016/03/21st-century-skills-future-jobs-students

Tate, W. F., & Rousseau, C. (2007). Engineering change in mathematics education: Research, policy, and practice. In F. K. Lester (Ed.), *Second handbook of research on mathematics teaching and learning* (pp. 1209–1241). Reston, VA: National Council of Teachers of Mathematics.

U.S. Department of Education. (2013). *For each and every child: A strategy for education equity and excellence*. Washington, D.C.: Author.

Vygotsky, L. S. (1962). *Thought and language*. Cambridge, MA: MIT Press. (Original work published 1934)

Vygotsky, L. S. (1978). *Mind in society: The development of higher psychological processes*. Cambridge, MA: Harvard University Press

Zwiers, J., & Crawford, M. (2011). *Academic conversations: Classroom talk that fosters critical thinking and content understandings*. Portland, ME: Stenhouse.

CHAPTER 1

Examining Key Uses of Academic Language

The verbal and nonverbal interaction in which the learner engages are central to an understanding of learning . . . they do not just facilitate learning, they are *learning in a fundamental way.*

—Leo van Lier (2000)

Teaching is a balance of reflection in action and reflection on action. We reflect in action when we respond to our students' needs in the moment. We reflect on action when we think about our students' overall strengths and goals. We plan for instruction and assessment based on our reflection on action while we react spontaneously during instruction and its embedded assessment based on our reflection in action. The conceptualization of key uses of academic language is a result of our own reflection on action. In our experiences, both in the classroom and in working with teachers, we have realized that great teaching is no accident but a result of deep reflection on action. Key uses are meant to guide teacher planning and reflection on action.

ASK

What is the nature of key uses of academic language? What is the language associated with each key use?

The overhaul of academic content standards in 2010 and beyond across the United States has increased the rigor of the curriculum, assessment, and instruction in classrooms. Consequently, students need to possess the language to think about and engage with content in classroom activities intended to mediate their learning. In reviewing the existing academic content standards, instructional materials, and linguistic theories, particular purposes for academic language use emerge: namely, *discuss, argue, recount,* and *explain* (DARE). These are the overall purposes we equate with DARE, and in doing so, we DARE teachers and school leaders to advocate for advancing key uses of academic language as an educational tool of practice.

Figure 1.1 depicts the four uses of academic language that form DARE and frame this book.

FIGURE 1.1 Key Uses of Academic Language

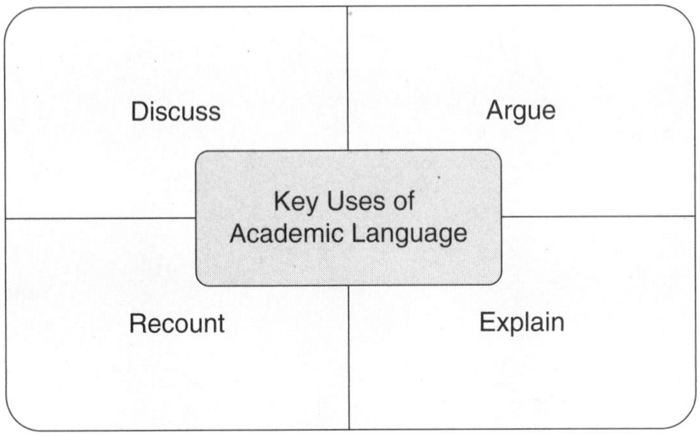

```
┌─────────────────────┬─────────────────────┐
│      Discuss         │        Argue         │
│         ┌───────────────────────┐          │
│         │      Key Uses of       │          │
│         │   Academic Language    │          │
│         └───────────────────────┘          │
│      Recount         │       Explain        │
└─────────────────────┴─────────────────────┘
```

Key uses of academic language are a focal point for organizing and promoting student interaction with content and with one another. In this chapter, we identify the linguistic features of each key use and point to how these defining characteristics are useful indicators of different genres across school disciplines. We use the term genre in this context to refer to the socially constructed ways in which we communicate for academic purposes. Examples of written genres in college and career readiness (CCR) standards in which key uses of academic language are strongly embedded, for example, include narrative, argumentative, and informational text. To guide our conversation, we invite teachers to take the DARE and do the following:

Discuss the concept of academic language use and its connection to academic achievement

Argue for DARE as a conceptual tool to enhance educators' focus on academic language use in planning curriculum, assessment, and instruction

Recount the individual and collective features of key uses of academic language

Explain how to highlight key uses of academic language across different contexts and activities

As we explore DARE-specific key uses of academic language, it is important to note that these are not the only purposes for language use in school. We have created these umbrella categories to ease educators into the practice of thinking about language use and its power when engaging in teaching complex academic concepts.

EXPLORE

When students go to school, they engage in many activities, from making friends, to negotiating meaning, to sharing what they know and how they know it. Language facilitates students' participation in all of these activities. The term academic language has been historically used to describe the processing and production of language used to share concepts, ideas, and information of the disciplines in school contexts (Bailey, 2007; Feldman & Kinsella, 2008; Gottlieb & Ernst-Slavit, 2014; Schlepegrell, 2004). In this book, we propose extending this definition to encompass all school-related activities in which students participate. When students interact with peers or their teachers and are involved in complex thinking, they do not necessarily use discipline-specific language, even though they may be using language for academic purposes. Such language can also be used to problem-solve, to collaborate, or to promote social justice. In other words, language use in schools does not fit into a traditional dichotomy of social and academic language. Language use is multifaceted, as the interaction among the contexts, participants, and activities that take place in school is complex and varied (Gee, 2004; Holland, 2005). This complexity is what we try to encapsulate in the term *academic language.*

Academic language, defined from a broader perspective as a means for students to engage in school, includes social interaction, making meaning, and accessing academic content. Many students who enter our classrooms bring with them experiences and ways of knowing and learning about the world that may differ from those described in challenging academic standards. As educators, one of our roles is to create connections between the two so that all students have the tools needed to meaningfully participate in learning. Making these connections with each and every student is one of the ways we can work toward equity in our classrooms.

Take the DARE

Reflect on or *discuss* with colleagues the role of language use in your school.

1. What opportunities do students have to use academic language every day?

2. How is language modeled in your school?

3. What models for language use exist in your classroom?

4. How do students and teachers use language with each other?

5. Is there an expectation for academic language use in your school? How is it conveyed?

6. Are students who are knowledgeable of multiple languages able to maximize their academic language use by being invited to communicate in more than one language?

A RATIONALE FOR KEY USES
FOR ACADEMIC LANGUAGE

As we have mentioned, in school, language serves as the vehicle for communicating ideas, information, and knowledge; it is also the tool for interacting with others as we learn new skills and engage in content area practices. The ultimate goal of this multiyear project initiated at WIDA, Wisconsin Center for Education Research, University of Wisconsin–Madison, was to support teachers' focus on oral and written language use in their content classrooms and to promote collaboration among teachers around the role of language in learning.

We shared the array of language uses we unearthed from extensive reviews of literature, examination of state academic content standards, analysis of instructional materials, and interaction occurring in classrooms with experts in the field of linguistics and language education, our colleagues, and practitioners. After arranging the many reasons for communicating (that is, identifying language functions, such as describe, compare and contrast, defend, and state) into categories, four key uses of academic language emerged as the most salient purposes. Having secured evidence from multiple data sources, we felt confident that the key uses of academic language would indeed help teachers and school leaders better grasp the important role of language in their disciplinary practices.

At first, three main academic purposes for language use were identified: *argue*, *recount*, and *explain*. A fourth key use, *discuss*, was added to highlight the increased attention to oral discourse, collaborative learning settings, and targeted interaction among students in today's classrooms. In our book, we make an acronym from these four overarching purposes for communication—*discuss*, *argue*, *recount*, and *explain*—DARE. We think that DARE serves our intent well, as we wish to challenge educators in consciously and intentionally infusing these key uses of academic language into teaching and learning. In DARE-ing educators, we hope that key uses of academic language can serve as a conceptual tool and an entry point for deeper conversations within and across the disciplines.

To make the terms more tangible, we use the following definitions for DARE:

Discuss: To interact with others or with content as a means of negotiating meaning, cocreating new knowledge, or sharing information.

Argue: To give opinions with reasons, make claims backed by evidence, or debate topics with the intent of persuading others.

Recount: To inform others; recall experiences or events; or display knowledge, information, or ideas.

Explain: To make ideas, situations, or issues clear through *how* or *why*; to account for cause or effect; or to describe complex relationships by providing details or facts.

LANGUAGE FUNCTIONS AND THEIR RELATION TO KEY USES OF ACADEMIC LANGUAGE

Each key use is broad in nature and encompasses various language functions descriptive of how we use language. Language functions help us organize how we speak or write around a message; in that way, language functions help us organize discourse and encompass specific sentence features that are part of the way we define academic language use (Gottlieb & Ernst-Slavit, 2014). Academic language functions refer to the purpose of language use or, put more simply, why we use language to communicate—how we might wish to identify, clarify, or paraphrase (among others) concepts and ideas.

Language functions often trigger specific discourses and types of sentences. For example, we use language to *describe* characters in a story, to *compare* two approaches to solving problems, or to *ask questions* about an event. *Describe*, *compare*, and *ask questions* are examples of language functions; each one indicates specific ways in which we communicate. When we *describe*, we may use language that includes adjectives and adverbs—language intended to create a mood or appeal to the senses. On the other hand, when we *compare*, we may use comparative and superlative forms (e.g., -er, -est, more than, or less than), noting similarities and differences. It is important to remember that the language function by itself does not shape language use. The context, intended audience, and other factors, including our own experiences and identities, also impact the specific ways in which we communicate with one another.

We can think of language functions as pieces of a puzzle that, together, show a more complete picture or landscape. Several language functions can be used together or build upon each other for a greater purpose, like DARE—*discuss*, *argue*, *recount*, or *explain*. During a *discussion*, for example, students may *ask and answer questions*, *summarize* others' ideas, or *elaborate* on particular topics. Similarly, we rarely *recount* only by *describing*, but we may also *compare and contrast*, *elaborate* on details, and even *ask questions* as part of a dialogue, to name a few. As we illustrated in the opening text on nutritional guidelines, DARE often represents multiple perspectives within a single passage.

There are many language functions, and each may be used for one or more key purposes. For example, *summarize* could be used to *recount* but could also be used to *argue*. Another example is *describe*, which could be used when trying to *explain* a process, *recount* a story, *argue* for the use of a particular technology, or *discuss* a particular topic in a small group. In attempting to decide on a language focus for instruction, the large number and variability of language functions can be overwhelming. Key uses of academic language, in representing the broadest of functions that are widely represented in learning at school, provide a more accessible approach to planning for infusion of language into instruction. Figure 1.2 is a table with some language functions that are associated with each key use of academic language in DARE.

As with other examples in this book, those in Figure 1.2 are only representative, not all inclusive. It is meant to further our understanding of each key use rather than to prescribe how to enact each one.

FIGURE 1.2 Example Language Functions Encompassed in DARE

DISCUSS	ARGUE	RECOUNT	EXPLAIN
• Ask and answer questions • Clarify what is written or said • Acknowledge or affirm others' ideas • Elaborate others' ideas • Summarize information • Evaluate others' ideas • Restate or paraphrase others' comments	• Persuade others • Compare and contrast viewpoints or perspectives • Agree and disagree with the status quo • Justify responses or positions • Critique issues, evidence, or claims • Confirm positions • State opinions	• Retell experiences or narratives • Paraphrase oral or written text • Summarize accounts or ideas • Report information • Recall events • Describe observations • Provide details	• Describe how something works • Sequence steps in processes or procedures • Define causes and effects • Enumerate and clarify different types • Detail components • Provide reasons why

Take the DARE

Select a unit of study or content topic that you will teach in the next few weeks. What are the expectations for language use in (a) readings, (b) activities, (c) assignments, and (d) assessment? Can you identify some of the key uses in DARE? Can you identify other language functions?

In understanding how to use DARE, we must use shift our assessment and instructional practices to encompass a language lens. While we continue to focus on academic content expectations for our instruction, DARE expands our view to include the language that accompanies content. So for example, as we ask students to *explain*, we are looking for the logic of their explanation and also for the language used to express that logic. To support this point, we offer Figure 1.3, which contains examples of language features associated with each key use of academic language and sample tasks.

It is important to note that key uses of academic language do not neatly occur independently from each other, as when we communicate, we seamlessly move across the various uses. While the tasks presented before typically include the key use to which they are connected in the figure, they may also include other key uses. For example, as one *explains* the cause of a natural phenomenon, such as an earthquake, one may need to inform the audience about the plates that form part of the crust of the earth, using the key use *recount*. One may also provide information (*recount*) about particular scientific theories and, in doing so, include claims and supportive evidence (*argue*) to be able to *discuss* causes for earthquakes from a particular scientific paradigm. In other words, key uses of academic language are often intertwined in text and talk.

FIGURE 1.3 Typical Language Features and Example Tasks Related to Key Uses

KEY USE	EXAMPLES OF LANGUAGE FEATURES	SAMPLE TASKS
Discuss	• Asking clarifying questions (e.g., "What do you mean by their corresponding fractions?") • Inviting others to the conversation (e.g., "What do you think? Do you agree?") • Building on others' ideas (e.g., "You said that the magnet would attract metals, so if you use the magnet to bring them together, you can also use it to keep the paper in place.")	• Working on lab experiments with a partner • Participating in literary circles • Contributing to online discussions
Argue	Introducing claims through the following: • Statements, typically in present tense (e.g., "Drugs are dangerous.") • Logical connectors to link ideas (e.g., however and therefore) Supporting claims with evidence through the following: • Sequential language (e.g., first, second, and finally) • Modals (e.g., possibly and may) Strengthening arguments through the following: • Emotive language to cause a reaction from the audience (e.g., critical and devastating) • Conditionals (e.g., "If . . . , we will")	• Participating in debates • Crafting persuasive essays • Presenting conclusions in lab reports
Recount	• Sequential language to organize stories (e.g., first, then, and finally) • Use of pronouns and referents to create cohesion across the composition (e.g., this event and he said) • Use of titles or subtitles when organizing expository text (e.g., "The Sun" or "Parts of a Cell") • Statements in past tense may include dependent and independent clauses to pack more information (e.g., "Mary, who was his number one fan, ran to meet him at the station.")	• Preparing reports on historical events • Composing short stories • Creating research briefs on particular topics
Explain	• Chronological connectors to sequence steps or sequence the explanation (e.g., to begin with, before the, and next) • Passive voice to create a sense of neutrality and present factual information (e.g., "Water is produced," and, "The two fractions are added.") • Simple present tense (e.g., "Our government has three branches.")	• Describing how to solve mathematical problems • Clarifying the causes or effects of natural phenomena • Elucidating the relationship between physical variables

Take the DARE

Keep a DARE journal, such as in Resource 1.1. Record in your journal the activities you design for your students, and identify the key use(s) for you and your students. At the end of the week, review your notes, and share the following with your students:

1. What are the key uses of academic language that appear most often?

2. What are the key uses you would like to focus on more?

3. What evidence have you collected that provides you information on how students use language?

4. How might you plan with your colleagues for gathering information on language?

Making language a priority in teaching and learning requires developing the ability to shift back and forth between attending to content and attending to language use. The following tools are intended to help you become more aware of language use in your classrooms.

ACADEMIC LANGUAGE IN KEY USES

For many, academic language is synonymous with academic vocabulary. As we suggested in our opening remarks about key uses, our vision of academic language use begins with disciplinary discourse that allows us to think deeply. The power of academic language does not reside in the particular words used but in the ways language portrays knowledge, the identities it confers on those who use it, and its power in connecting current knowledge to more complex ideas, concepts, and understandings. A functional approach to language learning means that the focus is, first and foremost, on the purpose for language use and how the language is shaped by factors in context. Figure 1.4 identifies some of the factors that impact language use in academic contexts.

Be advised: These factors do not work independently but interact with each other and work together to create unique situations and conditions for language use.

1. *Topics:* The topics are content bound; meaning is drawn from one or more disciplines and their related standards.

2. *Purpose:* Guided by the academic content standards, the topic, and their associated language, the overall purpose for academic language generally corresponds to DARE, or key uses.

3. *Activities:* Activities refer to the tasks or actions in which students engage when interacting with new ideas, knowledge, or content.

4. *Roles and Stances:* Students assume many identities in schools. Sometimes students listen to information from other, more knowledgeable experts, and at times, we ask them to be the more knowledgeable experts. Sometimes, we ask them to cocreate new knowledge with others, and sometimes, we ask them to seek information from other sources.

5. *Modalities:* By approaching communication through multiple modalities—orally, visually, tactilely, and/or in writing—students have unique opportunities for language use.

6. *Audiences:* The people involved in the communication influence the way the message is conveyed. The way students use language with peers, for example, is different from the way they use language with teachers. Thus, different audiences require different registers or degrees of formality.

FIGURE 1.4 Factors That Shape the Context for Communication

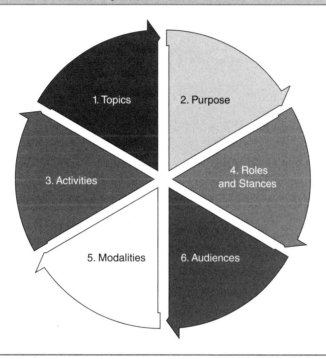

Take the DARE

How might you describe the context of communication in your school? Which factors mentioned in Figure 1.4 are taken into account in teaching and learning? Are there any unique factors that must considered for ELLs, long-term language learners, or students with disabilities? Do members of the school community engage in explicit conversations about the culture of the school? What are some spaces or structures that facilitate or have the potential of facilitating these conversations among students, teachers, and school leaders?

Use Resource 1.1 to gain insight into the potential of academic language use during instructional planning. This tool can also be considered as a springboard for conversations with grade-level teams or as a means to compare the variety of contexts in which your students learn. Don't forget that the icon of the two puzzle pieces coming together signifies that a blank template has been included at the end of the chapter for your personal use.

Use this tool to reflect and *discuss* with others the various factors impacting academic language use during teaching and learning.

Unit of Study: Exploring Weather Patterns **Grade Level:** K–2 **Timeline:** Two weeks	

Standards:	K-ESS2-1.
	Use and share observations of local weather conditions to describe patterns over time.
	CCSS.ELA W.K.7
	Participate in shared research and writing projects.
	CCSS. Mathematics
	K.MD.A.1.
	Describe measurable attributes of objects, such as length or weight. Describe several measurable attributes of a single object.
	WIDA English language development
	Standards 1-5, Integrated Strands, Grades K-5, Example Topic: Weather
Topic(s):	Local weather

ACTIVITY	MODALITIES	PURPOSE(S)— DARE	ROLE(S) OF STUDENTS	AUDIENCE(S)	OTHER
Daily weather conversations	Oral Digital	Discuss Recount	Information gathering	Peers	
Recording and graphing the weather	Tables and charts (Visual)	Recount Explain Discuss	Analyzing the weather Cocreating knowledge with others	Self Peers	
Reporting on the weather	Oral Written Digital	Recount Discuss	Expert	Peers Teacher Parents	
Video watching of weather segments	Digital	Recount Explain	Listener	Students	

LANGUAGE FEATURES IN KEY USES

In the previous section, we explained how the purpose for communication is one of the factors that impact academic language use. As we move through the various chapters of this book, we will continue to come back to this point through key uses of academic language. We propose specific key uses to enhance the academic language development of students in meaningful and relevant ways. In addition, we encourage you to reflect on and consider the sociocultural context in which interaction occurs. Part of being intentional about academic language use is identifying and being aware of DARE throughout the school day. In this section, we expand on the definitions of each key use of academic language and include specific examples of its features.

DISCUSS

Discuss, the *D* in DARE, highlights the importance of oral language development and social interaction in learning, to reinforce its role in literacy development, and to acknowledge its presence in academic content standards. Research has shown that proficiency in oral language provides children with a vital tool for thought and that structured oral language supports students' thinking processes (Bruner, 1983). As shown in Figure 1.5, oral discussions in classrooms may occur among students or between students and teachers around specific tasks.

Participation in these tasks alone is not enough to develop students' oral language. It is critical that educators make explicit the norms of working with partners or small groups. For some ELLs, for example, having access to the language needed to agree or disagree with others or to elaborate on others' ideas is a precursor to their participation in English-medium classrooms.

FIGURE 1.5 Examples of Oral Discussions

STAKEHOLDERS	EXAMPLE TASKS	WHAT STUDENTS DO WITH LANGUAGE DURING ORAL DISCUSSIONS
Student pairs	Lab experiments Problem solving Reading together	• Listen for or provide information • Ask and answer questions • Negotiate strategies or roles • Communicate ideas, information, or positions • Provide examples, details, or evidence • Agree or disagree with others • Clarify stances or views
Teachers and students	Writing conferences Guided reading Goal-setting conferences	
Groups of students	Presentations Large-group discussions Debates	

Promoting oral language development requires designing instruction around engaging content. This can be achieved by posing big questions that do not have easy answers yet provide opportunities for meaningful discussions, reading, and writing (Lesaux, 2012). Here are some ideas on how to achieve meaningful discussions:

- Select rich, complex texts that serve as platforms for learning
- Offer topic and language choices to students

- Engage in conversations about the impact of language choices
- Create spaces and design activities that engage students in collaborative learning in authentic situations
- Be creative and provide a variety of interactive activities, such as demonstrations, displays, debates, and role-plays

Take the DARE

Evaluate the effectiveness of the activities for a unit of study. How might you make these activities more interactive? What language resources are available for students to meaningfully participate? What opportunities exist to engage students in conversations about language use? How might you group students to support each other's language use in English and for ELLs from the same language background to allow their home language use to clarify or extend their learning?

Resource 1.2 is a record of students' individual contributions to discussions. You may change the features you wish to monitor once students consistently use the listed language strategies. You might also consider having different checklists for different groups of students.

RESOURCE 1.2 Monitoring Language Use During Group Discussions

Check the specific language strategies that each student uses to contribute to the discussion. Make sure the students are aware of the strategies and have practiced them in previous discussions.

Date: _____   ☑ Small-group discussion   ☐ Class discussion

Topic: <u>Discussion on Ch. 1-2 of The Giver</u>

NAME	INTRODUCES NEW TOPIC OR INFORMATION	ASKS QUESTIONS	RESPONDS TO A QUESTION OR COMMENT POSED BY OTHERS	BUILDS ON SOMEONE'S IDEA
Martin			✓	✓
Shameka	✓	✓	✓	✓
Wheaton	✓	✓		✓✓
Anna	✓✓	✓	✓	
Diego				
Ahmed			✓	

Notes:

Next time, I should pair Diego with another Spanish speaker, so he feels more comfortable.

Resource 1.3 is another tool that can be used as a source for discussion, in particular, to provide background information on particular topics and spark conversations among students.

RESOURCE 1.3 Resources for Promoting Discussions

One way to get students ready to *discuss* a topic is for them to do research, read specific resources, or watch movies together. Watching a video or movie, such as those associated with each topic of BrainPOP®, provides visual support and reinforcement for all students, including students who may have learning disabilities, students with interrupted formal education, or those who are in the process of developing English as an additional language.

Scan the QR code that leads to the BrainPOP® website. "Nutrition" is a featured movie that provides basic information related to healthful eating. After watching the movie, provide students with guiding questions, such as those below, that they can *discuss* in pairs or small groups.

Source: BrainPOP®, https://www.brainpop.com/health/nutrition/nutrition

Remember to be explicit about how students are to participate and contribute to the *discussion*. Later, the students might try to tackle the informational text on nutritional guidelines, such as those in the opening pages of the book.

Guiding Questions for Discussion About Nutrition

- What are some things that contribute to good nutrition? Why would you choose these?
- How do you balance what is nutritious and what is delicious?
- How might you plan a nutritious meal? What would you have to eat?
- What are some changes you can do or propose to others to make good choices related to nutrition?

As another way to encourage discussion of the guiding questions, direct students to the Make-a-Map® feature of BrainPOP's Nutrition topic. In pairs, ask students to *discuss* how they might answer one of the guiding questions in a concept map, and have them exchange information about their maps with each other.

Yet another feature of BrainPOP's Nutrition topic is Sortify®, a classification game. As pairs of students sort and categorize different elements of the food groups, they encounter new opportunities to engage in discussion about the topic.

An important aspect of discussion involves engaging students in monitoring their learning by setting up a series of "I can" statements with them based on individual student goals or the language expectations for a unit of learning.

ARGUE

Whether you are a student, teacher, or school leader, you probably have been asked to take a position, make a claim, and support it with specific evidence. These features are the ones most associated with the key use argue. In the context of school, arguments may be expressed in academic articles, persuasive speeches, convincing conversations, or even e-mails. Before you even respond to each of these scenarios, if you are to offer a rebuttal, you are most likely expected to (1) place yourself in the particular situation and recognize the audience, (2) evaluate text or the ongoing conversation, and (3) develop your position in relation to the situation.

Crafting arguments begins in kindergarten, when students indicate preferences and likes or dislikes, and continues through the end of high school, when students are expected to engage in sophisticated debates and create position papers and critiques. In school, we ask students to *argue* for the purpose of doing the following:

1. Supporting positions or points of view

2. Persuading others of particular courses of action

3. Showing someone the problems or difficulties with theories, approaches, or courses of action

To argue effectively, you need sophisticated language, but it pays off! Research has shown that learning to write arguments has positive impact on student learning. Students are able to build audience awareness, deepen understanding of content, better integrate ideas from multiple texts, and pay greater attention to information (Le Bigot & Rouet, 2007; Wiley & Voss, 1999). Typically, by middle school, students can identify and incorporate the following discourse and sentence features into oral or written arguments:

- An appeal to logic

- Facts, statistics, or specific examples as support for the claims

- Evidence of a research base

- Personal experiences to introduce or reinforce claims

- Counterclaims tied to evidence

- Use of linking phrases to build up a series of ideas

- Employment of emphatic words or expressions

- Repetition of key phrases

It is important for students to be aware of how the use of specific language shapes arguments so that they can intentionally choose language based on the purpose and the features of the key use. Inviting students to be decision makers means that they have choices as writers or speakers. For example, by having students determine whether to include the thesis statement at the beginning or at the end of the first paragraph, agency is shifted to them, along with the ownership of the tone and voice in the argument. DARE provides spaces for these conversations about how language works, which is often referred to as metalanguage. Metalanguage, or thinking and talking about language, encourages agency in students as it pushes students to think about the impact of their language choice on their message. In Figure 1.6, we provide examples of how features of language can be used for particular purposes in arguments.

FIGURE 1.6 Example Language Features of Arguments

FEATURES OF ARGUMENTS	EXAMPLES OF LANGUAGE FEATURES . . .	USED TO . . .
Stating claims or opinions	Using modals (e.g., may, could, should, or must)	Express certainty or uncertainty of claims or opinions
Providing supporting evidence	Including evaluative language with positive (e.g., important, significant, or impressive) or negative (e.g., questionable, insignificant, or weak) meaning	Strengthen stance
Offering counterarguments	Conceding language (e.g., while or even though)	Acknowledge other views without giving them power
Strengthening arguments	Using emotive language (e.g., critical, imperative, or inexcusable)	Evoke emotion in the audience

Even ELLs can engage in arguments if language is modeled and their level of English language proficiency is taken into account. For example, ELLs at English Language Proficiency Level 3 in Grades 4 and 5 can reasonably be expected to "identify evidence from multiple places within text" and "connect reasons to opinions supported by facts and details" in writing (WIDA, 2016).

Resource 1.4 is a checklist with examples for evaluating students' use of the language of arguments. This tool can be used by students in primary grades to identify the language of arguments in exemplary text, to provide feedback to others, or to self-assess their work. Teachers can also use the checklist to model in reviewing oral or written arguments or to assess student arguments.

Resource 1.5 is a checklist to evaluate the presence of the language of arguments. This tool can be used by students in intermediate grades to identify language useful in arguments in exemplary text, to provide feedback to others, or to self-assess their work. Teachers can also use the checklist to model in reviewing oral or written arguments or to assess student arguments.

Once students have practiced and have become familiar with how to use language to create strong arguments, it is important to provide them with opportunities to use their new skills. BrainPOP® has various resources, including movies, readings, interactive activities, and games, that provide students background knowledge on a variety of topics that could be the basis for argumentation. Resource 1.6 can be used as an activity for students to see the language used to *argue* in context.

Where is the language of argument? How are you using it? Put a check in the boxes to show what you did.

Name: _____   Date: _____

My Opinion: _____

☑ I state my opinion using

   ☑ complete thoughts

   ☑ opinion phrases (e.g., (I think,) I like, I want)

   Example: I chose "<u>I think</u>" because <u>it is my opinion and not a fact</u>.

☑ I give reasons using

   ☑ linking words (e.g., because, and, first, also, so)

   Example: I chose "first," "second," and "last" because I had three good reasons.

☑ I organize my ideas like this:

   1. Opinion
   2. Reason
   3. Reason
   4. Reason
   5. Conclusion

   Example: I chose this order because I wanted to give three reasons for my opinion.

Take the DARE

How might multimodal resources, such as those in BrainPOP®, enhance the learning experiences for ELLs, ELLs with disabilities, and other language learners? How can you maintain the students' high cognitive engagement in complex tasks, such as building claims and counterclaims for argumentation? Where would you insert these resources in the teaching and learning cycle?

RECOUNT

In DARE, recount includes a broad range of purposes, including to inform; retell experiences or events; or display knowledge, information, or ideas. Recount is the broadest of the key uses of academic language, as it includes both fiction and informational text types. In fiction, such as oral stories or written narratives, the goal, in most instances, is to entertain while in nonfiction text, whether oral or written, the goal is to share information. Figure 1.7 compares features of fiction and nonfiction *recounts*.

Use this checklist with examples to help you find or express the language of argument.

Name: _____   Date: _____

Topic of Argument: <u>Recycling</u>

In my argument,

☐ I state a claim using

    ☑ Helping words (e.g., must or should) <u>must</u>

    ☑ Evaluative language (e.g., important or critical) <u>crucial</u>

    ☑ Connectives (e.g., because or so that) <u>and</u>

    Example: I chose to state my claim using this language because <u>I wanted my audience to know this is very important.</u>

☐ I provide evidence using

    ☐ Connectives (e.g., first, but also, or finally)

    ☐ Markers

        ○ To cite evidence (e.g., "according to" or "research says")

        ○ To show agreement or disagreement (e.g., consequently or however)

    ☐ Evaluative language (e.g., important, significant, questionable, weak)

    Example: I chose to provide evidence using this language because <u>I cited research and used strong language to show the importance of recycling.</u>

☐ I include a conclusion using

    ☑ Connectives (e.g., therefore or so)

    ☐ Helping words (e.g., must or should)

    ☐ Evaluative language (e.g., important or critical)

    ☑ Connectives (e.g., because or so that)

RESOURCE 1.6 Accessing Multiple Modalities to Express an Argument

Scan the QR code that leads to the game "Time Zone X: International Space Station" in the BrainPOP® website. In pairs, ask students to *argue* for or against the placement of events on the timeline. "International Space Station" is a featured topic whereby students can learn more about space stations. The same topic provides a movie and other interactive activities for students to deepen their knowledge about the topic. It is suggested that students look for additional resources that pose different opinions about space exploration so that they can identify counterclaims and craft strong arguments. For some of the other BrainPOP® content area topics, students can take on different positions to create meaningful claims and evidence.

Source: BrainPOP®, https://www.brainpop.com/ games/timezonexinternational spacestation

FIGURE 1.7 Fictional and Nonfictional Recounts

RECOUNTS	FICTION OR NARRATIVE TEXT	NONFICTION OR INFORMATIONAL TEXT
Purpose	• To entertain	• To share ideas, concepts, or information
Examples	• Novels • Letters • Stories	• Reports • Research papers • Biographies
Language use	• Rich, descriptive language • Comparative and contrastive language • Action words • Past tense • Language of imagery	• Connectives to make text clear and coherent • Use of bullets and phrases, labeled graphics, and tables • Present tense • Factual language

Fictional *recounts* involve telling a story, often about personal events or other life experiences (e.g., novels, personal letters, and short stories). Awareness and use of fictional *recounts*, such as narratives, typically develop in early grades, often through storytelling experiences. Nonfictional *recounts*, on the other hand, involve conveying facts or describing procedures, sharing basic information, comparing processes, or stating points of view (e.g., essays or editorials). This type of writing typically is mastered later in the school years and tends to be more difficult to produce and comprehend for many students. Knowledge of how to *recount* while being developmental in nature has been related to reading comprehension and writing achievement (Olinghouse & Graham, 2009; Shanahan, 2006). Figure 1.8 presents some features and guiding questions associated with *recounts*.

FIGURE 1.8 Language Use in Recounts

PURPOSE FOR RECOUNTS	SOME FEATURES	GUIDING QUESTIONS FOR CONSIDERATION
Organizing the text (either oral or written)	• Connectives (e.g., first, before, then, and finally) • Adverbial phrases of time and place (e.g., "two days ago" or "in 1989")	Are you interested in a linear or nonlinear story?
Engaging your audience	• Feeling verbs (e.g., love, dislike, regret, or fear) • Verbs of sense (e.g., notice, feel, smell, taste, or hear)	What feelings do you want to evoke?
Creating a mood	• Perspective (e.g., first person or third person) • Time (e.g., use of various tenses)	How do you want the reader to connect with the characters?
Providing details	• Rich, descriptive, and specific language (e.g., languishing or grotesque) • Clauses and noun phrases (e.g., the last remaining dragon)	What pace and cadence do you want in your story?

Students need opportunities to play with language and use it in new creative ways. Using authentic literature as models for creativity in language use can be useful for students. Therefore, providing a variety of literature choices to students is important for expanding their repertoire and academic language use. Resource 1.7 can be used as an activity for students to see the language for *recounting* in context.

RESOURCE 1.7 Creating Recounts From Original Sources

Visit https://www.brainpop.com/socialstudies/famoushistoricalfigures/martinluther kingjr/activity/#=primary_source for the primary source activity from BrainPOP®'s topic on Martin Luther King Jr. Use these original newspaper articles to model and engage students in shared writing on how to create *recounts* from original sources. As an extension, have students bring an article from a local newspaper and create a *recount* of the current event using the article as an original source. Additionally, students who can express time and order graphically could construct a timeline to depict the events in recounts.

In DARE, nonfictional *recounts* include retelling and sharing information, concepts, or ideas. The organization and other language features vary depending on the particular *recount*. Figure 1.9 offers some examples.

FIGURE 1.9 Recounting to Inform in Nonfictional Text

EXAMPLE PURPOSES FOR NONFICTIONAL RECOUNTS	SOME FEATURES OF RECOUNTS	GUIDING QUESTIONS FOR LANGUAGE CHOICES
Reporting observations	• First or third person • Passive or active voice • Descriptive language • Absence of slang or idioms	• Is this a formal report? • What is the language that makes it formal? • Is the goal to sound objective or subjective? • Are details important?
Creating accounts of current or historical events	• Present or past tense • Dates and temporal adverbs • Specific language	• Is this a current or a historical event? • Is the goal accuracy of information or emotional appeal? • Who is the audience?
Sharing knowledge or information	• Titles and subtitles • Graphs, tables, or diagrams • Multiple paragraphs organized by topics and subtopics	• How much information will be shared? • How will it be organized? • What are the main ideas and important details?

Take the DARE

As you engage in conversations with students about language use, consider the following instructional activities:

- Select some *recounts* to share with your class. Identify relevant language features and the purpose for the author's choice in using them. Invite your students to do the same with other *recounts* that they select.

- Have students identify language choices in their own writing and defend those choices with their peers.

- Have students engage in shared writing experiences and think-alouds pertaining to their choice of language.

- Rewrite *recounts* using alternative language choices, and let your students discover how those language choices change the message or the tone of the pieces.

Resources 1.8 through 1.11 are checklists for evaluating language use in *recounts* for narrative and informative texts. The tools can be used by students to identify language useful in narrative text, to provide feedback to others, or to self-assess. Teachers can also use the checklists to model reviewing oral or written *recounts* or to interpret student *recounts*.

| RESOURCE 1.8 Language Use in Narratives: Primary Grades |

Name: _____ Date: _____

My Story: <u>The Big Hairy Hippopotamus</u>

Put a check or an X in the boxes that show how you wrote your story. Then, add to the sentence starters to share some things about your story.

☑ I have a beginning

- ○ I use language to begin the story. <u>"Once upon a time"</u>
- ○ I use words to describe the people and places in my story. <u>big, hairy</u>
- ○ I use language to organize my story.

☑ I have a middle

- ○ I use language to show what characters said.
- ○ I use language to describe what happened.
- ○ I use language to help the reader.

☑ I have an end

- ○ I use the past tense to show what happened in the story.
- ○ I use specific language to end my story.

Notes:

_____

Name: _____ Date: _____

My Narrative: _____

Use the following organizer to help you think about your language use in your written narrative. Underline the language uses you see.

Put a ✓ to show the elements you have included in each story element.

✓	STORY ELEMENT	SAMPLE LANGUAGE USES
✓	Opening	• Language that indicates the beginning of a story (e.g., "Once upon a time") • First- or third-person language to indicate point of view • Past tense
	Setting	• Descriptive language for characters, objects, or places • Comparative language to provide details about settings and create imagery • Variety of sentence beginnings
	Problem	• Words and phrases with specific or nuanced meanings • Connective language to organize the timeline of the story • Careful use of adjectives and adverbs
	Resolution	• Cause-and-effect language • Emotive language
✓	Closing	• Transitions • Conclusions (e.g., "and they all lived happily after")

Notes:

In this story, I focused on my opening and closing and used interesting language in them.

_____

Name: _____ Date: _____

Title: Report on Cats

Put a check mark or X in the boxes that show what you wrote about.

☑ My writing is about cats.

    ☑ It has two main ideas.

    ☑ It has details about my ideas.

    ☑ It has examples.

Notes:

I wrote about cats, and I wrote about my cat. I drew some pictures of cats and my cat.

_____

Name: _____ Date: _____

Title: <u>Life in the Thirteen Colonies</u>

Use this checklist to help you think about how you used language. Put a check mark or an X in the boxes that describe your writing.

☐ I organized my text using

    ☑ Titles and subtitles

    ☑ Pictures with captions

    ☑ Graphs and tables

☐ I provided information using

    ☑ Definitions

    ☑ Details

    ☑ Examples

    ☐ Connecting words

        ○ To compare and contrast

        ○ To show cause and effect

        ○ To order information

    ☐ I used specific language

        ○ Related to the topic

        ○ With precise words

        ○ With specialized terms

Notes:

I wrote about life in the colonies. I used language about transportation and how people traveled in colonial times. I made a graph on how far colonists could travel on foot, on horse, and in wagons.

As with all the resources in this book, feel free to adapt or modify them to meet your needs. In this case, the checklists may be too long for some students, and for others, more detail may be necessary. For ELLs, ELLs with disabilities, and other language learners, it might be more productive to read the checklists aloud to them. The tools are meant to inspire you and your students to reflect on language use, so make them your own.

EXPLAIN

The key use explain can be challenging because we often use the word *explain* in everyday conversations to mean to describe or to elaborate (e.g., "Explain how you got to school," or, "Explain where you went after school"). In DARE, *explain* means the following:

1. How something mechanical or natural works (e.g., *how* an engine operates or *how* an earthquake occurs)

2. Why things happen (e.g., *why* water expands when frozen)

3. What similarities and differences between objects exist (e.g., how animal cells compare with plant cells)

4. How a problem to be solved can be approached (e.g., addition of fractions)

5. What the causes or effects of actions, processes, or events are (e.g., the effects of introducing a new species into an ecosystem)

6. What the relationship between characters, numbers, or components is (e.g., the relationship between decimals and fractions)

As with the other key uses for DARE, language choices help shape explanations. Figure 1.10 gives some examples of language features that can be used to *explain* and some purposes for their use, along with examples.

FIGURE 1.10 Language Features Associated With Explanations

FEATURES OF EXPLANATIONS	CAN BE USED TO	EXAMPLES
Complex noun groups	Build detailed descriptions	The vast land area of the Americas
Pronouns for words already introduced in the text	Support cohesion throughout oral or written text	A volcano is a rupture in the crust of the Earth. It allows hot lava, volcanic ash, and gases to escape.
Action verbs	Convey a cause	Started from and evolved into
Adverbial phrases of time and place	Tell where and when actions occurred	It is found in West Africa.
Connectives and time conjunctions	Link time in cause-and-effect sequences	So, as a consequence, therefore, and when
Passive voice and nominalization	Connect events through cause and effect	The discovery of penicillin saved many lives.
Technical terms or word chains about a subject	Provide specific information	Wolves belong to the biological family Canidae.
Labeled diagrams or visuals	Support ideas or information presented	A diagram of the water cycle

You can use Resource 1.12 with your students to help support their oral or written explanations.

Resource 1.13 on page 41 can be used with older students to reflect on the reasons for using specific types of language. Remember to model their options in their language and thinking. Also, find times for students to coconstruct explanations and to have them practice thinking about language before asking them to do this independently.

These questions can be used to guide conversations with students about explanations. Students can eventually use the questions on their own as descriptors for self- or peer assessment of written text.

Name: _____   Date: _____

My Explanation: _____

Planning an Explanation

1. What is going to be explained? Circle one.

   a. How something works
   b. Why something happened
   c. How to solve a problem *(circled)*
   d. How things are related to each other

2. How do you want to organize your explanation? Pick one.

   a. As a sequence
   b. As cause and effect *(circled)*
   c. Other:

3. How might you organize your ideas with a concept map or another graphic?

   I will use an if-then chart.

After you have planned your explanation, practice giving it to a friend.

REFLECT

This chapter introduces key uses of academic language—*discuss, argue, recount,* and *explain* (DARE)—as a conceptual tool to guide conversations about language with your students and colleagues. As you reflect on teaching and learning, our hope is that language is made more explicit for all of your students, with special attention to your ELLs, ELLs with disabilities, and other language learners who may require access to content in multimodal ways. Additionally, we hope to guide you in continually looking for ways to enhance and maximize your students' opportunities for meaningful engagement in language use in your classroom.

In this last section, we offer one more tool, Resource 1.14, to help you focus on language use in each unit of learning. We encourage you to record key uses of academic language that you address as part of curriculum, assessment, and instruction to ensure their balanced representation throughout the year.

Consider sharing this resource with your colleagues and engaging in conversation with them about how to attend to language across grade levels and units of learning.

Name: _____ Date: _____

My Explanation: _____

As you plan your explanation, think about language you would like to use, and record what is the effect you are trying to achieve.

FEATURES OF MY EXPLANATION	REASONS FOR THEIR USE	EXAMPLES
Technical or specialized terms	For precision	Common denominator Proper fractions
Sequence words	To name the steps in order	First Then Finally
Example problems	To show what I mean	$\frac{3}{4} + \frac{2}{6} =$

RESOURCE 1.14 Recording and Monitoring Language Use Throughout the School Year

Make time to identify and record your focus on language use throughout the year. Use this chart to help you and your grade-level team plan for and monitor a comprehensive and balanced coverage of the various key uses of academic language.

Teacher Team: _____ School Year: _____

KEY USE OF ACADEMIC LANGUAGE	UNIT 1	UNIT 2	UNIT 3	UNIT 4	UNIT 5	UNIT 6	UNIT 7	UNIT 8
Topic/Theme	Building a House							
Discuss	X							
Argue								
Recount								
Explain	X							

Invite other classroom teachers and school leaders, as well as specialists, including music, art, and physical education teachers, to engage in the dialogue about academic language use.

TAKE ACTION

As you begin your journey to build your students' academic language use and *take the DARE*, we would like to give you some advice. The road may be bumpy and may even seem overwhelming at times, but it is definitely worthwhile. Here are some ideas for taking first steps in this journey and things to remember along the way.

1. **Language is never neutral.** Whether your students are aware of it or not, the language they use contains messages about who they are, who they think their audience is, and what they want to say. Inviting students to go behind the scenes and be intentional about their language use provides them with agency over their own messages and unveils hidden messages behind those of others. Talking with your students about language is a first step to bringing awareness to their own language use. Challenge your students to bring up language use that they notice or that they find interesting. Make sure students have time to share their perceptions with others.

2. **Using language intentionally and meaningfully is hard work.** Do not take on this task alone. Find colleagues with whom to discuss academic language use in your teaching. Collaboration around language instruction within content is crucial in sustaining your work and in building capacity for your students. Make it part of your to-do list to identify a colleague with whom to collaborate around infusing academic language into instruction.

3. **Take one step at a time.** Trying to do too much too fast might be counterproductive. Choose one key use of academic language to focus on at a time, or pay attention to language use in your class before jumping right into language instruction. Take time to feel comfortable with each key use as you *take the DARE*. Then, reflect on which approaches work for you. Keep a journal of new things you try with language and how they work. Take this advice and apply it to your students; they too need time to process and produce language unique to key uses.

4. **There is no right sequence to language learning.** Language is best learned in context. For your students, the academic content being learned is the perfect context in which to also learn language. It is the content that shapes the language of instruction. In other words, DARE does not mean that students need to learn *discuss*, then *argue*, then *recount*, and, finally, *explain*. Ideally, *discuss* happens all the time, in a variety of formats, but whether you focus on *argue*, *recount*, or *explain* depends on the content being learned and the situation in which learning occurs. To reiterate, there is not one prescriptive language sequence. As you plan for each unit of instruction, identify the key use of academic language that is the most appropriate to tackle.

RESOURCE 1.1 Factors Impacting Language Use in Academic Contexts

Use this tool to reflect and *discuss* with others the various factors impacting language use during teaching and learning.

Unit of Study: Grade Level: Timeline:					
Standards:					
Topic(s):					

ACTIVITY	MODALITIES	PURPOSE(S)—DARE	ROLE(S) OF STUDENTS	AUDIENCE(S)	OTHER

RESOURCE 1.2 Monitoring Language Use During Group Discussions

Check the specific language strategies that each student uses to contribute to the discussion. Make sure the students are aware of the strategies and have practiced them in previous discussions.

Date: _____ ☐ Small-group discussion ☐ Class discussion

Topic: _____

NAME OF STUDENT	INTRODUCES NEW TOPIC OR INFORMATION	ASKS QUESTIONS	RESPONDS TO A QUESTION OR COMMENT POSED BY OTHERS	BUILDS ON SOMEONE'S IDEA

Notes:

LANGUAGE POWER

One way to get students ready to *discuss* a topic is for them to do research, read specific resources, or watch movies together. Watching a video or movie, such as those associated with each topic of BrainPOP®, provides visual support and reinforcement for all students, including students who may have learning disabilities, experienced formal interrupted education, or may be in the process of developing English as an additional language.

Source: BrainPOP®, https://www.brainpop.com/health/nutrition/nutrition

Scan the QR code that leads to the BrainPOP® website. "Nutrition" is a featured movie that provides basic information related to healthful eating. After watching the movie, provide students with guiding questions, such as those below, that they can *discuss* in pairs or small groups.

Remember to be explicit about how students are to participate and contribute to the *discussion*. Later, the students might try to tackle the informational text on nutritional guidelines, such as those in the opening pages of the book.

Guiding Questions for Discussion About Nutrition

- What are some things that contribute to good nutrition? Why would you choose these?

- How do you balance what is nutritious and what is delicious?

- How might you plan a nutritious meal? What would you have to eat?

- What are some changes you can do or propose to others to make good choices related to your nutrition?

RESOURCE 1.4 Language Use in Argument: Primary Grades

Where is the language of argument? How are you using it? Put a check in the boxes to show what you did.

Name: _____ Date: _____

My Opinion: _____

☐ I state my opinion using

    ☐ Complete thoughts

    ☐ Opinion phrases (e.g., I think, I like, or I want)

Example: I chose _____ because _____

_____

_____

_____

☐ I give reasons using

    ☐ Linking words (e.g., because, and, first, also, and so)

Example: _____

_____

_____

_____

☐ I organize my ideas like this:

1. Opinion
2. Reason
3. Reason
4. Reason
5. Conclusion

Example: _____

_____

_____

_____

RESOURCE 1.5 Language Use in Argument: Intermediate Grades

Use this checklist with examples to help you find or express the language of argument.

Name: _____ Date: _____

Topic of Argument: _____

_____

In my argument,

☐ I state a claim using

    ☐ Helping words (e.g., must or should)

    ☐ Evaluative language (e.g., important or critical)

    ☐ Connectives (e.g., because or so that)

    I chose to state my claim using this language because _____

    _____

    _____

    _____

☐ I provide evidence using

    ☐ Connectives (e.g., first, but also, or finally)

    ☐ Markers

        ○ To cite evidence (e.g., "according to" or "research says")

        ○ To show agreement or disagreement (e.g., consequently or however)

    ☐ Evaluative language (e.g., important, significant, questionable, or weak)

    I chose to provide evidence using this language because _____

    _____

    _____

    _____

☐ I include a conclusion using

    ☐ Connectives (e.g., therefore or so)

    ☐ Helping words (e.g., must or should)

    ☐ Evaluative language (e.g., important or critical)

    ☐ Connectives (e.g., because or so that)

RESOURCE 1.6 Accessing Multiple Modalities to Express an Argument

Source: BrainPOP®, https://www.brainpop.com/games/timezonexinternationalspacestation

Scan the QR code that leads to the game "Time Zone X: International Space Station" in the BrainPOP® website. In pairs, ask students to *argue* for or against the placement of events on the timeline. "International Space Station" is a featured topic whereby students can learn more about space stations. The same topic provides a movie and other interactive activities for students to deepen their knowledge about the topic. It is suggested that students look for additional resources that pose different opinions about space exploration so that they can identify counterclaims and craft strong arguments. For some of the other BrainPOP® content area topics, students can take on different positions to create meaningful claims and evidence.

RESOURCE 1.7 Creating Recounts From Original Sources

Visit https://www.brainpop.com/socialstudies/famoushistoricalfigures/martinlutherkingjr/activity/#=primary_source for the primary source activity from BrainPOP®'s topic on Martin Luther King Jr. Use these original newspaper articles to model and engage students in shared writing on how to create *recounts* from original sources.

As an extension, have students bring an article from a local newspaper and create a *recount* of the current event using the article as an original source. Additionally, students who can express time and order graphically could construct a timeline to depict the events in *recounts*.

RESOURCE 1.8 Language Use in Narratives: Primary Grades

Name: _____ Date: _____

My Story:_____

Put a check or X in the boxes that show how you wrote your story. Then, add to the sentence starters to share some things about your story.

☐ I have a beginning.

   ○ I use language to begin the story.

   ○ I use interesting words to describe the people and places in my story.

   ○ I use language to organize my story.

☐ I have a middle.

   ○ I use language to show what characters said.

   ○ I use language to describe what happened.

   ○ I use language to help the reader.

☐ I have an end.

   ○ I use the past tense to show what happened in the story.

   ○ I use specific language to end my story.

Notes:

RESOURCE 1.9 Language Use in Narrative Recounts: Intermediate Grades

Name: _____ Date: _____

My Narrative: _____

Use the following organizer to help you think about your language use in your written narrative. Underline the language uses you see in your narrative.

Put a ✓ to show the elements you have included in each story element.

✓	STORY ELEMENT	SAMPLE LANGUAGE USES
	Opening	• Language that indicates the beginning of a story (e.g., "Once upon a time") • First- or third-person language to indicate point of view • Past tense
	Setting	• Descriptive language for characters, objects, or places • Comparative language to provide details about settings and create imagery • Variety of sentence beginnings
	Problem	• Words and phrases with specific or nuanced meanings • Connective language to organize timeline of story • Careful use of adjectives and adverbs
	Resolution	• Cause-and-effect language • Emotive language
	Closing	• Transitions • Conclusions (e.g., "and they all lived happily after")

Notes:

Name: _____ Date: _____

Title: _____

Put a check mark or X in the boxes that show what you wrote about.

☐ My writing is about _____

☐ It has a main idea.

What is it?

☐ It has details about my ideas.

What are the details?

☐ It has examples.

What are your examples?

Notes:

Name: _____ Date: _____

Title: _____

Use this checklist to help you think about how you used language. Put a check mark or an X in the boxes that describe your writing.

☐ I organized my text using

  ☐ Titles and subtitles

  ☐ Pictures with captions

  ☐ Graphs and tables

☐ I provided information using

  ☐ Definitions

  ☐ Details

  ☐ Examples

  ☐ Connecting words

    ○ To compare and contrast

    ○ To show cause and effect

    ○ To order information

☐ I used specific language

  ☐ Related to the topic

  ☐ With precise words

  ☐ With specialized terms

Notes:

RESOURCE 1.12 Language Use in Explanations

These questions can be used to guide conversations with students about explanations. Students can eventually use the questions on their own as descriptors for self- or peer assessment of written text.

Name: _____ Date: _____

My Explanation: _____

_____

_____

_____

Planning an Explanation

1. What is going to be explained? Circle one.

   a. How something works

   b. Why something happened

   c. How to solve a problem

   d. How things are related to each other

2. How do you want to organize your explanation? Pick one.

   a. As a sequence

   b. As cause and effect

   c. Other:

3. How might you organize your ideas with a concept map or another graphic?

After you have planned your explanation, practice giving it to a friend.

RESOURCE 1.13 Documenting Features of Explanations

Name: _____ Date: _____

My Explanation: _____

As you plan your explanation, think about language you would like to use, and record the effect you are trying to achieve.

FEATURES OF MY EXPLANATION	REASONS FOR THEIR USE	EXAMPLES

RESOURCE 1.14 Recording and Monitoring Language Use Throughout the School Year

Make time to identify and record your focus on language use throughout the year. Use this chart to help you and your grade-level team plan for and monitor a comprehensive and balanced coverage of the various key uses of academic language.

Teacher Team: _____   School Year: _____

KEY USE OF ACADEMIC LANGUAGE	UNIT 1	UNIT 2	UNIT 3	UNIT 4	UNIT 5	UNIT 6	UNIT 7	UNIT 8
Topic/Theme								
Discuss								
Argue								
Recount								
Explain								

References and Further Reading

Van Lier, L. (2000). From input to affordance: Social-interactive learning from an ecological perspective. In P. J. Lantolf (Ed.), *Sociocultural theory and second language learning* (pp. 155–177). Oxford: Oxford University Press.

Academic Language

Bailey, A. L. (2007). (Ed.). *The language demands of school: Putting academic English to the test*. New Haven, CT: Yale University Press.

Feldman, K., & Kinsella, K. (2008). Narrowing the language gap: The case for explicit vocabulary instruction in secondary classrooms. In L. Denti & L. Guerin (Eds.), *Effective practices for adolescents with reading and literacy challenges* (pp. 3–24). New York, NY: Routledge.

Gee, J. P. (2004). *Situated language and learning: A critique of traditional schooling*. New York, NY: Routledge.

Gottlieb, M., & Ernst-Slavit, G. (2014). *Academic language in diverse classrooms: Definitions and contexts*. Thousand Oaks, CA: Corwin.

Holland, J. H. (2006). Studying complex adaptive systems. *Journal of Systems Science and Complexity, 19*, 1–8.

Schlepegrell, M. J. (2004). *The language of schooling: A functional linguistics perspective*. New York, NY: Routledge.

Multimodality

Baldry, A. P., & Thibault, P. (2006). *Multimodal transcription and text analysis*. London, UK: Equinox Publishing.

Denning, T., Griswold, W. G., Simon, B., & Wilkerson, M. (2006, February). *Multimodal communication in the classroom: What does it mean for us?* In Proceedings of the 37th Annual SIGCSE Technical Symposium on Computer Science Education, 219–223.

Gottlieb, M., & Ernst-Slavit, G. (2014). *Academic language in diverse classrooms: Definitions and contexts*. Thousand Oaks, CA: Corwin.

Jewitt, C. (2008). Multimodality and literacy in school classrooms. *Review of Research in Education, 32*(1), 241–267.

Kalantis, M., & Cope, B. (2015). Regimes of literacy. In M. Hamilton, R. Heydon, K. Hibbert, & R. Stooke (Eds.), *Negotiating spaces for literacy learning: Multimodality and govermentality* (pp. 15–24). London, UK: Bloomsbury.

O'Toole, M. (2011). *The language of displayed art* (2nd ed.). London, UK: Routledge.

Discuss, Argue, Recount, Explain

Bruner, J. (1983). *Child's talk: Learning to use language*. New York, NY: Norton.

Le Bigot, L., & Rouet, J. F. (2007). The impact of presentation format, task assignment, and prior knowledge on students' comprehension of multiple online documents. *Journal of Literacy Research, 39*, 445–470.

Lesaux, N. K. (2012). Reading and reading instruction for children from low-income and non-English-speaking households. *Future of Children, 22*(2), 73–88.

Olinghouse, N. G., & Graham, S. (2009). The relationship between the discourse knowledge and the writing performance of elementary-grade students. *Journal of Educational Psychology, 101*, 37–50.

Quinn, H., Schweingruber, H., & Keller, T. (Eds.). (2012). *A framework for K–12 science education: Practices, crosscutting concepts, and core ideas*. National Academies Press.

Shanahan, T. (2006). Relations among oral language, reading, and writing development. In C. A. MacArthur, S. Graham, & J. Fitzgerald (Eds.), *Handbook of writing research* (pp. 171–186). New York, NY: Guilford Press.

WIDA. (2016). *Can do descriptors: Key uses edition, grades 4–5*. Madison: Board of Regents of the University of Wisconsin System.

Wiley, J., & Voss, J. (1999). Constructing arguments from multiple sources: Tasks that promote understanding and not just memory for text. *Journal of Educational Psychology, 91*, 301–311.

Ideas and Inspiration

Planning for Integrating Key Uses of Academic Language

Everything we do in life is touched by language, so whether it is delivering or receiving it, we all must be proficient language users if we are to succeed.

—Mary Jo Fresch (2014)

We have examined the crucial role language plays in all learning by providing access to the content as well as the vehicle for students' meaningful participation in school. We have also made the case that an intentional focus on academic language use ensures that all students are included in teaching and learning. In this chapter, we deepen our exploration of language within the context of curriculum and instruction by putting these ideas into action. We discuss key uses of academic language as a conceptual tool for planning, thus helping educators and students increase their focus on the development of academic discourse.

ASK

How do we plan for the integration of key uses of academic language into our practice?

Planning for language instruction should not be separate from planning for addressing the specific knowledge, skills, and practices in curriculum, assessment, and instruction. Content and language planning go hand in hand and should be interconnected. The focus for language instruction emanates from the content focus of the lesson or unit of learning. Since the content focus typically comes from academic content standards, which contain the knowledge, skills, and practices that students are expected to learn, the language focus should also be anchored in standards.

Your curriculum design—that is, the specific activities and instructional resources you select to scaffold learning—should also be considered in planning the implementation of key uses of academic language. However, the most important elements of instruction reside in the students themselves and the resources they bring from home and the community. These, too, are part of planning for language instruction, as students bring a wealth of linguistic, cultural, and experiential capital about how to make meaning from the world around them. In fact, the learning context includes both students' and educators' resources. As we set to explore how to plan for integrating DARE into instructional planning, we focus on these resources as sources for inspiration and guidance. Figure 2.1 highlights some of the sources educators rely on in planning curriculum, assessment, and instruction with key uses in mind.

FIGURE 2.1 Planning for Integrating Key Uses of Academic Language

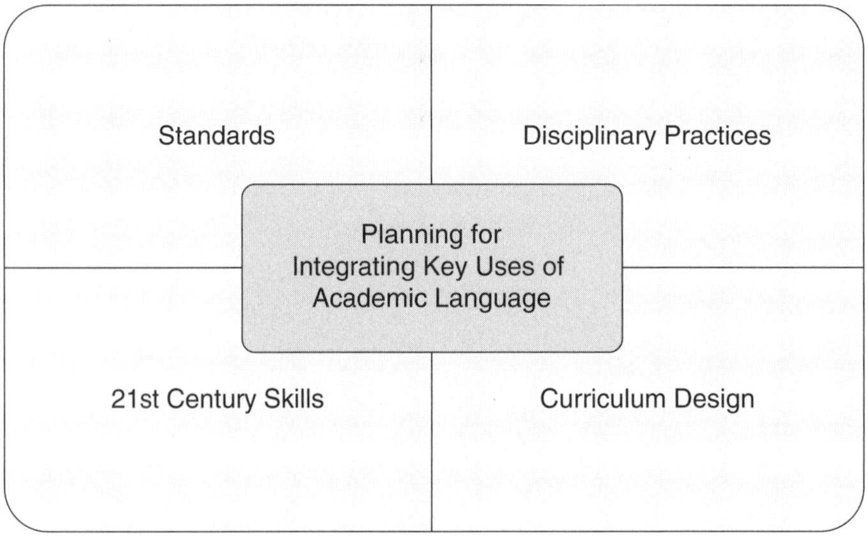

This chapter focuses on approaches for embedding key uses of academic language into classroom practices. We center on how teacher leaders can strategize for integrating key uses into school life by drawing from four primary sources. In it, we do the following:

Discuss the presence of key uses of academic language in the context of college and career readiness standards and language development standards

Argue for the value of intentional language use to support disciplinary practices

Recount how language is developed and used through engagement in 21st century skills

Explain how thoughtful curriculum design can support academic language development

As you plan to intentionally focus on key uses of academic language, we realize that the perspectives that we discuss in this chapter and are depicted in Figure 2.1 are not necessarily new to educators. What is new is the language lens we offer for analyzing the tools and sources associated with these perspectives. In this chapter, we invite you to join us in revisiting and reviewing these sources for curriculum, assessment, and instruction through a language lens.

For a long time, language has been recognized as a vehicle for learning (Dewey, 1916; Vygotsky, 1978). The ways in which language is used by students, teachers, and families have an impact on how children learn. Some researchers, for example, have attributed how well students do in school to the language patterns of particular social groups to which they belong (Bernstein, 1970; Heath, 1983). These studies highlight the unique ways of language use in school and the need to socialize students into those ways so that they can be academically successful. In spite of the existing research on the critical role that language plays in school, language development has not been fully integrated into the learning taking place in our classrooms. Key uses of academic language afford the opportunity for educators to focus and organize teaching and learning in a more manageable manner and to intentionally integrate language into content instruction.

Planning for teaching and learning includes (1) identifying what you want students to learn, (2) designing experiences for learning to ensure it is accessible and meaningful to all students, (3) checking for understanding, and (4) taking time to reflect in order to continuously improve the experience for all students. Language is critical at each stage of teaching and learning. We suggest a shift in curricular and instructional planning that includes questions about language, as depicted in Figure 2.2.

FIGURE 2.2 Questions Related to Language Within Teaching and Learning

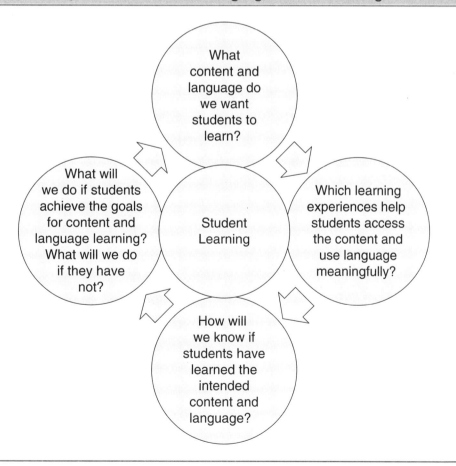

This chapter highlights the planning for language instruction using DARE as a conceptual tool for learning. Planning, in a sense, impacts every stage in the teaching and learning cycle. We plan for goals, activities, and assessment to help us collect information to guide our analysis of students' access to the intended content and academic language or the needed modification of our actions to enhance students' opportunities to meaningfully engage in learning. We carefully plan to ensure that learning is personalized so that students who may be challenged by the English language—ELLs, students with disabilities, students with interrupted formal education, and other language learners— have every chance to access grade-level content, participate, and achieve in school.

APPLY

In this section, we illustrate how DARE can help shape a language focus based on college and career readiness standards, including the disciplinary practices and 21st century skills. Subsequently, we show how to spotlight academic language use in curriculum design.

KEY USES OF ACADEMIC LANGUAGE IN STANDARDS

Academic Content Standards. As part of the accountability system for quality instruction, federal law has established the expectation that all states adopt internationally benchmarked college and career readiness standards. States have adopted or adapted the Common Core State Standards for English Language Arts and/or Mathematics (2010), the Next Generation Science Standards (2013), or developed their own college and career readiness standards. Additionally, some states address the College, Career, and Civic Life (C3) Framework for Social Studies State Standards (2013). These compendia of standards outline the knowledge, concepts, and practices that students are expected to demonstrate throughout their school experience, from kindergarten through 12th grade.

DARE, as a conceptual tool for language planning, can be used to support a large part of the interaction that takes place in the classroom. When aligned with the concepts, skills, and practices included in academic content standards, the key uses that form DARE allow students to participate meaningfully in classroom activities and show what they know. Including a focus on language during classroom instruction and assessment prepares students to participate in more complex tasks.

Key uses of academic language can help educators reflect on their language expectations derived from standards by answering the following questions:

1. How are students expected to process language to access the knowledge, skills, or practices included in this standard?

2. How are students expected to use language to demonstrate the knowledge, skills, or practices included in this standard?

Notice that the prior questions do not relate to specific grammatical forms (e.g., passive voice) or specific vocabulary but to the purpose for language use. Centering on the message makes language instruction meaningful and authentic, and content becomes part of the context in which language is used. Rather than treating academic language as an abstract subject of study, the subject remains the content, and content and language become intertwined.

Take the DARE

Reflect on the language required of the standards you address in your teaching:

- How are students expected to *discuss*?
- How are students expected to *argue*?
- How are students expected to *recount*?
- How are students expected to *explain*?

In some cases, the answer to this question is straightforward. For example, the standard may include the word *discuss*, *argue*, *recount*, or *explain*. Other times, the standard may include a word like *understand*, and unpacking the standard helps teachers identify or determine how students need to use language to be able to show that they have achieved the standard. Figure 2.3 shows examples of mathematics standards and how we have answered the questions related to the processing and use of language.

FIGURE 2.3 Determining a Language Focus for Units of Instruction

UNIT	STANDARDS	HOW ARE STUDENTS EXPECTED TO PROCESS LANGUAGE?	HOW ARE STUDENTS EXPECTED TO USE LANGUAGE?
Fractions	CCSS.MATH.CONTENT.4.NF.A.1 Explain why a fraction $\frac{a}{b}$ is equivalent to a fraction $\frac{n \times a}{n \times b}$ by using visual fraction models, with attention to how the number and size of the parts differ even though the two fractions themselves are the same size. Use this principle to recognize and generate equivalent fractions.	Understand explanations of others	Explain their own thinking
	CCSS.MATH.CONTENT.4.NF.B.3 Understand a fraction $\frac{a}{b}$ with $a > 1$ as a sum of fractions $\frac{1}{b}$.	Understand the procedure recounted by others	Recount their own procedure for solving problems about fractions

As we mentioned before, some standards may include more than one key use of academic language. Figure 2.4 shows examples of state academic standards from various content areas and accompanying key uses of academic language.

For units of learning, teachers match academic content standards to specific themes or topics. Resource 2.1 connects academic content standards, skills, and key uses of academic language to plan instruction.

FIGURE 2.4 Sample Academic Content Standards With Embedded Key Uses of Academic Language (DARE)

STANDARDS	DISCUSS	ARGUE	RECOUNT	EXPLAIN
Texas TEK §110.20. English Language Arts and Reading, Grade 8 10.C Students analyze, make inferences, and draw conclusions about expository text and provide evidence from text to support their understanding. Students are expected to make subtle inferences and draw complex conclusions about the ideas in text and their organizational patterns.		X		
CCSS.MATH.CONTENT.1.NBT.B.3 Compare two two-digit numbers based on meanings of the tens and ones digits, recording the results of comparisons with the symbols >, =, and <.				X
2-LS4-1. Make observations of plants and animals to compare the diversity of life in different habitats.			X	
Indiana WG.5.3 Map the occurrence and describe the effects of natural hazards throughout the world, and explain ways to cope with them.				X
Alaska Speaking and Listening Standards. Comprehension and Collaboration, Grade 5. 3. Summarize the points a speaker makes and explain how each claim is supported by reasons and evidence (e.g., use a graphic organizer or note cards completed while listening to summarize or paraphrase key ideas presented by a speaker).	X	X	X	

As you plan for your classes and map out the standards to address, use this tool to attend to academic language use illustrated by the key uses.

Teacher Team: _Grade 4 Science Team_   Date: _____

UNITS	STANDARDS	DISCUSS	ARGUE	RECOUNT	EXPLAIN
Fossils	Content 4-ESS1-1 Earth's Place in the Universe Identify evidence from patterns in rock formations and fossils in rock layers to support an explanation for changes in a landscape over time.	X			X
	Language WIDA-Grade 4-ELD Standard 4 Example Topic: Earth History/Materials	X			X
Animals	4-LS1-2 From Molecules to Organisms: Structures and Processes Use a model to describe that animals receive different types of information through their senses, process the information in their brain, and respond to the information in different ways.			X	X

As you see in Resource 2.1, you will soon notice that most units cover all key uses. In these cases, some decisions need to be made as to which is the primary key use. A suggestion is that once key uses of language have been identified for each unit in the school, you review their distribution; then, make choices to ensure there is a balance across all your units.

Take the DARE

In instructional teams or professional learning communities, create an aligned system for planning language instruction. Here are some ideas to begin the process:

1. Create a cross-disciplinary team to conduct the alignment process, including content area teachers, language specialists, special education teachers, literacy coaches, learning coordinators, and other experts in curriculum and instruction.

2. Use your existing curricular map to identify the sequence and organization of academic content standards throughout the school year.

3. Analyze each standard, individually applying key uses to answer the questions, "How are students expected to process language to access the knowledge, skills, or practices included in this standard?" and, "How are students expected to use language to show they have acquired the knowledge, skills, or practices included in this standard?"

4. Determine one or two key uses of academic language per unit so that there is an intentional focus on a particular language use.

5. Review the coverage and distribution of key uses throughout the year to ensure that each is adequately addressed in breadth and depth.

English Language Proficiency or English Language Development Standards. English language proficiency or English language development standards delineate language expectations within content-driven contexts, specifically for ELLs. Unlike academic content standards that identify specific knowledge, skills, and concepts, language standards offer developmental continua that illustrate how language scaffolds across progressive levels of language proficiency. Federal law mandates that state academic content standards and their language proficiency or development standards correspond to one another to facilitate continuity and coherence of ELLs' educational experiences. Thus, it is important in planning curriculum, assessment, and instruction that involves ELLs and ELLs with disabilities that language standards stand side by side with their corresponding content standards.

Two consortia and several large states, including Arizona, California, New York, and Texas, have designed English language proficiency or development standards. Those of the ELPA 21 consortium "highlight and amplify the critical language, knowledge about language, and skills using language that are in college-and-career-ready standards and that are necessary for English language learners (ELLs) to be successful in schools" (Council of Chief State School Officers, 2014, p. 1). The WIDA consortium has five English (and Spanish) language development standards; the features of academic language are overlaid onto (1) social and instructional language, (2) the language of language arts, (3) the language of mathematics, (4) the language of science, and (5) the language of social studies. It can be concluded that in the high-stakes environment in which schools operate, content and language standards must be joined in recognizing the value of academic language use for language learners.

KEY USES OF ACADEMIC LANGUAGE AND DISCIPLINARY PRACTICES

Another shift in academic content standards since 2010 is the increased attention to disciplinary practices. These practices refer to the activities in which students and teachers engage to construct knowledge, concepts, and skills in particular subject areas (Council of Chief State School Officers, 2012). In some standards, like the Next

Generation Science Standards (NGSS) and the Common Core State Standards (CCSS) for mathematics, they are called practices, whereas in the CCSS for English language arts, they are called performances. While there is increased attention to these practices, they are not new; all disciplines have specific student practices.

DARE is connected to specific practices because these practices address interaction with the content and with others for the purpose of learning. For example, as students problem-solve, which is a disciplinary practice, they need to process the language used to present or identify the problem, and they need to express language to propose solutions or share their thoughts.

For teachers trying to ensure that students are ready to participate in group work or problem solving, identifying essential language for students to communicate and express ideas, concepts, or information can be overwhelming. Key uses of academic language help to pinpoint the language focus by cutting across the academic content standard and disciplinary practice. For example, let's explore the following standard:

CCSS.MATH.CONTENT.3.MD.D.8

Solve real-world and mathematical problems involving perimeters of polygons, including finding the perimeter given the side lengths, finding an unknown side length, and exhibiting rectangles with the same perimeter and different areas or with the same area and different perimeters.

In this standard, students are expected to engage in problem solving, which also is the mathematical practice being addressed in the standard. What might be the language students need in order to participate meaningfully in problem solving? Without a tool to guide the task of identifying language, we could target vocabulary, such as *perimeter*, *hexagon*, or *meters*. We could also look at the particular language structures needed to use the vocabulary in ways that make sense to others, such as passive voice: "The length of one of the sides of the hexagon is multiplied by six." However, preferably, we could zero in on the sequential language needed to explain the procedure for calculating perimeter. Centering attention on one or two key uses adds an additional filter to tighten the focus of language instruction within a content area context.

Figure 2.5 shows some of these practices and key uses associated with them.

FIGURE 2.5 Examples of Content Area Disciplinary Practices and Corresponding Key Uses

DISCIPLINARY PRACTICE	KEY USES OF ACADEMIC LANGUAGE
CCSS ELA Practice 3: Construct valid arguments from evidence and critique the reasoning of others	Argue and discuss
CCSS for Mathematical Practice 4: Model with mathematics	Explain and discuss
NGSS Practice 3: Plan and carry out investigations	Recount, explain, and discuss

As educators plan for instruction, it is important to incorporate disciplinary practices. Resource 2.2 is a tool to help educators connect disciplinary practices to key uses of academic language.

RESOURCE 2.2 Identifying Key Uses of Academic Language in Disciplinary Practices

As you plan units of instruction, use this tool to add disciplinary practices or performances found in college and career readiness standards to key uses.

Teacher Team: _Grade 2 Social Studies Team_   Date: _____

UNIT	DISCIPLINARY-SPECIFIC PRACTICES	KEY USES OF ACADEMIC LANGUAGE			
		DISCUSS	ARGUE	RECOUNT	EXPLAIN
Personal Decisions	D1 Planning inquiries	X	X		X
Personal Consumption	D1 Asking compelling and supporting questions		X	X	X

Integrating standards and disciplinary practices helps you make some decisions in regard to selecting key uses of academic language. As shown in Resource 2.3, it is important to consider the match among key uses, academic content standards, and disciplinary practices.

Chapter 3 presents more details and information on the disciplinary practices and their relationship with assessment.

KEY USES OF ACADEMIC LANGUAGE AND 21ST CENTURY SKILLS

Another difference between previous academic content standards and this next generation of standards is a greater emphasis on 21st century skills. This knowledge and these skills, work habits, and character traits are related to collaboration, digital literacy, critical thinking, and problem-solving traits necessary to succeed in today's world. Key uses of academic language are the means to accomplish these most important skills; by honing in on specific uses of language, we are able to reach our goals with increased precision.

In designing a unit of instruction, lay out the academic content standards along with their corresponding disciplinary practices to select the most appropriate key uses of academic language.

Teacher Team: <u>Grade 6 Mathematics Instructional Team</u>   Date: _____

UNIT	STANDARD(S)	DISCIPLINE-SPECIFIC PRACTICE(S)	OVERLAPPING KEY USES OF ACADEMIC LANGUAGE			
			DISCUSS	ARGUE	RECOUNT	EXPLAIN
Polygons	CCSS.MATH.CONTENT.6.G.A.3 Draw polygons in the coordinate plane given coordinates for the vertices; use coordinates to find the length of a side joining points with the same first coordinate or the same second coordinate. Apply these techniques in the context of solving real-world and mathematical problems.	Make sense of problems, and persevere in solving them.	X			X
		Use appropriate tools strategically.	X		X	
		Attend to precision.	X		X	

According to the Partnership for 21st Century Learning, educators from diverse backgrounds must collaborate in order to provide a comprehensive, innovative, and robust education for students. When students work together, their learning experiences expand beyond acquiring knowledge to integrating various technologies, making real-world connections, and partaking of interactive experiences that result in relevant, personalized, and engaged learning.

Figure 2.6 provides examples of how 21st century skills are connected to various academic content standards.

FIGURE 2.6 Examples of 21st Century Skills Included in Various College and Career Standards

STANDARDS	EXAMPLES OF 21ST CENTURY SKILLS
Common Core State Standards for English Language Arts	**Collaboration** CCSS.ELA-LITERACY.CCRA.SL.1 Prepare for and participate effectively in a range of conversations and collaborations with diverse partners, building on others' ideas and expressing their own clearly and persuasively.
	Digital Literacy CCSS.ELA-LITERACY.CCRA.SL.5 Make strategic use of digital media and visual displays of data to express information and enhance understanding of presentations.
Common Core State Standards for Mathematics	**Critical Thinking** CCSS.MATH.CONTENT.1.OA.A.2 Solve word problems that call for addition of three whole numbers whose sum is less than or equal to 20, e.g., by using objects, drawings, and equations with a symbol for the unknown number to represent the problem.
	Problem Solving CCSS.MATH.CONTENT.6.RP.A.3 Use ratio and rate reasoning to solve real-world and mathematical problems, e.g., by reasoning about tables of equivalent ratios, tape diagrams, double number line diagrams, or equations.
Next Generation Science Standards	**Collaboration** MS-ETS1-2. Evaluate competing design solutions based on jointly developed and agreed-upon design criteria.
	Problem Solving HS-LS4-6. Create or revise a simulation to test a solution to mitigate adverse impacts of human activity on biodiversity.
Virginia Standards of Learning	**Critical Thinking** English SOL 4.6 f) Draw conclusions and make simple inferences using textual information as support.
	Digital Literacy English SOL K.13 CF Use available digital tools for reading and writing.
Alaska Standards for Culturally Responsive Schools	**Critical Thinking** A.5. Reflect through their own actions the critical role that the local heritage language plays in fostering a sense of who they are and how they understand the world around them.

STANDARDS	EXAMPLES OF 21ST CENTURY SKILLS
Alaska Standards for Culturally Responsive Schools	Problem Solving D.5. Identify and utilize appropriate sources of cultural knowledge to find solutions to everyday problems.
New Mexico Content Standards	Collaboration Physical Education 5–8 5–8 Benchmark 4: Work cooperatively with a group to achieve group goals
	Critical Thinking Social Studies 9–12 9–12 benchmark 1-D. Skills: Use critical thinking skills to understand and communicate perspectives of individuals, groups and societies from multiple contexts
National Core Art Standards	Critical Thinking Performing Anchor Standard #4. Analyze, interpret, and select artistic work for presentation.
National Association for Music Education Standards	Collaboration Rehearse, Evaluate and Refine MU: Pr5.1.3a—Apply teacher-provided and collaboratively developed criteria and feedback to evaluate accuracy of ensemble performances.

The various standards in Figure 2.6 illustrate the presence of collaboration, critical thinking, digital literacy, and problem solving for different purposes. Indeed, language is needed for students to participate meaningfully as they engage in learning around these standards. Resource 2.4 can further help you to reflect on the inclusion of 21st century skills in your planning.

Take the DARE

Game-based learning is an example of how 21st century skills and problem-based learning come together for students. Scan the QR code to access Guts and Bolts®, an online game about body systems. (Please note that this game is best played on a full-size screen.) GameUp® is BrainPOP®'s free game portal, hosting a curated collection of cross-curricular games. In Guts and Bolts®, students use critical-thinking and problem-solving skills to collaborate on designing a prototype of a body system.

Source: BrainPOP®, https://www.brainpop.com/games/gutsandbolts

If you already incorporate 21st century skills into your teaching, use Resource 2.5 to log the standards you teach and their associated skills as part of curriculum planning.

Use this tool to reflect on the presence of 21st century skills in your classroom. Decide the extent to which each skill is visible: consistently, sporadically, or not at all. Then, jot down ideas for next steps. While this tool can be completed individually, you can also use it for peer coaching. Ideally, the completion of this resource takes place after multiple observations over time.

Classroom: _____ Date: _____

SKILLS IN 21ST CENTURY CLASSROOMS	DEGREE OF IMPLEMENTATION IN MY CLASSROOM		
COLLABORATION IS EVIDENT THROUGH . . .	CONSISTENTLY	SPORADICALLY	NOT YET
Flexible grouping	X		
Explicit roles and responsibilities during group work			X
Academic and instructional language support, especially for language learners		X	
Other			
Next steps:			
DIGITAL LITERACY IS EVIDENT THROUGH . . .	CONSISTENTLY	SPORADICALLY	NOT YET
Equitable access to resources			
Meaningful use of technology	X		
Diversity of available resources			
Other			
Next steps:			
CRITICAL THINKING IS EVIDENT THROUGH . . .	CONSISTENTLY	SPORADICALLY	NOT YET
Challenging tasks and projects		X	
Open-ended questioning		X	
Use of multiple modalities		X	
Other			
Next steps:			
PROBLEM SOLVING IS SUPPORTED THROUGH . . .	CONSISTENTLY	SPORADICALLY	NOT YET
Inquiry-based instruction		X	
Interaction of students		X	
Multiple pathways to solutions			X
Other			
Next steps:			

LANGUAGE POWER

RESOURCE 2.5 Identifying 21st Century Skills and Standards in Your Curriculum Plan

Record the academic content standards and language proficiency or development standards addressed in each unit you teach. Include the corresponding 21st century skills.

Teacher Team: _____   Date: _____

UNIT/DATE	STANDARDS ADDRESSED	21ST CENTURY SKILLS
Personal stories	Content CCSS.ELA-LITERACY.RI.K.1 With prompting and support, ask and answer questions about key details in a text.	Collaboration—working with partners or in small groups
	CCSS.ELA-LITERACY.RI.K.2 With prompting and support, identify the main topic and retell key details of a text.	Critical thinking—analysis of text
	CCSS.ELA-LITERACY.RI.K.3 With prompting and support, describe the connection between two individuals, events, ideas, or pieces of information in a text.	Digital literacy—information gathered from multiple technology sources
	Language ELPA 21 ELP Standard K.2 An ELL can . . . participate in grade-appropriate oral and written exchanges of information, ideas, and analyses, responding to peer, audience, or reader comments and questions.	Problem solving through collaboration with peers

Take the DARE

After using Resource 2.5, here are some questions to consider:

1. Is there comprehensive coverage of 21st century skills throughout your units?

2. How can you increase your attention to 21st century skills?

3. What additional resources might you need to increase your attention on 21st century skills?

4. What special provisions must be made for ELLs, ELLs with disabilities, and other language learners to have access to and achieve 21st century skills?

Furthermore, you can collaborate with colleagues at your school or district to reflect on and address 21st century skills at your local level. Resource 2.6 can help you move this conversation forward.

Use this tool to identify 21st century skills that need attention in your school or district and the areas that can help you strengthen their implementation. Decide whether each skill is visible or applied consistently, sporadically, or not at all. Then, provide evidence for your answers, and jot down ideas for next steps. While this tool can be completed individually, it is more powerful if used to begin conversations among school teams or professional learning communities.

School or District: _____ Date: _____

SKILLS IN 21ST CENTURY CLASSROOMS	DEGREE OF IMPLEMENTATION IN MY SCHOOL OR DISTRICT		
COLLABORATION IS SUPPORTED THROUGH . . .	CONSISTENTLY	SPORADICALLY	NOT YET
Aligned curriculum	X		
Time and space for instructional teams to work together	X		
Opportunities for educators to observe and learn from each other		X	
Other			
Evidence of collaboration:			
Next steps:			
DIGITAL LITERACY IS SUPPORTED THROUGH . . .	CONSISTENTLY	SPORADICALLY	NOT YET
Equitable access to technology for all staff	X		
Professional learning opportunities for educators around the effective use of technology		X	
Students' meaningful engagement with a variety of digital tools		X	
Other			
Evidence of digital literacy:			

Next steps:			

CRITICAL THINKING IS SUPPORTED THROUGH . . .	CONSISTENTLY	SPORADICALLY	NOT YET
Attention to cognitive engagement of curricular tasks		X	
Advocacy for instructional supports or scaffolding so that students can access the content			X
Multimodal pathways for students, including use of languages other than English		X	
Other			

Evidence of critical thinking:			

Next steps:			

PROBLEM SOLVING IS SUPPORTED THROUGH . . .	CONSISTENTLY	SPORADICALLY	NOT YET
Teachers, families, school leaders, and support staff working together to ensure individual student success		X	
Collaborative data collection, analysis, and interpretation	X		
Shared technology resources to pool and store ideas		X	
Other			

Evidence of problem solving:			

Next steps:			

KEY USES OF ACADEMIC LANGUAGE IN CURRICULUM DESIGN

Standards, disciplinary practices, and 21st century skills all fold into curriculum design. As we move into the last perspective for this chapter, we would like to define curriculum, as it is one of those words that can have various meanings depending on the context. For us, curriculum is all encompassing, representing the sum of student experiences that occur during teaching and learning. The way we design curriculum and the choices we make set the direction in which our students will learn (Hale & Fisher, 2013).

While standards are the foundation upon which assessment and instruction are built, learning occurs through interaction with the experiences that educators craft and design around those standards. Participation in these experiences create opportunities for students to interact with the content and with each other to coconstruct knowledge and negotiate meaning. It is in these spaces that key uses of academic language become enacted by having teachers offer opportunities for students to use language in meaningful ways.

Multiple Modalities of Communication. In recent years, school and district curricula have expanded to embrace multimodalities. Multimodalities, or relying on multiple modes for communicating, is not a new phenomenon; we live, after all, in a multimodal society (Baldry & Thibault, 2006). Typical modalities of communication include oral (listening and speaking), written (paper or technology mediated), music, art, and dance. For example, news media is multimodal, as it includes auditory, visual, and textual information. In school, communication takes place in the form of oral discussions, online discussions, written formal discussions, and art processes, among many others. Being bombarded with these multiple sources and displays of information, our students have to be able to understand and flexibly use these many different modalities or ways of expression.

This variety of modalities of communication offers opportunities for educators and students in 21st century classrooms to engage in the exploration of new ways to express their thoughts and ideas outside of the traditional ones of listening, speaking, reading, and writing. Engaging in multimodal communication with students, especially those modalities that advantage in-class educational technologies, has the potential of offsetting the challenges of large class sizes, shyness on the part of some students, and ongoing data management for educators (Denning, Griswold, Simon, & Wilkerson, 2006). Being able to demonstrate learning in multimodal ways is also beneficial for historically marginalized students, including ELLs, students with interrupted formal education, and students of poverty whose expertise may lie outside of the traditional communication modes.

One of the central goals of multimodal approaches to learning is to expand the notion of literacy (think digital literacy, visual literacy, financial literacy, or assessment literacy, to name a few), along with an increased array of forms of representation and communication to help students negotiate a broader range of text types (Jewitt, 2008). In other words, the idea of text goes beyond the printed page to include paintings, architecture, sculpture, visual art, advertising, websites, and toys and games for making and sharing meaning (O'Toole, 1994/2011). According to Kalantis and Cope (2015), this new regime of multimodality is also bringing about new social power and new structures of student agency as expressions of equity.

Our hope is that as educators explore academic language through DARE, they experiment with approaches that engage students in multiple modalities. In other words, we hope that teachers invite students to pursue multimodal approaches to learning and expose them to the opportunities that expanded views of text and literacies afford. As a result, students who might struggle with traditional literacy-based modes of communication can be encouraged to demonstrate their achievement through additional pathways of personal interest.

Take the DARE

Take time to reflect and *discuss* with colleagues how to enhance your multimodal representation in teaching and learning.

- What are some modalities for communication that you already use with your students?

- Do some of these modalities appeal more to some students, especially your ELLs, students with disabilities, or other language learners? How so?

- What are some new modalities that you would like to introduce and your students would like to try?

- What support from administrators and coaches might you need to enhance multimodal approaches in your practice? How might families and communities help reinforce your efforts?

Resource 2.7 can be used to identify the various modalities of communication in curricular units and to evaluate the extent to which there is balance among the modalities in instructional activities. We encourage you to complete this tool individually and then share it with colleagues to ensure that all students engage in multimodal communication during their school day.

It is important for teachers to include both cognitive and linguistic expectations for the experiences they design. However, focusing on both new knowledge (in the form of content objectives) and new academic language (in the form of language objectives) simultaneously may not always be the most efficient way to learn. Therefore, a careful balance of using language to support meaning making and using content to provide a context for meaningful language use is necessary. For example, while students focus on problem solving, they may need language supports to engage cognitively. Requiring students to use precise academic language, especially when it is standard English, at the same time may not be feasible. Instead, once students have discovered particular approaches to addressing a problem, they may then turn their attention to thinking about the language needed to present their solutions and justify their choices. Being able to navigate and connect language and content seamlessly requires awareness on the part of the educator, as well as contingent feedback and support for the students.

Next, examples of some typical activities are presented, along with the key uses of academic language required for student engagement. The way language is used during these activities may look and sound different depending on the mental processing and the

For each activity for a unit of learning, such as the multidisciplinary one presented here, mark the modality of language use—oral, written, digital, visual, or other. Each activity may and probably will include more than one mode of communication, but as a whole, the unit should offer a balanced representation of multimodal approaches.

Unit of Study: Exploring Weather Patterns

Grade Level: K-2

Timeline: Two weeks

Standards:	Content
	K-ESS2-1. Use and share observations of local weather conditions to describe patterns over time.
	CCSS.ELA W.K.7 Participate in shared research and writing projects.
	CCSS.Mathematics K.MD.A.1 Describe measurable attributes of objects, such as length or weight. Describe several measurable attributes of a single object.
	Language WIDA English language development Standards 1-5, Integrated Strands, Grades K-5, Example Topic: Weather

Topic(s):	Local weather

ACTIVITY	ORAL	WRITTEN	DIGITAL	OTHER
Daily weather conversations	X (whole-group activity)		X (online search)	X (observation—looking outside)
Recording and graphing the weather (e.g., temperatures and precipitation)				X (tables and graphs)
Reporting on weather conditions	X (individual students)	X	X (video recording)	
Watching videos of weather segments			X	

language processing taking place. If students are engaged in demanding cognitive processing, the language representing the key use that the student produces may be imperfect—this is okay, as students are concentrating on making meaning of the concepts. However, once the students have achieved the cognitive level needed to accomplish the task, that attention is shifted to ensure they also acquire the more specific language associated with the key uses. This way, students are able to expand their language repertoire and engage in increasingly more complex tasks. To illustrate this point, Figure 2.7 exemplifies how DARE can be reflected in interactive activities, tasks, and projects.

FIGURE 2.7 Examples of Curricular Activities and Their Key Uses of Academic Language

PROJECT, TASKS, OR ACTIVITIES	DISCUSS	ARGUE	RECOUNT	EXPLAIN
Small groups working on representing multiplication as groupings of objects to determine multiple approaches to solving mathematical problems	X	X		X
Pairs conducting a lab experiment on boiling points of different substances	X		X	X
Teams participating in a debate		X		X
Individuals taking and sharing notes			X	X
Individuals or small groups making oral or multimedia presentations to the class		X	X	X

Note that two or more key uses have been identified for each activity in Figure 2.7. However, depending on the details of the activity, the key uses involved may shift. Most important, minimally, one key use of academic language should also correspond with the key use that has been identified for academic content. As with standards, the identification of a key use does not limit the language that is actually used during instruction, but rather, it focuses the attention of language instruction. Resource 2.8 is a tool that educators can use to focus on language associated with the activities that they design for their students.

We recommend that the initial decisions on key uses of academic language be made at the unit level. Doing academic language planning for a unit of learning ensures greater opportunity to balance the language focus across a series of lessons. Additionally, it allows for thinking about how all students can demonstrate attainment of standards through language, such as through multimodal ways. That way, at the lesson level, language can be differentiated for ELLs, ELLs with disabilities, and other language learners to better meet their individual needs.

RESOURCE 2.8 Key Uses of Academic Language in Curriculum

Use this organizer to identify key uses of academic language related to the activities in your lesson or series of lessons.

Unit: <u>Making Change: Counting, Adding, and Subtracting Money</u>

Time Period: _____

Standards: _____

Disciplinary Practice(s): _____

DATE	ACTIVITY	D	A	R	E	NOTES
9/15	Solving addition and subtraction problems related to cost and spending money created by students	X				
9/15	Presenting questions and answers to peers			X		
9/16	Reading "For Your Information" and viewing the movie from BrainPOP® on the topic of Money	X		X	X	
9/17	Playing the shopping game in small groups	X	X	X	X	
ongoing	Assessing accuracy of calculations (content) and academic language use during instruction with feedback to students			X		

Total Number of Instances of Key Uses: _____10_____

      Discuss: _____3_____

      Argue: _____1_____

      Recount: _____4_____

      Explain: _____2_____

Reflection on Key Uses of Academic Language:

It seems that I tend to rely on recount more than the other uses. In the next series of lessons, I will include more interactive activities so that students will have opportunities to discuss and explain assignments with each other.

Cognitive Functions. Curriculum design should include specific levels of cognitive engagement, often expressed as cognitive functions. Key uses of academic language, though compatible with cognitive functions, in essence, are quite different. We define cognitive functions as the mental activities that lead to knowledge while key uses correspond to the ways language is used for particular purposes. In Figure 2.8, we compare the features of cognitive functions and key uses of academic language.

FIGURE 2.8 Comparison Between Attributes of Cognitive Functions and Key Uses

COGNITIVE FUNCTIONS	KEY USES OF ACADEMIC LANGUAGE
Mental processes	Language processes
Take place inside one's mind	Help describe what takes place inside one's mind
Can be used to define learning goals or objectives	Can be used to demonstrate that learning goals or objectives have been achieved

While we refer to language and cognitive functions as two different concepts, there is a strong relation between the two. Notice that cognitive functions represent Bloom's revised taxonomy (see Figure 2.9). Here are some examples that show the relationship between cognitive functions and key uses of academic language:

- A student may *analyze* by comparing several options, but he or she may use language to persuade others (*argue*) to support one of options.

- A student may hear and *understand* an argument, but when engaging in activities, he or she may use language to summarize (*recount*) pieces of evidence.

Although Figure 2.9 shows some examples of cognitive functions that are matched with key uses of language to make that mental activity visible, note that there is *not* a one-to-one correspondence between the two. We do not only remember *recounts*. We may also remember *arguments*, *explanations*, or *discussions*. The table is meant to encourage you to intentionally reflect on the connection between mental processes and language use.

As you engage students in higher-order thinking, take the next step to plan for the language that will make that mental activity visible to others. Resource 2.9 can help you reflect on this.

FIGURE 2.9 Examples of Cognitive Functions and Key Uses

SAMPLE COGNITIVE FUNCTIONS (ANDERSON & KRATHWOHL, 2001)	POSSIBLE KEY USE	EXAMPLE
Remember	Recount	I can *recount* something that I remember.
Understand	Explain	I can *explain* something that I understand.
Apply	Discuss	I can *discuss* with peers how to apply something I know.
Analyze	Explain	I can *explain* a relationship between two characters that I analyzed.
Evaluate	Argue	I can *argue* for a position based on evidence that I evaluated.
Create	Discuss	I can *discuss* with peers how to create something new.

RESOURCE 2.9 Connecting DARE to Cognitive Functions

Use this resource to engage students in higher-order thinking according to Bloom's revised taxonomy. Then, record the key use of academic language you will ask students to demonstrate to make their thinking visible.

Unit: Point of View

I WILL ASK MY STUDENTS TO . . .	BY ENGAGING IN THIS ACTIVITY:	THEY WILL SHOW THEY DID IT BY DOING THE FOLLOWING:
Remember	Read Text A (pp. 13–16) and take notes	Recounting (in written form)
	Read Text B (pp. 21–22) and take notes	Recounting (in written form)
Understand	Listen carefully and follow the directions read orally from Text A for drawing a model	Explaining orally, step by step, how to construct a model
Apply	Use information from both Texts A and B	Explaining why events occurred from different perspectives
Analyze	Compare and contrast Texts A and B	Discussing with their reading buddy
Evaluate	Select their favorite text (A or B) and provide reasons for their choice	Arguing (using graphic organizers)
Create -	Create their own short story following the style of the text they selected	Recounting (in written form)

Highlighting cognitive functions in your planning can help ensure you pay attention to the depth of thinking of students throughout your unit. Categorize your activities and tasks to identify their cognitive rigor. Don't have all the fun by yourself; invite your colleagues. Norman Webb (1997) identified the following levels of cognition to explore and reflect on the depth of knowledge that you might consider in your analysis instead of Bloom's revised taxonomy.

Level 1: Recall and Reproduction. Tasks that require recall of facts or rote application of simple procedures.

Level 2: Skills and Concepts. Tasks that require some decisions about one's approach.

Level 3: Strategic Thinking. Tasks that require planning and evidence and in which thinking is more abstract.

Level 4: Extended Thinking. Tasks that require the most complex cognitive effort, including synthesis of information from multiple sources, often over an extended period of time, or transfer of knowledge from one domain to solve problems in another.

Instructional Materials in Curriculum Design. The careful selection of textbooks, digital technology, graphic supports, and other resources helps to round out a comprehensive plan for designing teaching and learning. (For a more in-depth discussion on the selection of instructional materials, see Chapter 4.) These materials afford students opportunities to use language meaningfully and engage students in using language in multimodal ways to support their development of academic language.

Once curricular activities identify the academic content, along with key uses, educators must look for ways to ensure students get a chance to see and hear models of academic language use, both through their own use of language—with teachers as models—and through the language in curricular materials. These models let students absorb the discourse of the discipline and the individual features of academic language that distinguish it from other disciplines.

Scan the QR code, go to "Unsolved Mysteries," and read the excerpt from a science text on unsolved mysteries of Mars, an activity in a unit on planets and the solar system. Overall, the intent of this text is to provide information to the reader about Mars, but within that larger purpose, there are many different configurations of scientific language. See if you can identify specific language features of this passage. (Hint: Some features are presented in the table that follows.)

Source: BrainPOP®, https://www.brainpop.com/science/space/mars/fyi/#tab=4

FIGURE 2.10 A Sample Science Text: Mars Unsolved Mysteries

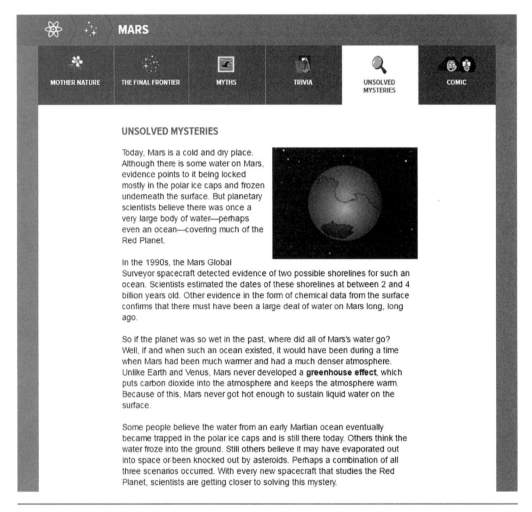

Source: BrainPOP®, https://www.brainpop.com/science/space/mars/fyi/#tab=4

Here are some of the language features in the text.

FEATURES OF LANGUAGE IN MARS TEXT	ACTUAL LANGUAGE IN THE TEXT
Use of declarative sentences, typically in simple present tense, to describe current state	"Today, Mars is a cold and dry place . . ."
Use of declarative sentences, in past tense, to describe what happened	"Mars never got hot enough to sustain liquid water on the surface . . ."
Use of connectives/clauses related to time to organize information	"Today, . . ." "In the 1990s, . . ."
Use of third person to infer neutrality	"The Mars Global Surveyor spacecraft detected . . ." "Scientists believe . . ."
Use of facts to describe	". . . between 2 and 4 billion years old."

From these features and using the information from Chapter 1, we can conclude that the key use of academic language of this text is *recount*. While the second paragraph provides evidence of water and the third paragraph hypothesizes about the existence of water, the overall purpose of the text is to provide facts about Mars. Identifying the language students are expected to process or produce is important, as it makes language use explicit, especially for ELLs, students with disabilities, or other language learners who find grade-level text challenging.

In Resource 2.10, we combine curricular resources, key uses of academic language, and language features for a unit of study, in this case, on asthma. This tool may help in planning for academic language use for a unit with colleagues.

RESOURCE 2.10 Representation of Key Uses of Academic Language in Curricular Resources

Make a list of the resources for a unit, and then match each resource with a key use of academic language. Record the particular language features associated with each key use that you would like to highlight during instruction.

Teacher Team: Grade 3 Instructional Team   Unit: Asthma

CURRICULAR RESOURCES	KEY USES OF ACADEMIC LANGUAGE				LANGUAGE FEATURES
	D	A	R	E	
Textbook			X	X	• Text organization • Coherence across text
Movie (i.e., BrainPOP®)	X	X			• Use of emotive language to argue • Summarizing others' points
Personal story			X		• Text organization • Sequence of events
Website		X	X		• Use of emotive language to argue

Note: Refer to the resources in Chapter 1 for specific features related to each key use.

Resource 2.11 of this chapter provides educators with a comprehensive plan for focusing on DARE as part of curriculum design.

REFLECT

Planning for curriculum and instruction is a dynamic and fluid process. Each year veteran and young professionals alike, with the support of school leaders, find it necessary to adjust and modify units of instruction to meet the needs of their students. As part of this annual curricular adjustment, teachers tap different linguistic, digital, and

Curricular activities and instructional materials provide opportunities for students to see and practice language in meaningful ways. For each activity, mark the level of cognitive engagement and the key uses of academic language to be highlighted.

Academic Content Area: _____

Grade Level: _____

Unit: _____ Time Span: _____

Unit Goal(s): _____

ACTIVITY OR INSTRUCTIONAL MATERIAL	LEVEL OF COGNITIVE ENGAGEMENT	FOCUS ON KEY USES OF ACADEMIC LANGUAGE			
		DISCUSS	ARGUE	RECOUNT	EXPLAIN
1. Building a model	Create	X			X
2.					
3.					
4.					
5.					
6.					
7.					
8.					

community resources to better match their students' interests. Think about what it takes to align curriculum to academic content standards, design effective curriculum around it, and, all the while, challenge your students to advance teaching and learning.

As you begin planning for integrating key uses of academic language into curriculum and instruction, identify sources for support and opportunities for collaboration in this endeavor.

1. What resources exist to support the implementation of curriculum and instruction?
    a. Academic content standards and language proficiency or language development standards?
    b. Disciplinary practices?
    c. 21st century skills?

2. What resources exist to support the following?
    a. Students? ELLs? Students with disabilities? Other language learners?
    b. Curriculum design?

3. What structures, such as professional learning communities or dedicated joint-planning time, exist for collaboration with colleagues around this work?

TAKE ACTION

Think about the various curricular activities in which students participate daily. How are expectations for language use by students, teachers, and others who participate in these activities made visible? For students, this would result in equitable access to meaningful participation. For teachers, this would mean a focused approach to ensure students' academic language development. For family and community members, this would open new opportunities for participation in their students' education. Having hopefully gleaned some ideas and inspiration from this chapter, how might you answer the following questions:

1. What do you consider the primary influence in shaping academic language use in school? How do you and your colleagues help shape it? How might you or you and your colleagues help enhance it?

2. How do you maximize students' opportunities for academic language learning? How do your disciplinary practices exemplify the role of DARE in learning?

3. To what extent is your classroom ready for 21st century learning? Which skills do you already incorporate into your curriculum, and which ones do you plan to tackle next?

4. How do you plan for curriculum to ensure student access to grade-level content, and how might you modify this planning to include opportunities for meaningful language use for each and every student?

RESOURCE 2.1 Identifying Key Uses of Academic Language in Content Standards and Language Standards

As you plan for your classes and map out the standards to address, use this tool to attend to academic language use illustrated by DARE.

Teacher Team: _____   Date: _____

UNITS	STANDARDS	DISCUSS	ARGUE	RECOUNT	EXPLAIN
	Content Language				

As you plan units of instruction, use this tool to add disciplinary practices found in college and career readiness standards to key uses.

Teacher Team: _____ Date: _____

UNIT	DISCIPLINARY-SPECIFIC PRACTICES	KEY USES OF ACADEMIC LANGUAGE			
		DISCUSS	ARGUE	RECOUNT	EXPLAIN

Chapter 2 Resources

RESOURCE 2.3 Aligning Language Foci With Academic Content Standards and Disciplinary Practices

In designing a unit of instruction, lay out the academic content standards, along with their corresponding disciplinary practices, to select the most appropriate key uses of academic language.

Teacher Team: _____ Date: _____

UNIT	STANDARD(S)	DISCIPLINE-SPECIFIC PRACTICE(S)	OVERLAPPING KEY USES OF ACADEMIC LANGUAGE			
			DISCUSS	ARGUE	RECOUNT	EXPLAIN

Chapter 2 Resources

Use this tool to reflect on the presence of 21st century skills in your classroom. Decide the extent to which each skill is visible: consistently, sporadically, or not at all. Then, jot down ideas for next steps. While this tool can be completed individually, you can also use it for peer coaching. Ideally, the completion of this resource takes place after multiple observations over time.

Classroom: _____ Date: _____

SKILLS IN 21ST CENTURY CLASSROOMS	DEGREE OF IMPLEMENTATION IN MY CLASSROOM		
COLLABORATION IS EVIDENT THROUGH . . .	CONSISTENTLY	SPORADICALLY	NOT YET
Flexible grouping			
Explicit roles and responsibilities during group work			
Academic and instructional language support, especially for language learners			
Other			
Next steps:			
DIGITAL LITERACY IS EVIDENT THROUGH . . .	CONSISTENTLY	SPORADICALLY	NOT YET
Equitable access to resources			
Meaningful use of technology			
Diversity of available resources			
Other			
Next steps:			
CRITICAL THINKING IS EVIDENT THROUGH . . .	CONSISTENTLY	SPORADICALLY	NOT YET
Challenging tasks and projects			
Open-ended questioning			
Use of multiple modalities			
Other			
Next steps:			
PROBLEM SOLVING IS SUPPORTED THROUGH . . .	CONSISTENTLY	SPORADICALLY	NOT YET
Inquiry-based instruction			
Interaction of students			
Multiple pathways to solutions			
Other			
Next steps:			

Chapter 2 Resources

RESOURCE 2.5 Identifying 21st Century Skills and Standards in Your Curriculum Plan

Record the academic content standards and language proficiency or development standards addressed in each unit you teach. Include the corresponding 21st century skills.

Teacher Team: _____ Date: _____

UNIT/DATE	STANDARDS ADDRESSED	21ST CENTURY SKILLS
	Content Language	

Use this tool to identify 21st century skills that need attention in your school or district and the areas that can help you strengthen their implementation. Decide whether each skill is visible or applied consistently, sporadically, or not at all. Then, provide evidence for your answers, and jot down ideas for next steps. While this tool can be completed individually, it is more powerful if used to begin conversations among school teams or professional learning communities.

School or District: _____ Date: _____

Chapter 2 Resources

SKILLS IN 21ST CENTURY CLASSROOMS	DEGREE OF IMPLEMENTATION IN MY SCHOOL OR DISTRICT		
COLLABORATION IS SUPPORTED THROUGH . . .	CONSISTENTLY	SPORADICALLY	NOT YET
Aligned curriculum			
Time and space for instructional teams to work together			
Opportunities for educators to observe and learn from each other			
Other			
Evidence of collaboration:			
Next steps:			
DIGITAL LITERACY IS SUPPORTED THROUGH . . .	CONSISTENTLY	SPORADICALLY	NOT YET
Equitable access to technology for all staff			
Professional learning opportunities for educators around the effective use of technology			
Students' meaningful engagement with a variety of digital tools			
Other			
Evidence of digital literacy:			
Next steps:			

(Continued)

Chapter 2 Resources

SKILLS IN 21ST CENTURY CLASSROOMS	DEGREE OF IMPLEMENTATION IN MY SCHOOL OR DISTRICT		
CRITICAL THINKING IS SUPPORTED THROUGH . . .	CONSISTENTLY	SPORADICALLY	NOT YET
Attention to cognitive engagement of curricular tasks			
Advocacy for instructional supports or scaffolding so that students can access the content			
Multimodal pathways for students, including use of languages other than English			
Other			
Evidence of critical thinking:			
Next steps:			

PROBLEM SOLVING IS SUPPORTED THROUGH . . .	CONSISTENTLY	SPORADICALLY	NOT YET
Teachers, families, school leaders, and support staff working together to ensure individual student success			
Collaborative data collection, analysis, and interpretation			
Shared technology resources to pool and store ideas			
Other			
Evidence of problem solving:			
Next steps:			

For each activity for a unit of learning, mark the modality of language use—oral, written, digital, visual, or other. Each activity may and probably will include more than one mode of communication, but as a whole, the unit should offer a balanced representation of multimodal approaches.

Unit of Study: Grade Level: Timeline:					
Standards:	Content Language				
Topic(s):					
ACTIVITY		**ORAL**	**WRITTEN**	**DIGITAL**	**OTHER**

Use this organizer to identify the key uses of academic language related to the activities in your lesson or series of lessons.

Unit: _____

Time Period: _____

Standards: _____

Disciplinary Practice(s): _____

DATE	ACTIVITY	D	A	R	E	NOTES

Total Number of Instances of Key Uses: _____

     Discuss: _____

     Argue: _____

     Recount: _____

     Explain: _____

Reflection on Key Uses of Academic Language:

Use this resource to engage students in higher-order thinking according to Bloom's revised taxonomy. Then, record the key use of academic language you will ask students to demonstrate to make their thinking visible.

Unit: _____

I WILL ASK MY STUDENTS TO . . .	BY ENGAGING IN THIS ACTIVITY:	THEY WILL SHOW THEY DID IT BY DOING THE FOLLOWING:

Chapter 2 Resources

Make a list of the resources for a unit, and then match each resource with a key use of academic language. Record the particular language features associated with that key use that you would like to highlight during instruction.

Teacher Team: _____ Unit: _____

CURRICULAR RESOURCES	KEY USES OF ACADEMIC LANGUAGE				LANGUAGE FEATURES
	D	A	R	E	

Note: Refer to the resources in Chapter 1 for specific features related to each key use.

Curricular activities and instructional materials provide opportunities for students to see and practice language in meaningful ways. For each activity, mark the level of cognitive engagement and the key uses of academic language to be highlighted.

Academic Content Area: _____

Grade Level: _____

Unit: _____ Time Span: _____

Unit Goal(s): _____

ACTIVITY OR INSTRUCTIONAL MATERIAL	LEVEL OF COGNITIVE ENGAGEMENT	FOCUS ON KEY USES OF ACADEMIC LANGUAGE			
		DISCUSS	ARGUE	RECOUNT	EXPLAIN
1.					
2.					
3.					
4.					
5.					
6.					
7.					
8.					

Chapter 2 Resources

References and Further Reading

Benson, D. J. (2012). *The standards-based teaching/learning cycle* (2nd ed.). Denver: Colorado Coalition for Standards-Based Education. Retrieved from https://www.cde.state.co.us/cdechart/standards-basedteachingandlearningcycle

Bernstein, B. (1970). Postscript. In D. M. Gahagan & G. A. Gahagan (Eds.), *Talk reform: Explorations in language for infant school children* (pp. 115–117). London: Routledge & Kegan Paul.

Dewey, J. (1916). *Democracy and education: An introduction to the philosophy of education*. New York: Macmillan.

Heath, S. B. (1983). *Ways with words: Language, life, and work in communities and classrooms*. Cambridge, England: Cambridge University Press.

Vygotsky, L. S. (1978). *Mind in society: The development of higher psychological processes*. Cambridge, MA: Harvard University Press.

Standards

Council of Chief State School Officers. (2014). *ELPA 21 English language proficiency standards with correspondences to K–12 practices and Common Core State Standards*. Retrieved from http://www.elpa21.org/sites/default/files/Final%204_30%20ELPA21%20Standards_1.pdf

National Council for Social Studies. (2013). *College, career, and civic life (C3) framework for social studies state standards: Guidance for enhancing the rigor of K–12 civics, economics, geography, and history*. Silver Spring, MD: Author.

National Governors Association Center for Best Practices & Council of Chief State School Officers. (2010). *Common Core State Standards for English language arts and literacy in history/social studies, science, and technical subjects*. Washington, DC: Authors.

National Governors Association Center for Best Practices & Council of Chief State School Officers (2010). *Common Core State Standards for mathematics*. Washington, DC: Authors.

NGSS Lead States. (2013). *Next generation science standards: For states, by states*. Washington, DC: National Academies Press.

O'Hara, S., Pritchard, R., & Zwiers, J. (2012). Identifying academic language demands in support of the Common Core Standards. *Best Practices for Teaching ELLs*, 7(17). Retrieved from http://www.ascd.org/ascd-express/vol7/717-ohara.aspx

Valdés, G., Menken, K., & Castro, M. (2015). (Eds.). *Common Core, bilingual and English language learners: A resource for educators*. Philadelphia: Caslon.

WIDA Consortium. (2012). *Amplification of the English language development standards, kindergarten–Grade 12*. Madison: Board of Regents of the University of Wisconsin System.

WIDA Consortium. (2013). *Los estándares del desarrollo del lenguaje español de WIDA, desde Kínder hasta el Grado 12* (Edición 2013). Madison: Board of Regents of the University of Wisconsin System.

Disciplinary Practices

Chauvin, R., & Theodore, K. (2015). Teaching content-area literacy and disciplinary literacy. *SEDL*, 3(1).

Council of Chief State School Officers. (2012). *Framework for English language proficiency development standards corresponding to the Common Core State Standards and the Next Generation Science Standards*. Washington, DC: Author.

Driscoll, M. (1999). *Developing algebraic habits of mind: A framework for classroom questions aimed at understandings thinking*. Retrieved from http://courses.edtechleaders.org/documents/Patterns/DriscollPart1.pdf

Hymes, D. (1964). *Language in culture and society: A reader in linguistics and anthropology*. New York: Harper & Row.

Robin, J., Chilla, N., & Gardner, M. (2015). *An educator's guide to disciplinary literacy*. New York, NY: NYC Department of Education.

21st Century Skills

National Education Association. (n.d.) *Preparing 21st century students for a global society: An educator's guide to the "Four Cs."* Retrieved from http://www.nea.org/assets/docs/A-Guide-to-Four-Cs.pdf

Partnership for 21st Century Skills. (2011). *P21 Common Core toolkit: A guide to aligning the Common Core Standards with the framework for 21st century skills.* Retrieved from http://www.p21.org/storage/documents/P21CommonCoreToolkit.pdf

Rotherham, A. J., & Willingham, D. (2009). 21st century skills: The challenges ahead. *Educational Leadership, 67*(1), 16–21

University of Houston. (n.d.) *New technologies and 21st century skills.* Retrieved from http://newtech.coe.uh.edu

Curriculum Design

Anderson, L. W., & Krathwohl, D. R. (Eds.). (2001). *A taxonomy for learning, teaching, and assessing: A revision of Bloom's taxonomy of educational objectives.* New York, NY: Longman.

Baldry, A., & Thibault, P. J. (2006): *Multimodal transcription and text analysis: A multimedia toolkit and coursebook.* London & Oakville, UK: Equinox.

Denning, T., Griswold, W. G., Simon, B., & Wilkerson, M. (2006). Multimodal communication in the classroom: What does it mean for us? *Proceedings of the 37th SIGCSE Technical Symposium on Computer Science Education* (pp. 219–223). Houston, TX: ACM Special Interest Group on Computer Science Education.

Hale, J. A., & Fisher, M. (2013). *Upgrade your curriculum: Practical ways to transform units and engage students.* Alexandria, VA: ASCD.

Jewitt, C. (2008). Multimodality and literacy in school classrooms. *Review of Research in Education, 32*(1), 241–267.

Kalantis, M., & Cope, B. (2015). Regimes of literacy. In M. Hamilton, R. Hayden, K. Hibbert, & R. Stoke. *Negotiating spaces for literacy learning: Multimodality and governmentality* (pp. 15–24). London: Bloomsbury.

O'Toole, M. (2011). *The language of displayed art* (2nd ed.). London & New York: Routledge. (Original work published 1994).

Webb, N. L. (1997). *Criteria for alignment of expectations and assessments in mathematics and science education.* Washington, DC: Council of Chief State School Officers.

Attainment and Achievement

Assessing Key Uses of Academic Language Across the Content Areas

Mastery of academic language is arguably the single most important determinant of academic success for individual students. . . . It is not possible to overstate the role that language plays in determining students' success with academic content.

—David J. Francis, Mabel Rivera, Nonie Lesaux, Michael Kieffer, and Hector Rivera (2006)

When you hear the word *assessment*, what does it conjure up? What immediately comes to mind? How do assessment data impact your professional life? What does language have to do with it?

Assessment, by definition, implies a collection of data from multiple sources over time as a basis for decision making. We would like to extend that notion to be inclusive of multiple stakeholders—including students, families, teachers, and school leaders—and multiple modalities—oral, textual, graphic, and visual—across multiple content areas. In educational settings, we also must acknowledge that assessment occurs across multiple levels of implementation—from individual classrooms to schools to programs to districts to states and beyond.

ASK

How might we assess key uses of academic language in our content classrooms?

This chapter views assessment through an academic language lens. More specifically, it envisions assessment of key uses of academic language as a cornerstone for organizing and implementing curriculum and instruction. Through examples, we show how assessment can serve as a tool for advocacy and equity to advance educational opportunities and outreach for students and teachers. Figure 3.1 portrays the approach we take in this chapter to discuss assessment through a deeper exploration of how assessment practices look like across some of the typical subject areas in schools.

FIGURE 3.1 Assessing Key Uses of Academic Language Across Content Areas

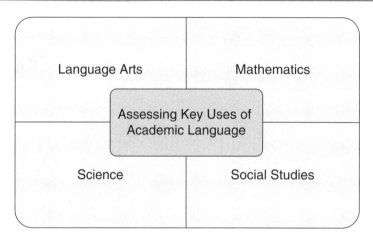

Alongside its concepts and practices, each content area or discipline represents and exemplifies key uses of academic language. In this chapter, we explore assessment that naturally occurs within the confines of instruction—hence instructional assessment as the backdrop for examining key uses in the content areas. We also speak to how performance assessment can be expressed by multimodalities associated with DARE in units of learning. Our goal is to lead stakeholders to rethink and reimagine how assessment and reporting of data can represent language in tandem with content. In it, we DARE teachers, school leaders, and teacher educators to do the following:

Discuss the role of key uses of academic language as a conceptual tool for assessing content area concepts

Argue for the use of multiple measures and multiple modalities to highlight academic language use within disciplinary practices

Recount ideas related to instructional assessment around key uses of academic language

Explain how key uses of academic language can be integrated into content assessment for language arts, mathematics, science, and social studies

Teachers, teacher teams, or professional learning communities should have dedicated time to coplan, coassess, and use evidence from assessment to improve teaching and learning. When teachers are able to work together in collaborative partnerships, instruction and assessment are strengthened and become more cohesive, which, in turn, benefits students and teachers alike (Honigsfeld & Dove, 2010).

When we say assessment, we do not mean multiple-choice tests, matching activities, or fill-in-the-blank exercises, although, at times, those kinds of measures do have their place. What we are referring to is performance assessment—that is, having students be a part of the process and having them show what they can do with content and language in relevant, meaningful ways.

PERFORMANCE ASSESSMENT

In performance assessment, students express learning through real-life, authentic situations. Performance assessment connects students' experiences with curriculum through active participation in hands-on activities and tasks. This approach to assessment allows students to do the following:

- Use multiple modalities or multiliteracies to express themselves, rather than being confined to paper-and-pencil tasks

- Access supports such as visuals, graphics, and manipulatives that are part of scaffolded instruction to make meaning during assessment

- Work and interact with partners or in small groups to problem-solve yet express their thoughts independently

- Reflect on their learning (Gottlieb, 2016)

In today's classrooms, with their eclectic mix of students, assessment as instruction has to be flexible in order to maximize each student's opportunities for academic success. As each content area has its own way of thinking and doing, so too are key uses of academic language applied in distinct ways. Assessment has to reflect that reality; for example, the language of citing evidence in a mock trial as part of an argument is much different from indicating evidence of a correct procedure in recounting a mathematics problem. In fact, when designing instructional assessment tasks, there are many language-related options to consider, as shown in Figure 3.2.

Take the DARE

Using Figure 3.2, circle your most important language considerations in planning classroom instruction and assessment. Think about your students and how you would incorporate or embed these language choices into your lessons and units of learning. Share your thinking with your grade-level colleagues.

STUDENT-CENTERED ASSESSMENT

Throughout their years at school, students assume many identities—mathematicians, scientists, journalists, and anthropologists, for example—yet when it comes time for assessment, their voices are often muted. We believe that student agency is integral to

FIGURE 3.2 Drawing Upon Language-Related Options for Assessment Planning

CONSIDERATIONS FOR LANGUAGE USE IN INSTRUCTIONAL ASSESSMENT	CHOICES IN DESIGN
1. Multiple modes for input and output	Oral or written language along with images and gestures
2. Multiple domains for input and output	Receptive (listening, reading, and viewing) or productive (speaking and writing)
3. Multiple languages	English and additional languages
4. Multiple representations by students	Visual, tactile, kinesthetic, or linguistic
5. Multiple language models to draw upon	Personal, family members, other adults, or peers
6. Multiple supports or scaffolds	Textual, auditory, sensory, or linguistic
7. Multiple audiences	Peers, teachers, family members, or others (e.g., journalists, authors, mathematicians, scientists, or historians)
8. Multiple key uses of academic language	*Discuss, argue, recount,* and/or *explain*

becoming independent and responsible learners, and we attempt throughout the book to honor student choice. Such is the case of the Expeditionary Learning schools. Not only are their practices student centered, but they often require students to analyze and present their own learning to others across the content areas. The practices include the following:

- Formulating learning targets

- Checking for understanding

- Providing models, critiques, and descriptive feedback

- Using data with students

- Reporting with standards-based grading

- Celebrating learning

- Engaging in student-led conferences

- Presenting learning exhibitions or student portfolios (Berger, Rugen, & Woodfin, 2014)

Figure 3.3 illustrates ways in which students might reflect on their performance tasks or projects, organized by DARE with example student reflections.

FIGURE 3.3 Key Uses of Academic Language Associated With Performance Assessment Along With Student Self-Assessment Based on Criteria for Success

KEY USE OF ACADEMIC LANGUAGE	SAMPLE PERFORMANCE ASSESSMENT	EXAMPLE STUDENT REFLECTION
Discuss (with others)	• Paired questions and answers • Academic conversations • Interactive book talks • Interviews between students or students and adults • Two-way tasks	• I share my thoughts with my group. • I give information to my partner. • I add to others' thoughts and information.
Argue	• Position statements or papers • Debates on issues, events, or policies • Editorials or op-ed pieces • Critiques of videos, games, movies, or websites • Research findings	• I make claims or give opinions with supporting evidence or reasons. • I state my stance on the issues. • I agree or disagree with others' positions.
Recount	• Biographies • Multimodal reports • Content-based learning logs • Oral or written summaries • Note taking or outlining • Reenactments of scenes, genres, or events (e.g., folktales)	• I follow a timeline of events. • I illustrate what has happened (orally, visually, or in writing). • I relate my own experiences to others.
Explain	• Instructions to others • Demonstrations of "how to do" activities • Task analyses • Student-led conferences • Descriptions of how or why	• I provide step-by-step analyses of tasks. • I summarize why some things happen. • I describe how things happen, as in processes and procedures.

Take the DARE

Which of the performance assessment tasks in Figure 3.3 are you familiar with or are already part of your teaching repertoire? How might you extend these ideas to reflect a specific content area? How might you generate more projects or products from these tasks?

This rubric has wide applicability; you are welcome to make it discipline specific or to retain its more generalized criteria and use it as a collaborative tool among teachers. For language learners in dual-language or immersion programs, consider adding "in home language and English" to the descriptors.

Task: _____   Date: _____

Student: _____   Grade: _____

For the given performance task and selected key use, check the box to indicate the extent to which students can do the following:

KEY USE OF ACADEMIC LANGUAGE	ATTEMPTING	ADVANCING	APPROACHING	ATTAINING
Discuss by	Responding orally when prompted in brief segments	Participating in academic conversations when prompted	Engaging in academic conversations on a variety of content-related topics using discourse features of the disciplines	Engaging in extended academic conversations on a variety of content-related topics using grade-level discourse of the disciplines
	☐	☑	☐	☐
Argue by	Presenting, orally or in writing, brief claims or opinions	Organizing oral and written presentations around claims or opinions with evidence or reasons	Organizing oral and written presentations around claims or opinions supported by logical evidence or reasons	Organizing oral and written presentations around solid claims or opinions justified with strong evidence or reasons
	☐	☑	☐	☐
Recount by	Retelling, orally or in writing, brief personal experiences or events	Retelling with some description, orally or in writing, personal experiences or a series of events	Retelling with description, orally or in writing, personal experiences or sequences of events	Retelling with rich description, orally or in writing, personal experiences or logical sequences of events
	☐	☐	☑	☐
Explain by	Stating, orally or in writing, the *how* or *why* of phenomena in brief accounts	Describing with sketchy details, orally or in writing, the *how* or *why* of phenomena	Summarizing with details, orally or in writing, the *how* or *why* of phenomena	Summarizing with vivid details, orally or in writing, the *how* or *why* of phenomena
	☐	☐	☑	☐

How might you involve students in the process? How might you expand the examples for each key use of academic language with your students or even convert them into a checklist?

A project that is agreed upon by teachers across classrooms, such as by grade or department, and that is interpreted using the same criteria can be considered common assessment. Defined from the vantage point of teachers, common assessment sets a collective vision and attainable instructional targets for students, generally corresponding with a unit of learning. It represents what teachers value, what has been taught, and what data are meaningful in making grade-level or schoolwide decisions (Gottlieb & Nguyen, 2007). Oftentimes, student work on common assessment tasks or projects is interpreted with rubrics, such as the one in Resource 3.1, which focuses on DARE across the content areas. It articulates general descriptors for each key use of academic language for four performance levels.

Take the DARE

How might you adapt this rubric so it reflects the range of students in your classroom? For example, ELLs may better express DARE initially through oral language than through written language, especially when instruction is in English. Some students with visual disabilities may need large-size print; others may have to have directions reread to them. Still other language learners may need to listen to multiple language models to gain a sense of the use of academic language in varying contexts.

APPLY

In this section, we exemplify how teachers can integrate key uses of academic language into instructional assessment in four content areas: language arts, mathematics, science, and social studies. Drawing from disciplinary practices and performances introduced in Chapter 2, we illustrate their applicability to assessment and provide a broad range of performance tasks that center on each key use.

ASSESSING KEY USES OF ACADEMIC LANGUAGE IN LANGUAGE ARTS

Let's enter a language arts classroom where students are in small groups busily exchanging information in academic conversations. When students are actively engaged in learning and assessment is embedded into instruction, the two become intertwined. In Figure 3.4, we see a variety of oral language tasks that are tied to key uses of academic language.

Take the DARE

Use the list in Figure 3.5 as a starting point for building a bank of performance assessment ideas. Take note of those tasks or projects in which you involve your students, and brainstorm how you might apply DARE to the tasks in additional content areas or disciplines. Share your ideas with your colleagues at grade-level meetings or with your professional learning community. Think about the applicability and relevance of these tasks for ELLs, students with disabilities, and other language learners.

FIGURE 3.4 Key Uses of Academic Language in Oral Language Arts Activities

KEY USE(S) OF ACADEMIC LANGUAGE	EXAMPLE INSTRUCTIONAL ASSESSMENT TASKS FOR SPEAKING
Recount	Book talks that include characters, setting, and events
Argue	Debates on school-related topics or current issues
Discuss	Dialogues among students on social or culturally related topics
Discuss	Interviews between students or between students and adults
Explain or recount	Presentations or reports on content-related research
Recount	Role-plays or dramatizations of current events or literature
Recount, explain, argue, or discuss	Speeches or talks based on students' topics of interest
Explain	Task analyses or demonstrations on how to do activities, processes, or procedures
Recount	Story (re)telling from illustrations or personal experiences
Explain	Student-led conferences on how original work was created or selected for their portfolios
Recount or explain	Think-alouds (personal reactions to reading) on articles, stories, or poetry
Discuss	Two-way tasks involving maps or missing information between partners
Argue	Critiques of videos, games, or movies

Source: Adapted from Gottlieb (2016).

As we have noted in Chapter 2, one of the primary sources for key uses of academic language is challenging academic standards, such as college and career readiness standards, and the supporting practices of the disciplines. As a result, the content area of language arts has come to embrace multiple genres inclusive of both narrative text (e.g., stories, folktales, and legends) and informational text (e.g., reports, biographies, and learning logs). These multiple means of expression—visual, oral, and written—serve as a backdrop for DARE, our key uses of academic language. Figure 3.5 is the first in this chapter that shows the intersection of content, supported by disciplinary practices of English language arts (Council of Chief State School Officers, 2012), and academic language use, as depicted in DARE, to assess that content.

FIGURE 3.5 College and Career Readiness Practices for English Language Arts and Suggestions for Assessment of Key Uses of Academic Language Associated With Those Practices

ENGLISH LANGUAGE ARTS "PRACTICES" (AS CITED IN THE ELPD FRAMEWORK, P. 11)	WHAT STUDENTS NEED TO DO IN LANGUAGE ARTS WITH KEY USES OF ACADEMIC LANGUAGE: IMPLICATIONS FOR ASSESSMENT
1. Support analyses of a range of grade-level complex texts with evidence.	*Argue* for academic language use in a variety of grade-level genres, and make claims about the use of discourse, sentences, and specific words and phrases, along with evidence from text.
2. Produce clear and coherent writing in which the development, organization, and style are appropriate to the task, purpose, and audience.	*Discuss* discourse features, such as connecting sentences with related ideas, in original pieces of writing with grade-level peers.
3. Construct valid arguments from evidence, and critique the reasoning of others.	*Argue* different points of view or issues using evidence, and evaluate the thinking of others orally, visually, or in writing.
4. Build and present knowledge through research by integrating, comparing, and synthesizing ideas from texts.	*Recount* what has been learned from research after connecting, comparing, and crafting ideas from texts.
5. Build upon the ideas of others and articulate one's own when working collaboratively.	*Recount* ideas gleaned from interaction and collaboration with others.
6. Use English structures to communicate context-specific messages.	*Explain* how language forms contribute to meaning in a variety of situations.

Teachers can document student performance within the instructional cycle in many ways. Figure 3.6 gives some examples of instructional assessment tasks that typify DARE and illustrates some ways to capture what students can do with language as they engage in sense making. Notice that scaffolds, such as graphic organizers, charts, or tables, may serve as the end products for some ELLs, which can redouble as documentation forms, while other students may produce essays or reports.

Take the DARE

Based on the exemplars throughout this chapter, use Figure 3.6 as a planning guide for assessing any single content area or combination of content areas. With your grade-level team, focus on one or more key uses of academic language, generate ideas for instructional assessment tasks, and identify documentation that reveals students' evidence of content and language learning. Don't forget to think about your ELLs, students with disabilities, and other language learners before acting.

KEY USE OF ACADEMIC LANGUAGE	IDEAS FOR INSTRUCTIONAL ASSESSMENT FOR LANGUAGE ARTS	SAMPLE DOCUMENTATION FORMS
Discuss (with others)	• Different perspectives or points of view • Ideas of different speakers on the same topic	Graphic organizers, such as Venn diagrams or T-charts, using comparative language
Argue	• For a favorite version of a folktale or fairy tale • For particular endings to mysteries	Charts with opinions and reasons
Recount	• Your personal story (memoir or autobiography) • The actions of the main characters throughout chapters or stories	Timelines with descriptions of significant events
Explain	• How characters evolve over time • The steps of how to do something (e.g., create a haiku)	Outlines or analysis sheets highlighting sequential language

Resource 3.2 is an extension of Figure 3.6. In it, we ask you to think of ideas for instructional assessment for key uses of academic language for your class or grade. Then, imagine how you might document students' academic language use for a specified theme in the content area of language arts or for an interdisciplinary project for the humanities, combining language arts and social studies.

RESOURCE 3.2 A Planning Sheet for Instructional Assessment of Key Uses of Academic Language

Here is a tool that can be applied to any content area. Independently or with colleagues, generate instructional assessment ideas for a series of related lessons or units of learning, along with potential accompanying documentation as part of performance assessment.

Grade Level: _____   Unit Theme: _____

KEY USE OF ACADEMIC LANGUAGE	IDEAS FOR INSTRUCTIONAL ASSESSMENT	SAMPLE DOCUMENTATION FORMS
Discuss (with others)	Small-group discussions	Checklists
Argue	Class presentations	Rating scales
Recount	Short biographies	Rubrics
Explain	Lab experiments with a partner	Anecdotal notes

Blogs. Blogs are a relatively new genre that has gained popularity across content areas in a wide variety of contexts. We introduce blogs here within language arts as a means of illuminating key uses of academic language to share with students.

As exemplars of multimodalities, blogs can take on many forms: photo blogs, video blogs, audio blogs, cartoon blogs, and, yes, even text-based blogs. Blogs can also be expressions of DARE, as in students' self-reflections of group interactions (*discussions*), critiques of political or social positions (*arguments*), and personal narratives, such as book reviews (*recounts*) or rationales for why something happened (*explanations*). Resource 3.3 offers additional ideas for blogs based on each key use and asks you to think about how students might use this genre as a platform for peer and self-assessment.

RESOURCE 3.3 Exemplifying Key Uses of Academic Language Through Blogging

What kinds of instructional assessment might go along with the different blog ideas? For each key use, generate some ways, with your colleagues and with your students, to move learning forward with student-generated assessment.

KEY USE	IDEAS FOR BLOGS	SUGGESTIONS FOR STUDENT PEER OR STUDENT SELF-ASSESSMENT
Discuss	• Pose different positions • Weigh potential resolutions to problems from different vantage points • Question others' ideas • Seek clarification from others	Analyze the interaction among students in recordings of conversations on issues.
Argue	• Give personal opinions • Critique issues • Challenge reasoning of others • Defend varying perspectives • Persuade others of your stance	Throughout the project, keep a journal evaluating the strength of your position, your claims, and your evidence.
Recount	• Narrate personal experiences • Describe past events • Report information • Produce multimedia documentaries (e.g., with photos or video snippets)	Make an annotated photo album.
Explain	• Offer advice on how to do something • Share why class norms are necessary • Show cause-effect relationships • Summarize how some things work	Show how something is put together or how to solve a mystery by demonstrating what to do, step by step.

Let's go a bit more in depth about blogging. Resource 3.4 illustrates how to couple text-based literacy with visual literacy for a multimodal experience. This movie on blogs and blogging highlights how students might gain knowledge about how language works (building their metalinguistic awareness) while immersed in literacy.

Scan the QR code that leads to the BrainPOP® website's featured movie about blogs, and have students, either individually or in pairs, watch it.

In pairs, have students discuss, orally or in writing, what they notice about the language of blogging. Then, produce a class list from the examples.

Source: BrainPOP®, https://www .brainpop.com/english/writing/blogs

---

Once students are introduced to and learn about the history and purposes of blogs in the BrainPOP® movie, they are invited to couple their multimedia experience with text (see the *recount* blog about Michael Jackson later in the chapter). Eventually, students become bloggers on their own, taking on topics of personal interest or school-related issues.

Discussions in Language Arts Classrooms. Authentic discussions are oral interactions among students or between students and teachers where participants present and consider multiple perspectives and, in contributing to the group, often incorporate or expand upon others' ideas. With student-to-student interaction initiated by discussions, students are able to gain insight into their peers' perspectives while simultaneously expanding their own interpretation of literature or text (Hadjioannou, 2007). Two naturally occurring activities in the language arts classroom that center on oral discussions among students are book talks and literature circles. Resources 3.5 and 3.6 are checklists of student self-reflections that assess their level of participation in small-group discussions.

Name: Analleli _____   Date: _____

Use this checklist after you have had a discussion with your classmates. Read each sentence. Decide if you did what it says or not. Put a check in one of the two boxes.

THINGS TO REMEMBER TO DO IN A DISCUSSION	I DID IT!	OOPS, NOT THIS TIME
1. I had more than one turn to talk.	☺	
2. I let everyone in my group have their turn.	☺	
3. I listened to the others in my group talk.	☺	
4. I understood everyone's ideas.		✕
5. I added to others' ideas.		✕
6. I respected my peers' ideas.	☺	
7. I was polite and did not interrupt my peers.	☺	
8. I presented my own ideas.	☺	
9. I used text or other evidence to back up my ideas.		✕

Here is a similar self-assessment checklist for *discussions* that has been designed for middle school students.

RESOURCE 3.6 Student Self-Assessment for Participating in Discussions: A Checklist for Grades 5–8

Name: _Diep_____   Date:_____

Students in My Group: _Kasha, Ivan, and Paulo_

Use this checklist after you have had a discussion with your peers. Read each sentence. Decide if you did what it says or not. Then, put a check in one of the two columns.

IN MY DISCUSSION GROUP,	I DID	NOT THIS TIME
1. I had more than one opportunity to speak.	X	
2. I acknowledged others' contributions to the group.	X	
3. I listened carefully to the others in my group.	X	
4. I understood others' ideas.		X
5. I asked clarifying questions to help me better understand.		X
6. I accepted differences in opinions or points of view.	X	
7. I contributed to and built on others' ideas.		X
8. I maintained a respectful tone and did not criticize my peers.	X	
9. I responded politely and did not interrupt my peers.	X	
10. I made self-to-text connections and shared them with my peers.	X	

Oral Arguments. Debates or persuasive speeches provide students opportunities to argue in favor of their side of an issue. To increase students' attention to the points and counterpoints, have them engage in peer assessment that includes a summary of each side's argument. Resource 3.7 is a sample checklist of the features of debates or persuasive speeches that invites students to document what is said.

Take the DARE

How might you convert this expanded checklist that interprets oral arguments to one that captures the features of written arguments? With a team of teachers, reconfigure this form so that it reflects text-based arguments in persuasive essays. Have students try it out and give you feedback on its effectiveness.

Some students might be adept at oral arguments; others might prefer to produce their arguments in writing. Moving from one mode to the other, college and career readiness anchor standards for writing identify key uses of academic language and thread them

RESOURCE 3.7 A Peer Assessment Checklist for Debates or Persuasive Speeches

Use this checklist when listening to debates with two sides or persuasive speeches given by one person. You will need to decide whether the speaker(s) include(s) the features for *argue*; then, give the evidence you hear.

Your Name: _____   Date: _____

Speaker or Team 1's Name: _____

Speaker or Team 2's Name: _____

FEATURES OF DEBATES OR PERSUASIVE SPEECHES: THE SPEAKER	SIDE 1: THE ISSUE:			SIDE 2: THE OPPOSING ISSUE:		
	YES	NO	WHAT SPEAKER 1 SAYS	YES	NO	WHAT SPEAKER 2 SAYS
Identifies his or her position	X			X		
States a claim	X			X		
Provides facts, not opinions, about the claim	X			X		
Offers relevant evidence to support the claim	X			X		
Uses persuasive language to convince others of his or her position	X				X	
Summarizes the claim and supporting evidence		X			X	

throughout the document. In regard to argument, students are expected to "write arguments to support claims in an analysis of substantive topics or texts using valid reasoning and relevant and sufficient evidence" (Common Core State Standards Initiative, 2010). We suggest combining oral language and literacy in creating tasks and rubrics for argumentation. (As suggested in *Take the DARE*, the documentation form in Resource 3.7 can readily be converted to written arguments).

For example, a project might entail having students research a topic and being able to report their initial claims and evidence in a variety of ways. Some students might choose to keep electronic files while ELLs might prefer to create graphic organizers; other language learners might use interviews as a means of collecting information. From there, students can take a side to more fully develop their case and then prepare oral arguments. The final step, which would reinforce their speech, would be to write a persuasive piece based on their stance. What an easy and natural way of building in multimodalities around a common theme!

Recounts. In *recounts*, one relives experiences or events orally or in writing. There are several different types:

1. *Personal recounts* describe what you as a writer or orator have witnessed or have been involved in, which might be expressed as diary entries or personal incidents.

2. *Factual recounts* state what has happened, usually in chronological order, as in reports or biographies.

3. *Procedural recounts* name the steps from beginning to end, such as in conducting investigations.

4. *Literary recounts* retell a series of events for the purpose of entertaining the reader.

The following excerpt from a news blog represents a type of factual *recount*. Follow it to uncover the series of events.

RESOURCE 3.8 A Blog About the Death of Michael Jackson

First, make sure the students (fourth graders and older) know a bit about the life of Michael Jackson, and perhaps play a YouTube excerpt of some of his songs and dances. After the introduction, use the QR code to access the blog from BrainPOP® (click "Real Life"); then, have the students read it twice. The first time is to gain a general understanding of the role and impact of blogging, typical of a factual *recount*. The focus of the second read is to identify its unique metalinguistic features (see Resource 3.9 on metalinguistic awareness).

Source: BrainPOP®, https://www.brainpop.com/english/writing/blogs/fyi

> For more than an hour, the only place people could learn about (Michael) Jackson's death was a Hollywood entertainment blog called TMZ.com. Jackson was officially pronounced dead at 2:26 p.m. PDT—a full six minutes *after* TMZ broke the story.
>
> Newspapers and TV networks held off on reporting the death until they received confirmation from multiple sources. But as *The New York Times* reported the next day, TMZ "seemed to have sources everywhere—at Mr. Jackson's mansion; in the ambulance; and in the corridors of the U.C.L.A. Medical Center."
>
> TMZ's scoop spread around the Web like wildfire. Across the entire Internet, traffic was 11 percent higher than normal. Fans typed "Michael Jackson" into Google so many times that the site's operators thought they were being hacked. Nearly 1 million users visited Wikipedia's "Michael Jackson" page within one hour, while 15 percent of all Twitter posts—an average of 5,000 new tweets every minute—mentioned Jackson.
>
> The event was a great example of how blogging has changed how journalism works in the 21st century. Nowadays, reporters can file articles instantaneously through blog posts and microblogs like Twitter. As a result, the public can keep informed about an event as it's happening.

Take the DARE

What are the advantages of having students being exposed to multiple modes on blogging—that is, how does the text-based news blog reinforce or complement the BrainPOP® movie? How is this strategy effective for your ELLs, ELLs with disabilities, and other language learners? Would you consider flipping your lesson and having the students watch the movie, let's say, as an assignment to see what they can unearth in terms of new expressions and terminology related to this 21st century genre? How might the Language article from the "FYI" section or the "Vocabulary" page from the "Activities" section from BrainPOP® support this work? Would you consider having your students create and maintain a blog on their own interests, let's say, sports or fashion? How might they use the graphic organizer provided in the "Activities" section of BrainPOP® to help them take and organize their notes?

If students are unfamiliar with the notion of metalinguistic awareness, where they reflect on and manipulate the features of language, introduce some of the categories that are descriptive of the different ways in which language is presented in the text on blogging, as in Resource 3.9.

RESOURCE 3.9 Metalinguistic Awareness

Have the students reread the blog post on Michael Jackson for its unique metalinguistic features; then, ask them to complete the blank resource at the end of the chapter in small groups. Some groups of students may wish to add features that they saw, heard in the accompanying blogging movie, or have used themselves.

KNOWING ABOUT LANGUAGE (METALINGUISTIC AWARENESS)	EXAMPLES OF LANGUAGE FROM THE NEWS BLOG
Words with multiple meanings	Scoop, Internet traffic
Idiomatic expressions	Spread like wildfire
Newly created technical words or phrases	Blog posts, microblogs
Social media references	Twitter, tweet

Explanations. Producing explanatory text is very much a part of college and career readiness, as Anchor Standard 2 for writing calls for students to "write informative/explanatory text to examine and convey complex ideas and information clearly and accurately" (CCSSI, 2010). In the lower grades, this standard may be exemplified by having students produce a series of facts about a topic or the steps in cycles. Building on this foundation, in the middle and upper grades, students may be analyzing and synthesizing information from multiple sources in order to generate text that sheds new light on the *how* or *why* of concepts, processes, or procedures.

Cause-and-effect explanations are also very much part of language arts. Students can begin to gain a sense of the relationship between cause and effect by drawing on their personal experiences. BrainPOP Jr.® (geared to Grades 1–3) offers a wealth of suggestions for students, teachers, and family members (see https://educators.brainpop.com/lesson-plan/cause-and-effect-activities-for-kids). As students move into deepening their understanding through content, they can consider how if–then expressions can represent multiple points of view, take on multiple perspectives, or be applied to making predictions. ELLs and ELLs with disabilities must come to understand specific language structures that are triggered by cause and effect (in this case, conditionals). For example, you might ask, "*If* you were to rename one of the seven dwarfs (let's say from Dopey to Brainy), how *would* the story change?" What might you do to assess the academic language of cause and effect as applied to the actions of the character and the content of language arts?

ASSESSING KEY USES OF ACADEMIC LANGUAGE IN MATHEMATICS

You may think that mathematical symbols and notation are a language unto themselves, but they are not—achievement in this discipline, as others, is highly influenced by text and context. Thinking and communicating mathematically involves teachers and students taking the DARE by *discussing* how to approach problems, *arguing* for one operation or another, *recounting* what has been learned and relating that information to a specified audience, and *explaining* how to solve problems step by step. According to Kenney, Hancewicz, Heuer, Metsisto, and Tuttle (2005), presentation of mathematical concepts through graphic representations, classroom discourse, and literacy is more stimulating, sparks student interest, and improves student understanding.

So let's look at the mathematical practices suggested by college and career readiness standards and their application to key uses of academic language. Moschkovich (2013) contends that these practices reflect a complex view of mathematical language that includes not only specialized and technical vocabulary but also how language is organized in sentences and communicated through discourse. Figure 3.7 juxtaposes the standards for mathematical practices with instructional assessment around key uses of academic language and gives an example of their application.

Resource 3.10 is intended for students who have experience with DARE and with self- or peer assessment. If they are not familiar with key uses of academic language, you may wish to pull items from the checklist one by one as a starting point for introducing them within mathematics discourse.

Working in pairs or individually, students will better remember academic language use if they have opportunities to engage in multiple modalities, such as listen, speak, read, write, and even draw. You might model the academic language that is associated with mathematical problem solving. Have students keep a notebook or journal of their notations of the different language forms that they hear modeled or that they see in their textbooks, using Resource 3.11. We have inserted some grade-level topics and examples in the key uses boxes, but you are welcome to use this Resource for a single class or grade level throughout the year. You may also wish to take observational notes on your students' entries and give them written feedback based on the features of DARE.

STANDARDS FOR MATHEMATICAL PRACTICES (AS CITED IN THE ELPD FRAMEWORK, P. 20)	WHAT STUDENTS NEED TO DO IN MATHEMATICS WITH KEY USES OF ACADEMIC LANGUAGE: IMPLICATIONS FOR ASSESSMENT
1. Make sense of problems and persevere in solving them.	*Discuss* problem-solving strategies with classmates to develop metacognitive and metalinguistic awareness.
2. Reason abstractly and quantitatively.	*Explain* how to analyze and carry out a variety of mathematical procedures.
3. Construct viable arguments and critique the reasoning of others.	*Discuss* mathematical thinking, *argue* using the language of mathematical solutions as evidence, and evaluate others' reasoning.
4. Model with mathematics.	*Recount* mathematically. *Explain* how to apply mathematics to everyday life.
5. Use appropriate tools strategically.	*Explain* how and why mathematical tools are used for specific purposes.
6. Attend to precision.	Identify and *recount* the language that expresses accuracy and exactness of measurement.
7. Look for and make use of structure.	Identify and *explain* strategies for seeking solutions for given patterns, equations, or figures.
8. Look for and express regularity in repeated reasoning.	*Explain* the reasoning (the *why*) behind mathematical patterns, equations, or figures that occur in logical sequence.

RESOURCE 3.10 A Checklist to Apprentice Students Into Math Discourse Through Key Uses of Academic Language

This checklist is intended for students who are working with partners to solve mathematical problems together. For ELLs, you may wish to pair speakers of the same language together so that they can use their home language to clarify or elucidate the task.

Names: <u>Maria and Jaime</u>   Date: _____

A SEQUENCE OF KEY USES TO HELP SOLVE MATH PROBLEMS WITH A PEER WE . . .	DONE!	STILL WORKING ON IT
1. *Recount* what the problem asks in our own words, and show what it says with drawings or real objects.	X	
2. *Explain* how to get the answer, step by step, to ourselves.	X	
3. *Recount* the steps to each other to see if we agree with one another.	X	
4. *Discuss* any differences the two of us might have and, together, decide on a solution pathway.		X
5. *Explain* how we came to an agreement on how to solve the problem.		X
6. Justify (*argue*) our solution and defend our reasoning to others in our class.	X	

Source: Adapted from Avalos, Medina, and Secada (2015, p. 19).

Name(s): _____

EXAMPLES OF LANGUAGE USED IN *DISCUSSIONS*	EXAMPLES OF LANGUAGE USED IN *ARGUMENTS*
Topic: Telling Time Grade: 2 Date: _____	Topic: Ratio and Proportion Grade: 7 Date: _____
1. I go to bed at 7:30. What about you? 2. I get up at 6:45. What about you? 3. On Saturday, I go to bed at half past 8. What about you? 4.	1. 2. 3. 4.

EXAMPLES OF LANGUAGE USED IN *RECOUNTS*	EXAMPLES OF LANGUAGE USED IN *EXPLANATIONS*
Topic: Algebraic Thinking Grade: 5 Date: _____	Topic: Base 10 Thinking Grade: 1 Date: _____
1. 2. 3. 4.	1. Because 10 plus 10 plus 10 is 30 2. You put one pile of tens, then another pile and another one. 3. I drew 30 happy faces. Then, I put a circle around groups of 10. I made 3 circles! 4.

Figure 3.8 is a mock-up of how you might think about instructional assessment and its corresponding documentation for a hypothetical unit on "How Much Money Does a Family Spend Each Month?" Notice how DARE helps strengthen the language focus of the project. Note: If this topic is too sensitive for your class, please adapt or change it.

ASSESSING KEY USES OF ACADEMIC LANGUAGE IN SCIENCE

The notion of scientific practices introduced in *A Framework for K–12 Science Education* (National Research Council, 2012) underscores the importance of social interaction with oral and written discourses that help build scientific understanding in classrooms. Student engagement in scientific and engineering practices is a twofold endeavor: It requires scientific sense making alongside academic language use. Thus, a practice-oriented science classroom can serve as both a rich language-learning and science-learning environment (Quinn, Lee, & Valdés, 2012).

FIGURE 3.8 Ideas for Instructional Assessment Tasks and Documentation Forms for a Mathematics Project on Family Expenses

KEY USE OF ACADEMIC LANGUAGE	SAMPLE INSTRUCTIONAL ASSESSMENT TASKS FOR MATHEMATICS	SAMPLE DOCUMENTATION FORMS EMBEDDED IN INSTRUCTION
Discuss (with others)	Collect, analyze, and report data on family expenses with peers in a small group.	Interview questions and data gathered from family members
Argue	Take a stance on the expenses per month for a family, and defend it.	A table with calculations of total expenses matched to evidence to justify the stance
Recount	State steps in formulating an expense sheet, and share the sequence with peers.	An outline with a description of each step
Explain	Determine and describe how expenses are allocated (e.g., categories such as housing, food, clothing, gas, electricity, phone, and entertainment) and the amount of money assigned to each.	A pie chart or other representation of percentage of expenses in each category along with how each is determined

In order for students to be confident in their role as budding scientists, teachers have to create a classroom climate that is safe for students to explore and DARE to be wrong as they work toward articulating more complete explanations and arguments. To show how language permeates content, Figure 3.9 pairs practices for science and engineering with relevant key uses of academic language and give examples of how they might be reflected in assessment.

Take the DARE

How might you or your grade-level team combine disciplinary practices and key uses of academic language with curricular planning and assessment for a unit of learning? Using the figures in this chapter, take an example from the grade you are most familiar with, and *discuss* with your team how you might integrate discipline-related content and language into classroom assessment.

Explanations in Science. Two practices, in particular, that emphasize the close tie between key uses of academic language and the reasoning behind scientific ideas are (1) engaging in argument from evidence and (2) obtaining, evaluating, and communicating information (Reiser, Berland, & Kenyon, 2012). Scientific investigation should be built on explanations and arguments, where students are invited to provide reasons for their ideas and thinking rather than relying only on conceptual accuracy (Sutherland, McNeill, Krajcik, & Colson, 2006).

FIGURE 3.9 Scientific and Engineering Practices and Suggestions for Assessment of Key Uses of Academic Language Associated With Those Practices

SCIENTIFIC AND ENGINEERING PRACTICES (AS CITED IN THE ELPD FRAMEWORK, P. 26)	WHAT STUDENTS NEED TO DO IN SCIENCE AND ENGINEERING PRACTICES WITH KEY USES OF ACADEMIC LANGUAGE: IMPLICATIONS FOR ASSESSMENT
1. Asking questions (for science) and defining problems (for engineering)	*Explain* by asking questions (e.g., to hypothesize) and describing the *how* or *why* of engineering problems
2. Developing and using models	*Explain*, *discuss*, and *describe* scientific phenomena with others
3. Planning and carrying out investigations	*Recount* and *explain* steps in scientific investigations
4. Analyzing and interpreting data	*Explain* the *why* behind scientific data
5. Using mathematics and computational thinking	*Explain how* and *why* to compute the steps in problem solving
6. Constructing explanations (for science) and designing solutions (for engineering)	*Explain* relationships (e.g., cause and effect) and *discuss* how they lead to solutions
7. Engaging in argument from evidence	*Argue* for particular stances or positions based on claims and evidence
8. Obtaining, evaluating, and communicating information	*Discuss* with partners rationales and justification of choices based on multiple sources of information

A scientific explanation is a written, oral, or graphic (visual) response to a question that generally requires students to analyze data, interpret data, and report the findings. Explanations in scientific communities are generally causal in that they link theory with answering the *why* behind observed phenomena. In producing a chain of cause-and-effect relationships, students may engage in academic conversations around a series of language functions whose purposes are wrapped around explanations, including the following:

- Defining the concepts

- Asking and answering questions that have multiple plausible answers

- Describing processes or procedures

- Comparing and contrasting information

- Evaluating ideas that answer *why* using scientific models

- Summarizing events that lead to a conclusion

These purposes can readily be presented as a checklist to remind students of how to participate in scientific explanations and serve as a self-assessment tool. Older students might also give examples of their academic language use alongside each purpose. For ELLs who are newcomers, each purpose could be represented by an icon; these students would most likely begin with definitions and questioning in English but most likely could also engage in conversations, if buddies are available, in their home language.

Teachers and students have to have a shared vision of what constitutes sound scientific explanations for given sociocultural contexts, along with their conceptual and language expectations. In investigating scientific phenomena, students need to have opportunities to probe deeply into uncovering and mastering the concepts and the language of science and assessment, and the teacher, in turn, has to measure those expectations, taking into account the characteristics of the students and how they have approached the task. For example, fourth graders could *explain* how water changes state as it moves through the water cycle in a variety of ways: by demonstrating or acting out the cycle, drawing and labeling the stages, constructing a model of a water cycle, writing a narrative about what happens to a drop of water, or making an oral presentation on the water cycle.

Arguments in Science. Argument centers on the precept that scientists make claims that are justifiable yet often challenged. As a result, alternatives are posed, with counterclaims that are backed by opposing evidence. There is much interaction in elaborating both sides of a scientific argument. For example, third graders might decide whether or not an animal of their choice could survive being placed in a new environment or ecosystem, determine what features the animal might possess that would help it survive or not, and locate evidence based on their research of illustrated text or videos.

Scientific arguments contain a wealth of academic language. Students must be able to grasp the many purposes for language use, including the following:

- Describing the controversy of scientific thought
- Agreeing or disagreeing with scientific statements backed by reasons
- Evaluating claims from investigations and evidence from both sides
- Defending or justifying a stance based on analysis of data
- Persuading others of the stance or position
- Reflecting on the position taken and its outcome

Take the DARE

Just as in explanations, the purposes for argumentation can be converted into a checklist for assessing their usage. Try developing a checklist for either one or both of these key uses of academic language, using language that is appropriate for your grade level. Then, share it with your students, and have them give examples that they could keep as models. Once the students gain familiarity with each purpose, encourage them to engage in self-assessment.

As with the other disciplines, key uses of academic language are part of the scientific community. Figure 3.10 is a sampling of instructional assessment tasks for science and how the learning process might be documented for key uses of academic language.

FIGURE 3.10 Applying Key Uses of Academic Language to Instructional Assessment Tasks and Documentation Forms for Science

KEY USE OF ACADEMIC LANGUAGE	SAMPLE INSTRUCTIONAL ASSESSMENT TASKS FOR SCIENCE	SAMPLE DOCUMENTATION FORMS EMBEDDED IN INSTRUCTION
Discuss (with others)	Content or topics to research with rationales and justifications	Annotated citations and references
Argue	For or against scientific issues (e.g., climate change)	Graphic organizers of points of view and evidence (e.g., T-charts)
Recount	Scientific thinking and learning from observations or experiences through ongoing journal writing	Criterion-referenced feedback on science standards and practices that are addressed
Explain	The *why* behind scientific investigations	Rich descriptions in charts or graphs (e.g., cause and effect)

For those of you who work with ELLs or ELLs with disabilities, knowing their level of language proficiency, whether in English or an additional language, is a starting point for documenting their academic language use. Become familiar with the criteria specified for each level of language proficiency that are framed around key uses of academic language. Then, use the checklist in Resource 3.12 as a means of documenting the students' academic language use and representation when they are involved in scientific investigation.

Ecosystems is a scientific theme that tends to spiral throughout the elementary school years. Units of learning on this theme tend to touch upon many key uses of academic language. Using Resource 3.13 as a starting point and an exemplar, determine which key uses are best represented in your units (whether from science or other disciplines), when they are covered, and how each one is documented. You may also wish to add a column either stating the applicable content standards or concepts that match each key use.

ASSESSING KEY USES OF ACADEMIC LANGUAGE IN SOCIAL STUDIES

As with other content areas, social studies is anchored in a set of standards that reflects key uses of academic language. The *College, Career, and Civic Life (C3) Framework for Social Studies State Standards* "emphasize[s] the disciplinary concepts and practices that support students as they develop the capacity to know, analyze, explain and argue about the interdisciplinary challenges in our social world" (National Council for the Social Studies, 2013, p. 6). In fact, the fourth dimension of the inquiry arc, "Communicating Conclusions and Taking Informed Action," also accentuates the

RESOURCE 3.12 An Assessment Checklist for ELLs and Other Language Learners Based on DARE for Scientific Investigation

Name: _____ Grade: _____

Investigation: <u>Volcanoes</u>   Date: _____

Language of Performance: <u>English</u>

Oral Performance: _____X_____   Written Performance:_____

Visual Representation: _____X_____

Given the scientific experiment or experience, check how the student demonstrates key uses of academic language by placing an X on criteria from Level 1, "On the Ground," to Level 5, "The Summit." Note: It is possible to cross multiple language proficiency levels, depending on the task, the context, and the student's familiarity with the content.

LANGUAGE PROFICIENCY LEVEL	LANGUAGE EXPECTATIONS FOR SCIENTIFIC INVESTIGATION FOR LANGUAGE LEARNERS THE STUDENT . . .
Level 5 The Summit	☐ *Argues* results of scientific investigation using claims matched with evidence ☐ *Explains* by connecting cause and effect based on results of scientific investigation ☐ *Recounts* by summarizing each step to reach the results of scientific inquiry
Level 4 Summit Sighting	☐ *Explains* with details how the scientific questions or hypotheses relate to the conclusions ☑ *Recounts* the steps in the inquiry process in short scientific reports ☐ *Discusses* the impact of scientific questions under varying conditions (e.g., if, then) with others
Level 3 Halfway Up	☑ *Explains* how scientific questions lead to conclusions ☐ *Recounts* steps in conducting scientific inquiry using sequential language ☑ *Argues* pros and cons of possible results of investigation
Level 2 Base Camp	☐ *Explains* why by stating scientific questions and conclusions ☐ *Argues* by making statements to be verified or negated ☐ *Discusses* research questions or hypotheses with peers
Level 1 On the Ground	☐ *Recounts* with labeled illustrations that are descriptive of scientific questions and conclusions ☐ *Explains* by distinguishing the language of claims from the language of evidence

Source: Adapted from Gottlieb (2016, p. 165).

role of language in the discipline. It acknowledges how "explanations and making and supporting arguments" can take on multimodalities to

> include a range of venues and a variety of forms, such as essays, discussions, debates, policy analyses, video productions, and portfolios. Moreover, the manner in which students work can also vary from individual endeavors, to interactions with partners, in small groups, and the whole class. (p. 19)

RESOURCE 3.13 A Checklist Focused on Key Uses of Academic Language for a Science Unit on Ecosystems

When students are studying ecosystems and demonstrate a key use of academic language, note the date and the evidence they give, whether oral, written, or visual.

Student: _____   Teacher: _____

Oral Evidence: _____X_____   Written Evidence: _____X_____

Visual Evidence: _____X_____

KEY USES OF ACADEMIC LANGUAGE IN A SCIENCE UNIT ON ECOSYSTEMS STUDENTS WILL . . .	DATE(S)	DOCUMENTATION OF DARE
1. *Discuss* animal and plant adaptations in various ecosystems in small groups		Individual summaries of discussion points made by your partners in science notebooks
2. *Argue* and provide evidence of positive or negative changes in various ecosystems		Infographics or graphic organizers stating claims for the type of change along with their pieces of evidence
3. *Recount* detailed characteristics of various ecosystems.		Ecosystems posters
4. *Explain* how animals and plants adapt to various ecosystems		Step-by-step depiction of the adaptation process from the perspective of plants or animals

Teachers must become aware that the content area of social studies in the United States, in large part, is filled with sociocultural assumptions that are largely Anglocentric in their orientation (e.g., "westward expansion" and "the Vietnam War") that spill over onto assessment. It is full of vocabulary that carries double meanings (think of *party, lobby, table top, house,* or *period,* to name a few examples), abstract concepts (e.g., *free will, the rights of the people,* and *democracy and justice*), and grammatical structures that are difficult to interpret (e.g., the use of passive voice—"America was discovered by"—or complex noun phrases, such as a *two-chamber legislature*). How do teachers and students begin to make sense of it all?

As an introduction to assessing key uses of academic language in the context of social studies, examine Figure 3.11. In it, you will see similar forms of documentation, such as graphic organizers and timelines, useful for collecting evidence from assessment, but here, they are applied social studies themes.

FIGURE 3.11 Applying Key Uses of Academic Language to Instructional Assessment Tasks and Documentation Forms for Social Studies

KEY USE OF ACADEMIC LANGUAGE	SAMPLE INSTRUCTIONAL ASSESSMENT TASKS FOR SOCIAL STUDIES	SAMPLE DOCUMENTATION FORMS EMBEDDED IN INSTRUCTION
Discuss (with others)	Comparing and contrasting the value of different forms of governments with a partner	Venn diagrams with similarities and differences or T-charts with comparative features
Argue	Providing claims and counterclaims with evidence on immigration	Two-sided templates for anecdotal notes
Recount	Relating the changing demographics of different regions	Graphs (e.g., histograms or line) or charts (e.g., pie or scatterplot)
Explain	Tracing how the concept of *revolution* has changed over time	Timelines with accompanying tables, including definitions, descriptions, and examples

You may be filled with ideas for history projects or products but may be challenged by specific wording that would spark students to *take the DARE*. Figure 3.12 offers some suggestions for initiating oral language, written, and multimodal projects associated with key uses of academic language within historical contexts. You are welcome to invite students to pick and choose from the list and then generate criteria for success or project descriptors for them.

Explanations in history often involve making cause-and-effect connections. By the time students reach the middle grades, causes and effects, the seeds of explanations in historical contexts, move from being explicit to implicit. Zwiers and Crawford (2011, p. 142) list a series of topics in which cause-and-effect patterns are present and suggest using them as a basis for students to engage in academic conversations in history.

Figure 3.13 is a summary of historical topics that lend themselves to explanation that is expressed through cause and effect. For each topic, there is an instructional assessment idea that begs students to engage in conversations with each other or to work in small groups to produce solutions to issues that pertain to social justice or for taking social action. Many of these ideas are also conducive for students to band together to produce written or oral briefs.

Take the DARE

Do any of the topics in Figure 3.13 particularly resonate with you, or are they emphasized in your history curriculum? How might you take this figure and make it more specific for your setting by integrating key uses of academic language into your social studies instruction?

FIGURE 3.12 A Jump Start for Assessing DARE in History Classes

DARE IN HISTORICAL CONTEXTS	SUGGESTIONS FOR PARAGRAPH OR ESSAY PHRASE WALLS OR TO JUMP-START ACADEMIC CONVERSATIONS	IDEAS FOR PERFORMANCE ASSESSMENT
Historical **D**iscussion	• On one hand _____, but on the other hand . . . • There are several points of view represented . . . • What do you think is the issue behind . . . ? • Tell me the pros and cons of . . . • When is the best time to . . . ?	• Recording exchanges among students • Producing summaries of shared ideas • Collecting, sharing, and comparing information from virtual communities (e.g., classrooms around the world)
Historical **A**rgument	• The evidence for _____ points to . . . • From our point of view, we are convinced that . . . • We base our claim on the primary source document . . . • In my opinion . . . • I think it would be better if . . .	• Engaging in formal debates with artifacts • Producing multimedia presentations or short videos with documented evidence • Creating and acting out scenes of plays or scripts
Historical **R**ecount	• Starting in or with (e.g., the 21st century) . . . • Past experience shows that . . . • The trend over the past years indicates . . . • A long time ago . . . • At the beginning . . .	• Reenacting historical events • Producing fictional accounts in stories, poems, or raps • Making montages or murals of events and their impact on history
Historical **E**xplanation	• Looking at the cycle (e.g., of poverty), first . . . • The causes of . . . ? • The changes in . . . (e.g., city life) over time show . . . • To describe the importance of . . . (e.g., community), we • The effects of . . . (e.g., election results) will . . .	• Constructing models • Creating posters • Producing displays or exhibits • Making detailed timelines

FIGURE 3.13 Historical Topics and Instructional Assessment Ideas for Cause and Effect

CAUSE AND EFFECT IN HISTORICAL TOPICS	EXAMPLE INSTRUCTIONAL ASSESSMENT IDEAS BASED ON KEY USES OF ACADEMIC LANGUAGE
Racism	Trace (*recount*) racism from *Brown v. Board of Education of Topeka* to the civil rights movement
Fear	*Explain* how fear grips you, and give examples
Religion	Compare and contrast (*explain*) the tenets of different religions
Compassion	*Discuss* feelings toward different historical events with peers (e.g., nomination of the first female for the U.S. presidency)
Desire for power	*Explain* how different forms of government view power
Lust for fame	*Argue* which general, president, or governor had the greatest lust for fame with claims and evidence
Desire for freedom	*Recount* the events that led to people's freedom (e.g., the right to vote)
Natural events	*Explain* how natural disasters have impacted demography (e.g., the flight of people)
Desire for knowledge	*Recount* research on an abstract concept, such as revolution, democracy, or justice

There are many ways to organize key uses for each content area. Resource 3.14 shows a chart to help students work through explanations in social studies. For students to *explain*, input is given orally, seen in video or multimedia, or read in text.

REFLECT

In this chapter, we come to value key uses of academic language as we carefully plan assessment of DARE in our content classrooms. We peek into four content areas—language arts, mathematics, science, and social studies—to envision their relationship with DARE and think about how we might be more diligent in organizing instructional assessment around concepts and language. Through myriad instructional assessment ideas, we see how easy it is to pair academic language use with content area topics. Additionally, by building a strong relationship of disciplinary practices with DARE, we become aware of how pervasive academic language should be in our schools.

As a summary, we reserve Resource 3.15 for grade-level or department teacher teams to complete in order to record their distribution of DARE in their content classes throughout the year. Perhaps it could be enlarged to chart size, where teachers could place their ideas for instructional assessment on sticky notes (one color for each content area or one

Imagine you are a leader or president of a country. Give reasons why an important historical event occurred during your reign or administration, how it changed over time, and how it concluded. Make sure you give answers from your identity and point of view.

Student: _Hector Villanueva_____   Time Frame: _1840s_____

Topic or Historical Event: _Mexican-American War or the Invasion of Mexico_____

Date: _____   Historical Figure: _____

EXPLANATION OF WHY PEOPLE OR HOW EVENTS CHANGE OVER TIME	EVIDENCE (WHAT DID I HEAR OR SEE AS CONFIRMATION OR PROOF?)	ANALYSIS (WHY DID YOU DO WHAT YOU DID, OR HOW DID THIS EVENT HAPPEN?)	RELEVANCE (HOW DOES THE ANALYSIS SUPPORT YOUR INTERPRETATION?)
In the Beginning: What was your reason(s) for fighting a war or leading a revolution? To protect my people What event(s) triggered the conflict? The U.S. annexation of Texas in 1845!			
Point of Change: When and how did your reason(s) for fighting the war or revolution change? When Polk was elected President of the U.S. in 1844, all he wanted to do was to expand U.S. territories. What events produced change in fighting the war or revolution? U.S. troops invading Coahuila, Mexico.			
In the End: What was your reason(s) for ending the war or revolution? Mexico could not afford to lose any more of its precious land. What was the event that ended the conflict? I reluctantly agreed to sign the Treaty of Guadalupe Hidalgo.			

Source: Adapted from https://blueprintforhistory.files.wordpress.com/2012/03/cw5-7-historical-interpretation.pdf

RESOURCE 3.15 A Summary Chart of Key Uses of Academic Language:
Ideas for Instructional Assessment Across the Content Areas

Review all of the ideas presented throughout the chapter for instructional assessment by key use of academic language. Decide which ones are most relevant and useful for your context and grade by content area. Note your ideas or those that you generate with your colleagues in the chart and revisit them on a monthly basis.

DARE Sticky Notes

Grade Level: _____ School Year: _____

Teacher Team: _____

Image source: ©iStockphoto
.com/Rawpixel Ltd

KEY USE OF ACADEMIC LANGUAGE	INSTRUCTIONAL ASSESSMENT OF MATHEMATICS	INSTRUCTIONAL ASSESSMENT OF LANGUAGE ARTS	INSTRUCTIONAL ASSESSMENT OF SCIENCE	INSTRUCTIONAL ASSESSMENT OF SOCIAL STUDIES
Discuss	Pose solutions to problems in small groups.			
Argue		Defend your point of view.		
Recount			Summarize this month's weather.	
Explain				Compare and contrast the foreign policies of two U.S. presidents.

color for each key use of academic language, depending on how you would like to organize the task). Those of you who prefer to work paperlessly are welcome to create a spreadsheet to document your classroom assessment of DARE within the content areas.

One of the messages we have tried to communicate throughout these pages is that both teachers and students should be encouraged to be active participants in their own learning who make decisions on their own behalf. To maximize attainment and achievement of school success, we DARE assessment to be integral to teaching and learning.

Key uses of academic language is a conceptual tool for accentuating language in content learning. Thinking of teachers and their interactions with students, we have tried to illustrate the ease in identifying the purpose (the *why* or the *how*) for communication in conjunction with each discipline's concepts (the *what*). Although this book is devoted to four key uses, its intent is not to necessarily make them inclusive but simply exemplary of how language impacts content throughout the school day. We invite you to suggest others, substitute one for another, or combine several key uses in your work. Most important, though, we hope that every time you approach a new content topic or theme, you immediately say to yourself, "How am I going to ensure that my students can access, express, and achieve these concepts through language in meaningful ways?"

TAKE ACTION

The disciplinary practices associated with today's challenging academic content standards offer teachers, teacher educators, and school leaders opportunities to reconceptualize the critical role of language in content teaching and learning. But what do students need to do with language as teachers implement the content-driven practices for each discipline, and what are their implications for assessment? Here are some questions to ponder and take action as we close our discussion on ways to assess key uses of academic language.

1. How might you incorporate key uses of academic language into performance assessment at a particular grade cluster or school level? How might you insert key uses into what is already in place in your curriculum so it is present alongside essential conceptual understandings? How might you incorporate key uses into culminating projects for your units so that students have opportunities to take social action?

2. How might you collect and store evidence of students' uses of academic language in content area classrooms? How might language and content teachers work together to ensure that language is taught through content and that content is taught through language? How might this collaboration be a stimulus for ongoing reciprocal teaching and use of common data for decision making?

3. How might you and your colleagues compare and contrast strategies for assessing key uses of academic language within and across the content areas? Which key uses of academic language do you tend to rely on for content-based assessment? How might you balance the representation of DARE in curriculum, assessment, and instruction?

4. Which content area would you examine first to ascertain the presence of DARE? Would you begin at specific grade levels or make it a whole-school initiative? Specifically, where in your curriculum do you need to address key uses of academic language, and how might you make provisions for their assessment?

This rubric has wide applicability; you are welcome to make it discipline specific or to retain its more generalized criteria and use it as a collaborative tool among teachers. For language learners in dual-language or immersion programs, consider adding "in home language and English" to the descriptors.

Task: _____   Date: _____

Student: _____   Grade: _____

For the given performance task and selected key use, check the box to indicate the extent to which students can do the following:

KEY USE OF ACADEMIC LANGUAGE	ATTEMPTING	ADVANCING	APPROACHING	ATTAINING
Discuss by	Responding orally when prompted in brief segments ☐	Participating in academic conversations when prompted ☐	Engaging in academic conversations on a variety of content-related topics using discourse features of the disciplines ☐	Engaging in extended academic conversations on a variety of content-related topics using grade-level discourse of the disciplines ☐
Argue by	Presenting, orally or in writing, brief claims or opinions ☐	Organizing oral and written presentations around claims or opinions with evidence or reasons ☐	Organizing oral and written presentations around claims or opinions supported by logical evidence or reasons ☐	Organizing oral and written presentations around solid claims or opinions justified with strong evidence or reasons ☐
Recount by	Retelling, orally or in writing, brief personal experiences or events ☐	Retelling with some description, orally or in writing, personal experiences or a series of events ☐	Retelling with description, orally or in writing, personal experiences or sequences of events ☐	Retelling with rich description, orally or in writing, personal experiences or logical sequences of events ☐
Explain by	Stating, orally or in writing, the *how* or *why* of phenomena in brief accounts ☐	Describing with sketchy details, orally or in writing, the *how* or *why* of phenomena ☐	Summarizing with details, orally or in writing, the *how* or *why* of phenomena ☐	Summarizing with vivid details, orally or in writing, the *how* or *why* of phenomena ☐

Here is a tool that can be applied to any content area. Independently or with colleagues, generate ideas for sample instructional tasks for a series of related lessons or units of learning along with potential accompanying documentation as part of performance assessment.

Grade Level: _____   Unit Theme: _____

KEY USE OF ACADEMIC LANGUAGE	IDEAS FOR INSTRUCTIONAL ASSESSMENT	SAMPLE DOCUMENTATION FORMS
Discuss (with others)		
Argue		
Recount		
Explain		

What kinds of instructional assessment might go along with the different blog ideas? For each key use, generate some ways, with your colleagues and with your students, to move learning forward through student-generated assessment.

KEY USE	IDEAS FOR BLOGS	SUGGESTIONS FOR STUDENT PEER OR STUDENT SELF-ASSESSMENT
Discuss		
Argue		
Recount		
Explain		

Scan the QR code that leads to the BrainPOP® website's featured movie about blogs, and have students, either individually or in pairs, watch it.

In pairs, have students discuss, orally or in writing, what they notice about the language of blogging. Then, produce a class list from the examples.

Source: BrainPOP®, https://www
.brainpop.com/english/writing/blogs

Reprinted from *Language Power*: *Key Uses for Accessing Content* by Margo Gottlieb and Mariana Castro. Thousand Oaks, CA: Corwin, www.corwin.com. Reproduction authorized only for the local school site or nonprofit organization that has purchased this book.

Chapter 3 Resources

Name: _____   Date : _____

Use this checklist after you have had a discussion with your classmates. Read each sentence. Decide if you did what it says or not. Put a check in one of the two boxes.

THINGS TO REMEMBER TO DO IN A DISCUSSION	I DID IT!	OOPS, NOT THIS TIME
1. I had more than one turn to talk.		
2. I let everyone in my group have their turn.		
3. I listened to the others in my group talk.		
4. I understood everyone's ideas.		
5. I added to others' ideas.		
6. I respected my peers' ideas.		
7. I was polite and did not interrupt my peers.		
8. I presented my own ideas.		
9. I used text or other evidence to back up my ideas.		

Name: _____   Date: _____

Students in My Group: _____

Use this checklist after you have had a discussion with your peers. Read each sentence. Decide if you did what it says or not. Then, put a check in one of the two columns.

IN MY DISCUSSION GROUP,	I DID	NOT THIS TIME
1. I had more than one opportunity to speak.		
2. I acknowledged others' contributions to the group.		
3. I listened carefully to the others in my group.		
4. I understood others' ideas.		
5. I asked clarifying questions to help me better understand.		
6. I accepted differences in opinions or points of view.		
7. I contributed to and built on others' ideas.		
8. I maintained a respectful tone and did not criticize my peers.		
9. I responded politely and did not interrupt my peers.		
10. I made self-to-text connections and shared them with my peers.		

Chapter 3 Resources

Use this checklist when listening to debates with two sides or persuasive speeches given by one person. You will need to decide whether the speaker(s) include(s) the features for *argue*; then, give the evidence you hear.

Your Name: _____   Date: _____

Speaker or Team 1's Name: _____

Speaker or Team 2's Name: _____

FEATURES OF DEBATES OR PERSUASIVE SPEECHES: THE SPEAKER	SIDE 1: THE ISSUE:			SIDE 2: THE OPPOSING ISSUE:		
	YES	NO	WHAT SPEAKER 1 SAYS	YES	NO	WHAT SPEAKER 2 SAYS
Identifies his or her position						
States a claim						
Provides facts, not opinions, about the claim						
Offers relevant evidence to support the claim						
Uses persuasive language to convince others of his or her position						
Summarizes the claim and supporting evidence						

Chapter 3 Resources

First, make sure the students (fourth graders and older) know a bit about the life of Michael Jackson, and perhaps play a YouTube excerpt of some of his songs and dances. After the introduction, use the QR code to access the blog from BrainPOP® (click "Real Life"); then, have the students read it twice. The first time is to gain a general understanding of the role and impact of blogging, typical of a factual *recount*. The focus of the second read is to identify its unique metalinguistic features (see Resource 3.9 on metalinguistic awareness).

Source: BrainPOP®, https://www .brainpop.com/english/writing/blogs/fyi

> For more than an hour, the only place people could learn about (Michael) Jackson's death was a Hollywood entertainment blog called TMZ.com. Jackson was officially pronounced dead at 2:26 p.m. PDT—a full six minutes *after* TMZ broke the story.
>
> Newspapers and TV networks held off on reporting the death until they received confirmation from multiple sources. But as *The New York Times* reported the next day, TMZ "seemed to have sources everywhere—at Mr. Jackson's mansion; in the ambulance; and in the corridors of the U.C.L.A. Medical Center."
>
> TMZ's scoop spread around the Web like wildfire. Across the entire Internet, traffic was 11 percent higher than normal. Fans typed "Michael Jackson" into Google so many times that the site's operators thought they were being hacked. Nearly 1 million users visited Wikipedia's "Michael Jackson" page within one hour, while 15 percent of all Twitter posts—an average of 5,000 new tweets every minute—mentioned Jackson.
>
> The event was a great example of how blogging has changed how journalism works in the 21st century. Nowadays, reporters can file articles instantaneously through blog posts and microblogs like Twitter. As a result, the public can keep informed about an event as it's happening.

Chapter 3 Resources

If students are unfamiliar with the notion of metalinguistic awareness, where they reflect on and manipulate the features of language, introduce some of the following categories that are descriptive of different ways in which language is presented in the text on blogging. Have the students reread the blog post on Michael Jackson for its unique metalinguistic features; then, ask them to complete the table below. Some groups of students may wish to add features that they saw, heard in the accompanying blogging movie, or have used themselves.

KNOWING ABOUT LANGUAGE (METALINGUISTIC AWARENESS)	EXAMPLES OF LANGUAGE FROM THE NEWS BLOG
Words with multiple meanings	
Idiomatic expressions	
Newly created technical words or phrases	
Social media references	

This checklist is intended for students who are working with partners to solve mathematical problems together. For ELLs, you may wish to pair speakers of the same language together so that they can use their home language to clarify or elucidate the task.

Names: _____ and _____

Date: _____

A SEQUENCE OF KEY USES TO HELP SOLVE MATH PROBLEMS WITH A PEER WE . . .	DONE!	STILL WORKING ON IT
1. *Recount* what the problem asks in our own words, and show what it says with drawings or real objects.		
2. *Explain* how to get the answer, step by step, to ourselves.		
3. *Recount* the steps to each other to see if we agree with each other.		
4. *Discuss* any differences the two of us might have and, together, decide on a solution pathway.		
5. *Explain* how we came to an agreement on how to solve the problem.		
6. Justify (*argue*) our solution, and defend our reasoning to others in our class.		

Source: Adapted from Avalos, Medina, and Secada (2015, p. 19).

Name(s): _____

EXAMPLES OF LANGUAGE USED IN *DISCUSSIONS*	EXAMPLES OF LANGUAGE USED IN *ARGUMENTS*
Topic: _____	Topic: _____
Grade: _____	Grade: _____
Date: _____	Date: _____
1.	1.
2.	2.
3.	3.
4.	4.

EXAMPLES OF LANGUAGE USED IN *RECOUNTS*	EXAMPLES OF LANGUAGE USED IN *EXPLANATIONS*
Topic: _____	Topic: _____
Grade: _____	Grade: _____
Date: _____	Date: _____
1.	1.
2.	2.
3.	3.
4.	4.

Chapter 3 Resources

Name: _____   Grade: _____

Investigation: _____   Date: _____

Language of Performance: _____

Oral Performance: _____   Written Performance: _____   Visual Representation _____

Given the scientific experiment or experience, check how the student demonstrates key uses of academic language by placing a X on criteria from Level 1, "On the Ground," to Level 5, "The Summit." Note: It is possible to cross multiple language proficiency levels, depending on the task, the context, and the student's familiarity with the content.

LANGUAGE PROFICIENCY LEVEL	LANGUAGE EXPECTATIONS FOR SCIENTIFIC INVESTIGATION FOR LANGUAGE LEARNERS THE STUDENT . . .
Level 5 The Summit	☐ *Argues* results of scientific investigation using claims matched with evidence ☐ *Explains* by connecting cause and effect based on results of scientific investigation ☐ *Recounts* by summarizing each step to reach the results of scientific inquiry
Level 4 Summit Sighting	☐ *Explains* with details how the scientific questions or hypotheses relate to the conclusions ☐ *Recounts* the steps in the inquiry process in short scientific reports ☐ *Discusses* the impact of scientific questions under varying conditions (e.g., if, then) with others
Level 3 Halfway Up	☐ *Explains* how scientific questions lead to conclusions ☐ *Recounts* steps in conducting scientific inquiry using sequential language ☐ *Argues* pros and cons of possible results of investigation
Level 2 Base Camp	☐ *Explains* why by stating scientific questions and conclusions ☐ *Argues* by making statements to be verified or negated ☐ *Discusses* research questions or hypotheses with peers
Level 1 On the Ground	☐ *Recounts* with labeled illustrations that are descriptive of scientific questions and conclusions ☐ *Explains* by distinguishing the language of claims from the language of evidence

Source: Adapted from Gottlieb (2016, p. 165).

Chapter 3 Resources

When students are studying a science theme and demonstrate a key use of academic language, note the date and the evidence they give, whether oral, written, or visual.

Student: _____   Teacher: _____

Oral Evidence: _____   Written Evidence: _____   Visual Evidence: _____

KEY USES OF ACADEMIC LANGUAGE IN _____ STUDENTS WILL . . .	DATE(S)	DOCUMENTATION OF *DARE*
1. *Discuss*		
2. *Argue*		
3. *Recount*		
4. *Explain*		

Imagine you are a leader or president of a country. Give reasons why an important historical event occurred during your reign or administration, how it changed over time, and how it concluded. Make sure you give answers from your identity and point of view.

Student: _____ Time Frame: _____

Topic or Historical Event: _____

Date: _____ Historical Figure: _____

EXPLANATION OF WHY PEOPLE OR HOW EVENTS CHANGE OVER TIME	EVIDENCE (WHAT DID I HEAR OR SEE AS CONFIRMATION OR PROOF?)	ANALYSIS (WHY DID YOU DO WHAT YOU DID, OR HOW DID THIS EVENT HAPPEN?)	RELEVANCE (HOW DOES THE ANALYSIS SUPPORT YOUR INTERPRETATION?)
In the Beginning: What was your reason(s) for fighting a war or leading a revolution? What event(s) triggered the conflict?			
Point of Change: When and how did your reason(s) for fighting the war or revolution change? What events produced change in fighting the war or revolution?			
In the End: What was your reason(s) for ending the war or revolution? What was the event that ended the conflict?			

Source: Adapted from https://blueprintforhistory.files.wordpress.com/2012/03/cw5-7-historical-interpretation.pdf

Review all of the ideas presented throughout the chapter for instructional assessment by key use of academic language. Decide which ones are most relevant and useful for your context and grade by content area. Note your ideas or those that you generate with your colleagues in the chart and revisit them on a monthly basis.

DARE Sticky Notes

Grade Level: _____   School Year: _____

Teacher Team: _____

Image source: ©iStockphoto .com/Rawpixel Ltd

KEY USE OF ACADEMIC LANGUAGE	INSTRUCTIONAL ASSESSMENT OF MATHEMATICS	INSTRUCTIONAL ASSESSMENT OF LANGUAGE ARTS	INSTRUCTIONAL ASSESSMENT OF SCIENCE	INSTRUCTIONAL ASSESSMENT OF SOCIAL STUDIES
Discuss				
Argue				
Recount				
Explain				

References and Further Reading

Francis, D. J., Rivera, M., Lesaux, N., Kieffer, M., & Rivera, H. (2006). *Research-based recommendations for instruction and academic interventions*. Portsmouth, NH: Center on Instruction. Retrieved from http://www.centeroninstruction.org/files/ELL1-Interventions.pdf

Assessment

Berger, R., Rugen, L., & Woodfin, L. (2014). *Leaders of their own learning: Transforming schools through student-engaged assessment*. San Francisco, CA: Jossey-Bass.

Gottlieb, M. (2016). *Assessing English language learners: Bridges to educational equity: Connecting academic language proficiency to student achievement* (2nd ed.). Thousand Oaks, CA: Corwin.

Gottlieb, M., & Nguyen, D. (2007). *Assessment & accountability in language education programs: A guide for administrators and teachers*. Philadelphia, PA: Caslon Publishing.

Honigsfeld, A., & Dove, M. G. (2010). *Collaboration and co-teaching: Strategies for English learners*. Thousand Oaks, CA: Corwin.

Assessing Key Uses of Academic Language in Language Arts

Brisk, M. E. (2015). *Engaging students in academic literacies*. New York, NY: Routledge.

Common Core State Standards Initiative (CCSSI). (2010). *Common Core State Standards for English language arts & literacy in history/social studies, science, and technical subjects*. Retrieved from http://www.corestandards.org/ELA-Literacy

Council of Chief State School Officers. (2012). *Framework for English Language Proficiency Development Standards corresponding to the Common Core State Standards and the Next Generation Science Standards*. Washington, DC: Author.

Derewianka, B., & Jones, P. (2012). *Teaching language in context*. New York, NY: Oxford University Press.

Hadjioannou, X. (2007). Bringing the background to the foreground: What do classroom environments that support authentic discussions look like? *American Educational Research Journal, 44*(2), 370–399.

Schleppegrell, M. (2004). *The language of schooling: A functional linguistics perspective*. Mahwah, NJ: Erlbaum.

Assessing Key Uses of Academic Language in Mathematics

Avalos, M. A., Medina, E., & Secada, W. G. (2015). Planning for instruction: Increasing multilingual learners' access to algebraic word problems and visual graphics. In A. Bright, H. Hansen-Thomas, & L. C. De Oliveira (Eds.), *The Common Core State Standards in mathematics for English language learners* (pp. 5–23). Alexandria, VA: TESOL Press.

Kenney, J. M., Hancewicz, E., Heuer, L., Metsisto, D., & Tuttle, C. L. (2005). *Literacy strategies for improving mathematics instruction*. Alexandria, VA: ASCD.

Moschkovich, J. (2013). Principles and guidelines for equitable mathematics teaching practices and materials for English language learners. *Journal of Urban Mathematics Education, 6*(1), 45–57.

Tellez, K., Moschkovich, J., & Civil, M. (Eds.). (2011). *Latinos/as and mathematics education*. Charlotte, NC: Information Age Publishing.

Assessing Key Uses of Academic Language in Science

National Research Council. (2012). *A framework for K–12 science education: Practices, crosscutting concepts, and core ideas*. Washington, DC: National Academies Press.

Quinn, H., Lee, O., & Valdés, G. (2012). *Language demands and opportunities in relation to Next Generation Science Standards for English language learners: What teachers need to know*. Stanford, CA: Understanding Language Initiative. Retrieved from http://ell.stanford.edu/sites/default/files/pdf/academic-papers/03-Quinn%20Lee%20Valdes%20Language%20and%20Opportunities%20in%20Science%20FINAL.pdf

Reiser, B. J., Berland, L. K., & Kenyon, L. (2012, April/May). Engaging students in the scientific practices of explanation and argumentation: A framework for K–12 education. *Science Scope*, 6–11.

Sutherland, L. M., McNeill, K. L., Krajcik, J. S., & Colson, K. (2006). Supporting middle school students in developing scientific explanations. In R. Douglas, M. P. Klentschy, & K. Worth (Eds.), *Linking science and literacy in the K–8 classroom* (pp. 163–181). Arlington, VA: NSTA Press.

Assessing Key Uses of Academic Language in Social Studies

Library of Congress. (n.d.). Classroom materials. Retrieved from http://www.loc.gov/teachers/classroommaterials

National Council for the Social Studies. (2013). *College, career, and civic life (C3) framework for social studies state standards: Guidance for enhancing the rigor of K–12 civics, economics, geography, and history.* Silver Spring, MD: Author. Retrieved from http://www.socialstudies.org/system/files/c3/C3-Framework-for-Social-Studies.pdf

Seidlitz, J., & Perryman, B. (2010). *Navigating the ELPS in the social studies classroom: Using the standards to improve instruction for English learners.* Irving, TX: Seidlitz Education.

Zwiers, J., & Crawford, M. (2011). *Academic conversations: Classroom talk that fosters critical thinking and content understandings.* Portland, ME: Stenhouse.

CHAPTER 4

Efficacy and Equity

Implementing Key Uses
of Academic Language

Agency is the bridge that connects knowledge with transformative action.

— Alberto J. Rodriguez, 2002

What can we do internal to our classrooms to promote and sustain equity? How can we ensure that what we do as educators is worthwhile and makes a difference in the lives of the students we face each day? We suggest that by instilling language power as a classroom norm, students and teachers can work together as a community with a shared vision and realization of academic success.

ASK

What are some viable ways of embedding key uses of academic language into classroom life so that learning is equitable for all students?

In this chapter, we highlight four perspectives that shed light on the implementation of key uses of academic language in equitable ways. In it, we underscore the positive relationships that can be forged between students and teachers around open communication through student voice, agency, and participation in learning. Additionally, we see how the interaction of students with authentic instructional materials that treat language and content together can be facilitated by scaffolding instruction. Elevating the status of students by gradually increasing their responsibility for their own learning coupled with the legitimacy of academic language use as a vehicle for learning ultimately paves the way to more equitable educational practices. Figure 4.1 depicts these perspectives, which serve as an organizational frame for this chapter.

FIGURE 4.1 Implementing Key Uses of Academic Language in Classrooms

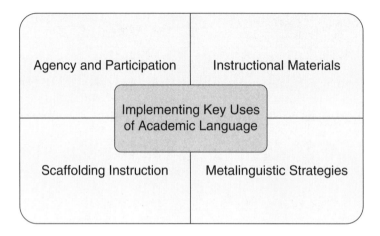

In enacting key uses in our classrooms, we ask teachers and school leaders to *take the DARE* to do the following:

Discuss student agency and the role of students as engaged implementers of key uses of academic language.

Argue for instructional materials and digital resources as sources of rich academic language for classrooms.

Recount ideas for scaffolding instruction in implementing key uses of academic language.

Explain how metalinguistic strategies can promote student awareness of academic language use.

Implementing key uses of academic language revolves around the interaction among students and teachers to maximize opportunities for success in school. The four perspectives presented in Figure 4.1 come together in classrooms during their implementation. We invite educators to reflect as they intentionally implement key uses of academic language in their practice.

EXPLORE

In planning curriculum based on backward design, assessment is a prelude to instruction (Wiggins & McTighe, 2005). Having identified potential student performances and documentation that are suggested by standards, teachers can more readily craft experiences to equip students to be able to demonstrate learning. That is the approach we have taken in this book. Having addressed instructional assessment across the content areas in the previous chapter, we now turn our attention to introducing aspects of implementing DARE in student-centered classrooms. But before we begin, we would like to take a moment to recap how we have reenvisioned teaching and learning around key uses of academic language.

Figure 4.2 illustrates the larger frame of reference for key uses of academic language. Knowing we always begin with students, along with their families and other stakeholders, we move to the planning phase for embedding key uses of academic language into school life. From planning, we venture outward and think about how we might weave assessment within and across the content areas. Lastly, we implement DARE through instructional and disciplinary practices that promote student participation and agency.

> ### FIGURE 4.2 A Frame of Reference for Teaching and Learning Inclusive of Key Uses of Academic Language

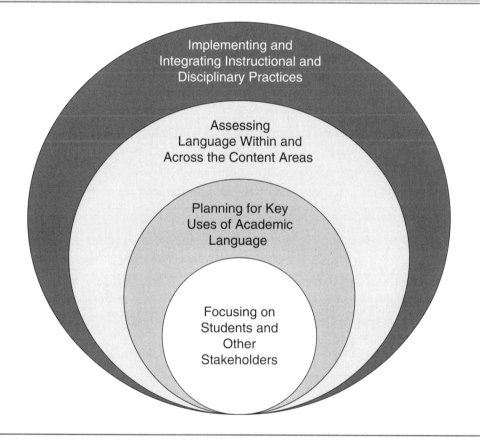

APPLY

In implementing DARE, we challenge you to expand student voice in decision making and give students choice in how and what they learn. By selecting challenging instructional materials that reflect your students' interests, scaffolding instruction to meet their individual needs, and adding metalinguistic strategies to your teaching repertoire, you will be better equipped to take the DARE and embed key uses of academic language use in your instruction.

ENSURING AGENCY AND PARTICIPATION

Agency can be defined as the capacity and desire to take purposeful initiative in shaping ones' actions; in schools, it applies to all stakeholders: students, families, teachers, and school leaders. Let's briefly touch on school leaders and teachers as agents before moving into the realm of students. A recent research study suggests that in the context of professional learning, educational leaders need to pay greater attention to the importance of teacher agency, which is "the capacity of teachers to act purposefully and constructively to direct their professional growth and contribute to the growth of their colleagues" (Calvert, 2016, p. 4). School leaders are pivotal players in prompting teachers to become engaged in improving their practice. Principals, in particular, can provide teachers with dedicated time to collaborate with each other, support teacher-led structures such as professional learning communities or grade-level teams, encourage their participation in learning networks, and offer options in helping teachers contribute to solving pressing issues—all of which helps to move teachers along the continuum of agency.

While for teachers, agency, in part, refers to making learning choices to achieve their goals, so too does this principle apply to students. Students who possess agency tend to seek meaning in their world and act with determination and persistence to reach desired goals for themselves and others (Vander Ark, 2015). The development of student agency is acquired under the watchful eye of the teachers who nurture their students' development day in and day out, urging each and every one to reach his or her full potential. We encourage you to watch the short YouTube video (www.youtube.com/watch?v= VyZZQqXFoR0) for a concise summary of the defining features of student agency and the role of the teacher as facilitator.

Student agency must be captured and embodied in curriculum that is enacted in schools. Curriculum must "present students with socially relevant and challenging new knowledge so that they—in collaboration with their teachers—can engage in meaningful dialogue and become more active members of their communities" (Rodriguez, 2002, p. 1020). Teaching practices must be synchronized with curriculum and geared to promoting independence of learning by students.

Take the DARE

With your grade-level team, review a unit of learning through the eyes of your students. To what extent do your students have opportunities to have input in the following?

a. Identifying applicable standards and making them student friendly

b. Formulating learning targets from the standards using student-friendly language

c. Suggesting ideas for crafting or deciding on final projects for units of learning

d. Selecting from an array of materials and technologies (in the language of their choice)

e. Helping to determine criteria for success for final projects

f. Participating in self- and peer assessment

Where might you begin to make your projects more student centered? How might you make students more aware of their language use and control over their own learning?

Strategies that tend to foster student agency include having students define their own goals, question while they learn, use metacognitive strategies, and self-monitor their learning. Figure 4.3 contrasts teaching practices associated with traditional classrooms with practices that reflect student agency. As is evident in the figure, the foundation for student agency is teacher agency. With teachers as agents, learning environments are set up that honor students and endorse assessment *as* learning—where teachers trust and support students in gradually taking on responsibility for and monitoring and showing evidence of their own learning (Gottlieb, 2016).

FIGURE 4.3 Comparison Between Classrooms of Traditional Practice and Those of Agentic Practice

Notice the distinct roles of teachers and students in these two sets of practices.

IN EMPLOYING TRADITIONAL PRACTICE, TEACHERS . . .	IN EMPLOYING AGENTIC PRACTICE, TEACHERS . . .
Select standards for assessment and instruction	Facilitate converting standards into student-friendly ones
Craft content and language objectives	Guide the crafting of content and language objectives with students
Determine activities and tasks	Create a menu of activities and tasks or approve of students' ideas
Construct criteria for success	Coconstruct criteria for success with students
Share data among themselves	Share data with students and family members
Provide standards-referenced feedback	Encourage students to self- and peer assess on standards-referenced tasks and projects
Formulate student goals	Approve and give feedback on goals formulated by students
Monitor student performance	Monitor student performance in conjunction with student self-monitoring
Communicate with students	Interact with and empower students

It is rather challenging to illustrate student agency and participation, as each student is indeed unique. That said, we try to show teachers how to instill more of these virtues in their practices. The following series of resources offer a variety of approaches for increasing student agency and student participation in classroom contexts. Let's start with Resource 4.1, which may serve as a needs assessment and a planning sheet for determining how students can play a more active role in the teaching and learning cycle.

RESOURCE 4.1 Signs of Student Agency in Teaching and Learning

To what extent is student agency promoted in your classroom? Complete the rating scale as a needs assessment to determine the ways in which your students exhibit agency. Discuss your results with colleagues; then, team up, and brainstorm ideas as to how students can play a greater role in initiating and engaging in learning. Don't forget to share your findings with students for their approval.

Teacher: _____   Date: _____

AS AGENTS OF LEARNING, STUDENTS . . .	SOME-TIMES	MOST TIMES	ALL THE TIME
1. Have a voice in classroom decision making	X		
2. Display original work all over the room		X	
3. Choose partners to work with		X	
4. Help (re)arrange the classroom	X		
5. Make suggestions in regard to activities and tasks	X		
6. Advocate the learning style that best suits them	X		
7. Have access to technologies (e.g., through centers) and contribute to evolving phrase/concept/learning walls and other classroom and school displays		X	
8. As representatives of their community, are involved in outreach and social action through classroom projects	X		
9. Are liaisons to families and advocates on their behalf		X	
10. Have time to reflect on their learning and to help set next steps		X	
11. Feel secure in freely participating in class			X
12. Exert independence of thought and action		X	

The checklist in Resource 4.2 offers ways of incorporating language-focused ideas for student agency in instructional practices. Used in conjunction with Resource 4.1, it might be useful for teachers to plan next steps for student participation.

When classrooms are set up as communities of practice, student agency is inevitable, as each member of the community is valued. Here is where students have ongoing opportunities to work together in a safe place and where they respect each other's ideas to reach common understandings. It is in this nurturing environment that students interact in shared activities, help each other to succeed, and build relationships (Lave & Wenger, 1991). From the safety of communities of practice, students gradually become practitioners of language and content on their journey to independence.

Are these language-centered strategies present in your classroom, or would you consider implementing them? This checklist is inspired by Ferlazzo and Hull Sypnieski's (2016) ideas for promoting student agency.

Teacher(s): _____   Date: _____

STUDENT-CENTERED CLASSROOM STRATEGY	YES	NO
1. Setting Content and Language Goals: Students		
• agree on goals with teachers	X	
• periodically review and evaluate their goals	X	
• revise their goals based on evidence	X	
2. Heightening Awareness Through Self-Talk: Students		
• communicate *what* they are thinking (metacognitive awareness)	X	
• communicate *how* they use language (metalinguistic awareness)		X
• communicate *what* they know about culture and *how* it affects the message (metacultural awareness)		X
3. Teaching Others: Students		
• participate in content-related activities, become experts on an aspect of learning, and share it with others in their group (e.g., jigsaw activities)	X	
• tutor younger students or purposefully interact with them (e.g., story reading)		X
• partner and collaborate with peers	X	
4. Encouraging Students' Language Development: Teachers		
• emotionally support students in their academic language development	X	
• offer feedback on students' academic language use to push them forward		X
• model to illustrate what students are expected to do with language	X	

Within this collaborative learning environment, students are able to assume more expanded roles as decision makers. Resource 4.3 is a scale for teachers to pinpoint the extent to which students are reflective learners in becoming agents who can be advocates on behalf of themselves.

Take the DARE

Which of your management and instructional strategies promote and sustain student engagement and participation? With your colleagues, discuss some of the issues surrounding each of the four categories descriptive of student engagement (in Resource 4.2), and

Based on the anchors that describe student roles, place an X along each continuum that marks the placement of students on the road to becoming agents of their own learning.

Teacher: _____   Date: _____

STUDENTS AS RESPONDERS TO LEARNING / STUDENTS AS AGENTS OF LEARNING

1. Feedback: Students

Receive feedback from teachers

Receive and give feedback to peers and others

———————————————————————————x———————————————

2. Assessment: Students

Take teacher-made and commercial tests

Engage in self-and peer assessment

———————————————————x———————————————————————

3. Activities, tasks, and projects: Students

Follow teacher directions

Choose from a menu or self-select with teacher approval

————————————————————————x———————————————————

4. Learning style: Students

Work alone

Collaborate and interact with peers

———————————————————————————————————x————————

5. Learning projects or products: Students

Produce right/wrong or constructed responses

Create original work

———————————————————————————————————x————————

6. Conferencing with teachers or family members: Students

Do not participate

Lead the discussion

———————————————x—————————————————————————————

come up with a plan of how you might try to maximize students' interest and participation in academic tasks that revolve around key uses of academic language.

Students must feel secure and safe in their classrooms in order to learn; they must have a sense of belonging and believe in themselves as capable learners. At the same time, teachers must value and seek student participation and provide ongoing opportunities to DARE students: to *discuss* important issues, *argue* for their position or offer their opinions, *recount* important events or experiences in their lives, and *explain* how or why some things happen. So in essence, in the development of agency, key uses of academic language provide the avenue for students to express themselves in self-fulfilling ways. In doing so, students can begin to take ownership and become empowered individuals.

To optimize learning, teachers must encourage students to actively engage in challenging academic tasks (Boykin & Noguera, 2011). According to Federicks, Blumenfield, and Paris (2004), three types of engagement occur in classrooms.

1. Behavioral engagement includes students who display attributes such as paying attention, staying on task, and seeking clarification or assistance when necessary.

2. Cognitive engagement involves students diving into stimulating problems, having strategies for understanding new concepts, and pursuing higher-order thinking tasks.

3. Affective engagement entails students taking interest in learning, exhibiting curiosity to pursue learning, and having a positive attitude toward learning.

Although these are admirable traits, they are often hidden for English language learners (ELLs), who may not have enough English language proficiency to persevere grade-level academic demands in a new language, and other students in need of language support. Therefore, we would like to suggest an additional type of engagement—namely, linguistic engagement—and apply it to all students.

4. Linguistic engagement encompasses capitalizing on the languages of the students as resources, the language(s) of instruction to match those of the students, the use of academic language (focusing on DARE), and opportunities for students to interact with each other in academic situations.

Similarly, linguistic engagement alone or coupled with other types of engagement might affect students with language or communication-related disabilities—for example, students who have difficulty with auditory processing of language, who may appear to lack attention or focus (behavioral engagement). Others who may have been diagnosed with dyslexia and struggle with literacy may appear disinterested (affective engagement) when confronted with text. Teachers who know the students best and are aware of their unique characteristics need to apply specific strategies to maximize their classroom engagement.

Student engagement is multifaceted, and each type of student engagement has distinctive characteristics. Resource 4.4 identifies these features and asks you to determine their presence in your classroom.

Examining the four types of student engagement, use this checklist as a reflective tool to evaluate the extent to which you are maximizing students' opportunities to participate in learning.

Teacher: _____   Date: _____

TYPES OF STUDENT ENGAGEMENT AND THEIR ATTRIBUTES	PRESENT IN MY CLASSROOM	NOT AS MUCH AS I WOULD LIKE
1. Behavioral Engagement: Students . . .		
• Pay attention and are not easily distracted	X	
• Remain on task	X	
• Exert effort to learn	X	
• Seek assistance to carry out tasks		X
2. Cognitive Engagement: Students . . .		
• Comprehend complex concepts (with or without scaffolding)	X	
• Are academically challenged by higher-order thinking tasks		X
• Have opportunities to solve thought-provoking problems		X
• Gain subject matter expertise that they apply to new situations	X	
3. Affective Engagement: Students . . .		
• Have interest in the academic tasks	X	
• Have a positive attitude toward learning	X	
• Are curious in seeking information and ideas	X	
• Feel safe and comfortable in pursuing challenges		X
4. Linguistic Engagement: Students . . .		
• Have opportunities to interact with each other	X	
• Express themselves visually, orally, and in writing		X
• Ask clarifying questions to peers and adults		X
• Practice key uses of academic language in each content area		X
• Rely on multiple languages as resources, when appropriate		X

Student participation goes hand in hand with student choice and agency; as the more students are involved in having a say in what they will learn and how they will learn it, the more motivated they will be to carry out a task to its completion. According to Anderson (2016), having student choice yields a host of benefits, including students

- Engaging in deeper, richer learning

- Displaying more on-task behavior

- Connecting to their strengths

- Pursuing their interests

- Taking ownership for what they do

- Purposefully interacting with others

- Enjoying the pursuit of learning and being vested in it

- Contributing to a more collaborative learning environment

There are a number of strategies that teachers can initiate to foster student participation in academic language practices. They are based on the premise that what students say has meaning and that teachers can help solidify and deepen this meaning by offering different options for communicating, including (1) coshaping conversations, (2) rephrasing student responses, (3) having students paraphrase their own thoughts, and (4) prompting students to enrich classroom talk (Zwiers, 2008).

Resource 4.5 offers some ideas for having students actively participate in the teaching and learning cycle. See which of these appeal to you and your grade-level team, and then, try them out.

SELECTING INSTRUCTIONAL MATERIALS

Learning is a social activity that occurs in school through the interaction of students with their peers and teachers. The selection of instructional materials has also been shown to have a powerful influence on student learning. Although, admittedly, there are many factors that impact students' lives, in large part, they learn by engaging in cognitive processes that are triggered and shaped by interacting with people and instructional materials (Chingos & Whitehurst, 2012). We believe that when key uses of academic language are paired with student interaction and instructional materials, learning becomes more focused and intentional.

Although commercially produced instructional materials still dominate the marketplace, today's classrooms are no longer bound to solely to print as a source for learning. Rather, more and more instructional materials represent multiliteracies where students have opportunities to express themselves through multiple modes, often including multimedia and technologies (Gottlieb & Ernst-Slavit, 2014). By relying on a variety of materials that include audio (listening), video (viewing), and tactile-kinesthetic (doing) segments, students are able to derive more meaning from content and connect with each other in more genuine ways.

Discuss what you might do to be more inclusive of students participating in teacher-facilitated activities that address key uses of academic language in authentic ways throughout the teaching and learning cycle.

Unit of Instruction: _____   Grade: _____

PHASE IN THE TEACHING AND LEARNING CYCLE	IDEAS FOR LANGUAGE-CENTERED STUDENT PARTICIPATION
1. Identify applicable standards	• Guide students in translating standards into student-friendly ones • Encourage students to formulate and *recount* their content and language expectations
2. Formulate learning targets	• Have students *explain* (or *argue*) which key use of academic language would best fit the standard and why • Pair students to *discuss* expectations associated with content and language targets
3. Craft a final project	• Allow students to brainstorm projects they would like to pursue that fit the standards and learning targets • Ask students to take a stance (*argue*) for their choice and give reasons why
4. Select instructional materials	• Let students *discuss* the pros and cons of instructional materials in small groups • Allow students to make selections from different categories of instructional resources
5. Determine criteria for success	• Coconstruct performance criteria with students for projects based on language and content expectations • Prompt students to *argue* in favor of or against their application of criteria and the corresponding evidence in their work
6. Participate in self- and peer assessment	• Direct students in applying the criteria for success to their own work and that of their classmates • Have students *explain* how the feedback they provide to their peers matches the criteria for success

Selecting materials that support the goals of instruction is an important part of curricular alignment. Instructional materials that offer opportunities for students to interact with language in meaningful ways and that engage students in using language through listening, reading, talking, writing, viewing, and thinking help support the development of academic language. We encourage teachers to always contemplate how to incorporate DARE associated with content topics so that students' language and conceptual development co-occur. In that way, key uses of academic language enable teachers and students to focus on the primary purposes for communicating in content classrooms.

Take the DARE

Return to Chapter 1 to identify the features associated with key uses of academic language: *discuss*, *argue*, *recount*, and *explain*. Then, with your grade-level colleagues, select text or media from any of the content areas that exemplifies each key use, remembering that oftentimes, more than one will be present. You may wish to create a chart for each key use, along with an accompanying text, such as in Resource 4.6. Another option is to keep a grade-by-grade catalog of text and media selections, along with their principal key use so that you can pair them with content area topics.

RESOURCE 4.6 Evidence of Key Uses in Instructional Materials

Analyze the instructional materials for each of your units of study to identify key uses of academic language. Indicate how each key use is exemplified in text, audio, or video. Include the references in your unit plan.

Let's use an excerpt from a BrainPOP® passage on "Gadgets" (as part of a unit on angles) as an example of DARE in instructional materials, in this instance, text.

> Today, ships use Global Positioning System (GPS) devices to navigate the oceans. But from the 18th through 20th centuries, ship navigators had to use a device called a sextant to find their latitude (north or south location).
>
> Here's how it worked: To find your latitude, you had to measure the angle between the sun and the horizon at 12:00 noon. To do that, you'd pull out your sextant, which consisted of two mirrors. One of these mirrors was semitransparent—you could see through it. The other was attached to a movable arm.

Source: BrainPOP®, https://www .brainpop.com/math/geometryand measurement/angles/fyi/#tab=2

Content Topic: <u>Gadgets</u>   Grade: _____

DARE	DESCRIPTIONS OF KEY USES OF ACADEMIC LANGUAGE WITHIN CONTENT	INSTRUCTIONAL MATERIALS—PAGE NUMBER OF TEXT OR REFERENCE (E.G., URL)
Discuss	Ways to navigate the ocean	
Discuss		
Argue	Best gadget to navigate the ocean	
Argue		
Recount	The history of Global Positioning Systems	
Recount		
Explain	How the sextant worked	
Explain		

Once curriculum has been designed to include academic content targets, as well as a focus on particular key uses, educators must look for ways to ensure students have opportunities to systematically see and hear models of academic language use, lesson by lesson. Teachers are language models, as are instructional materials. The careful selection of textbooks, digital technology, graphic supports, and other instructional tools contributes to the designing of rich teaching and learning experiences for the students.

There is a range of instructional materials for teachers to consider in their lesson design that take students' preferences into account. One overarching consideration in material selection in our increasingly diverse classrooms is whether the materials represent a Universal Design for Learning (UDL) and are inclusive of all students and their learning styles (Voltz, Sims, & Nelson, 2010). In adhering to the UDL principles, instructional materials should give students (1) multiple means of representation of concepts (to demonstrate *what* they have learned), (2) multiple means of action and expression (to show *how* they have learned), and (3) multiple means of engaging in learning concepts (to show the *why* of learning).

RESOURCE 4.7 Representation of the Principles of Universal Design for Learning in Instructional Materials

For each instructional material you or your team selects, either check those principles of UDL (and perhaps the page numbers or URLs for websites) that are present, or provide examples of each principle of UDL. Then, assess the extent to which UDL principles are present, and devise an action plan.

Teacher Team: _____   Grade: _____

INSTRUCTIONAL MATERIAL (TEXT, AUDIO, OR DIGITAL)	PRESENCE OF PRINCIPLES OF UNIVERSAL DESIGN FOR LEARNING		
NAME OR TYPE	1. MULTIPLE MEANS OF REPRESENTATION OF CONCEPTS	2. MULTIPLE MEANS OF ACTION AND EXPRESSION	3. MULTIPLE MEANS OF ENGAGING IN LEARNING CONCEPTS
Video excerpt	X (audio, visual, textual)		X (audio, visual, textual)

Take the DARE

The three principles of UDL are foundational to instructional materials and disciplinary practices in today's classrooms. To what extent are they evident in the materials you and your students use? By incorporating these principles, how might the materials be improved? Use the chart in Resource 4.7 to document the presence or absence of UDL principles in your everyday classroom materials. For those that are present, complete the figure by providing the means by which the UDL principles are exhibited.

Instructional materials should include multimodal ways for students to access and demonstrate meaning. As shown in Resource 4.8, key uses of academic language can offer multiple means of representation and expression in interactive, visual, and kinesthetic ways.

RESOURCE 4.8 Strategies for Engaging Students in Key Uses of Academic Language Inclusive of Multiple Learning Styles and Materials

The following chart illustrates one curricular idea for each key use—DARE—as an exemplar that includes interactive, visual, and kinesthetic modes of support.

Unit: Space Exploration   Grade: _____

AUDITORY (LISTENING AND SPEAKING)	INTERACTIVE	VISUAL	KINESTHETIC
Discuss issues related to space exploration	with a small group of peers	using photographs	and manipulatives
Argue for STEAM in constructing project designs rather than STEM	in a debate	with a multimedia presentation	reinforced with gestures and exemplars
Recount stories from your most favorite authors	and share with a friend	then together draw a sequence of events	and act them out
Explain how to build models to scale	to a partner	and videotape the step-by-step process	to see if your partner can re-create it

Instructional materials help teachers shape their lessons and units of learning. It is important to select materials in a thoughtful manner to ensure that they meet your instructional goals and exemplify the standards you have identified. Resource 4.9 is useful tool for determining the appropriateness of materials for adoption and use.

Instructional materials inherently address key uses of academic language; it is teachers who must bring DARE to the forefront. In Resource 4.10, students are asked to view the movie "Digital Etiquette" from BrainPOP® as an exemplar of *recount*. As many students already have a sense of the language of social media, the movie could even be presented as a flipped lesson, where they are assigned to watch it as homework (providing all students have access to technology). Students may wish to watch the movie several times to see how many facts they can uncover and *discuss* their digital etiquette with their peers.

Use this rating scale to evaluate instructional materials; share it with your colleagues to determine the extent to which they agree with your judgment. You may wish to select some of the items to include in an Excel spreadsheet to maintain an ongoing inventory of instructional materials by topic or theme for yourself or for your grade-level team.

Name of instructional material: _Fish Is Fish script_

Source or publisher: _ReadWriteThink website_

Retrieved from _www.readwritethink.org/files/resources/30629_script.pdf_

Theme: _Multiple points of view_

Year of publication or production: _2010_

Grade level(s): _4–5_

Type of instructional material:

- ☐ Textbooks
- ☐ Articles
- ☐ Trade books
- ☐ Original source documents
- ☐ Apps for a handheld device or computer
- ☐ Videos
- ☐ Illustrations, diagrams, or cartoons

- ☐ Other:
- ☑ Online resources
- ☐ Multimedia (e.g., PPTs, Prezis)
- ☐ Audio (e.g., podcasts)
- ☐ Illustrations, diagrams, or cartoons
- ☑ Other: _Script_

THE INSTRUCTIONAL MATERIAL	SELECT ONE		
	CONSISTENTLY	INCONSISTENTLY	NOT AT ALL
1. Addresses your instructional goals and objectives		X	
2. Presents information in a manner that is accessible and achievable by your students	X		
3. Organizes information in an intuitive manner that makes it easy for students to navigate		X	
4. Builds continuity in students' development of concepts and information, skills, and practices	X		
5. Has a balance of coverage in higher-order thinking skills			
6. Includes learning activities that are engaging, authentic, and relevant			
7. Integrates visual and graphic scaffolding related to the content into the learning activities		X	
8. Models use of academic language (including DARE) for a variety of purposes	X (recount or explain)		
9. Includes language that is familiar and accessible when presenting complex ideas and concepts	X		
10. Provides opportunities for students to partake in 21st century skill development	X		
11. Represents ideas that are actionable			
12. Respects students' different learning styles and rates of learning by providing a variety of options for reaching the same outcome			
13. Considers the range of student performance			X
14. Highlights academic language development in conjunction with conceptual development	X		
15. Is inviting, welcoming, and, at the same time, challenging to students		X	

RESOURCE 4.10 *Recount* (and Discuss) a Movie on Digital Etiquette

Scan the QR code to watch the BrainPOP® movie. The overall purpose of this movie is to provide information to the watcher about digital etiquette. The following are features of the key use *recount*. Match the features with examples from the movie; don't be surprised, however, if there is not an example of each feature. Share your findings with colleagues, and consider how you might replicate this exercise for your students.

Source: BrainPOP®, https://www.brainpop.com/socialstudies/culture/digitaletiquette

Teacher or Teacher Team: _____   Date: _____

FEATURES OF THE KEY USE *RECOUNT*	EXAMPLES FROM THE MOVIE "DIGITAL ETIQUETTE"
State experiences	
Relate a series of facts	
Describe a sequence of events	
Summarize what happened	
Recall details related to personal events or experiences	
Reflect or comment on the experiences	"Wow, I didn't know that I needed to use digital etiquette with social media!"

The movie "Digital Etiquette" can serve as a precursor to having students read a related text on the topic. The passage, "Language," from the "FYI" section of BrainPOP®'s "Digital Etiquette" topic (see Resource 4.11) introduces the key use *argue* in a real-life situation.

Take the DARE

Based on the text, how might you have students formulate an argument about the value of texting as a metalinguistic strategy—that is, being able to understand language in order to convert it to instant messaging or tweets? What information can they glean from the movie to use as reasons or evidence? Consider having students use both types of instructional materials to complete the chart. Carrying this topic even further, after completing the graphic organizer, students could form sides and orally debate the issue, produce a persuasive essay, or even create a rap or poem on social media.

Language

OMG, it wuz gr8! Catch u l8r!

You know you've seen it, whether chatting online or texting on a cell phone. But is texting language good or bad for kids' learning?

A number of parents and teachers are concerned that the rise in popularity of IMing and text messaging among kids might be hurting their written language skills. Could this be true?

On one hand, more and more teachers in the United States have discovered "text-speak" or "textisms" in the formal schoolwork of their students. Students are actually including things like emoticons (smileys and such), acronyms ("LOL"), abbreviations ("ru going?"), and numeric short cuts ("l8ter 2day") in their written assignments.

Many teachers consider texting language to be conversational slang for the tech-savvy generation. And they consider it a bad habit that could hurt students if, for instance, they use such language in an inappropriate setting (say, on a written exam or in a job application).

But on the other hand, at least one study has shown that kids who use such texting language do not have poorer written language skills. In fact, they were actually *better* readers and writers than kids who didn't use the abbreviations!

According to the researchers from the study, it's possible that wacky symbols and text spellings actually give kids a better appreciation for language sounds, which is a key part of reading. And contrary to popular belief, there doesn't seem to be any connection between texting and a child's normal spelling ability; in other words, kids who text a lot still know how to spell correctly!

What do you think?

Source: BrainPOP®, https://www.brainpop.com/socialstudies/culture/digitaletiquette/fyi/#tab=0

Student or Student Team: _____   Date: _____

For each feature of *argue*, find an example or two from the text, or supply one based on your own opinion on digital etiquette.

FEATURES OF THE KEY USE *ARGUE*	EXAMPLES FROM THE TEXT "LANGUAGE"
State the issue (often in the form of a question)	Do you view texting language as an advantage or disadvantage in students' learning?
Give your opinion or claim based on the issue	
Provide reasons for your opinion or claim	Texting illustrates students' metalinguistic awareness.
Substantiate or defend your position with evidence and support	Findings of a study point to the fact that students who text are more literate than those who don't.
Use a persuasive tone	
Summarize your reasoning	

One other type of instructional material that we should consider using for instruction and assessment, especially for ELLs, is real-life objects or manipulatives. The content areas of mathematics, social studies, and science lend themselves to making learning concrete and experiential with a variety of authentic materials. Resource 4.12 is set up so that each feature of an explanation is grounded in a content area topic and example objects or materials. Why don't you try it out with a group of colleagues?

RESOURCE 4.12 *Explain* Using Real-Life Objects and Materials

Teacher or Teacher Team: _____   Date: _____

For each feature of *explain* and suggested content area activity, provide some examples of real-life objects or materials that might be useful for instruction and classroom assessment. You will find some ideas waiting for you.

FEATURES OF THE KEY USE *EXPLAIN*	SUGGESTED ACTIVITIES BY CONTENT AREA	EXAMPLES OF OBJECTS OR MATERIALS
Sequence a series of steps in events, processes, or cycles	Science: describe mitosis	String or lima beans
Connect the steps in the sequence in a logical order	Mathematics: find the perimeter	Yardstick or measuring tape, rectangular books, desks, or tables
Answer *why* something happens		
Answer *how* something works	Science: build a circuit	Wooden base 2 1.2 volt lightbulbs 1 lamp holder 1 battery holder for a D-size battery 1 simple switch 4 screws to mount the switch and the lamp holder Insulated solid copper wire
Show a cause-and-effect relationship		
Describe phenomena	Mathematics: sort by sizes and shapes	Vegetables or fruits

Take the DARE

How might you capitalize on different types of instructional materials to maximize students' exposure to and reinforcement of concepts? For example, besides movies, there are a variety of supplemental materials on topics found on the BrainPOP® website

(Make-a-Map®—BrainPOP®'s concept-mapping tool; a graphic or comic—a visual representation; Challenge—a series of digital cognitive tasks about the topic; and text-based activities, to name some). These materials offer students opportunities to work with multimodal forms of linguistic expression and different forms of representing meaning throughout a unit. How might you expand upon the types of instructional materials that you rely on?

Identifying the academic language students are expected to process or express in class is important, as it makes language use explicit. The instructional materials from which academic language use is drawn must also be relevant for students. Instructional materials might be analyzed in light of their linguistic and cultural responsiveness, as shown in Resource 4.13, to determine their usefulness for your classroom.

SCAFFOLDING INSTRUCTION

Scaffolds are a metaphoric concept (think scaffolding on a building used as support) for the assistance provided by adults and peers to enable learners to engage in learning, such as in solving problems or carrying out tasks, that would otherwise be unattainable (Fisher & Frey, 2010; Heritage, 2007). The concept of scaffolding is integral to teaching so that every student is duly challenged but yet is able to achieve within his or her zone of proximal development (Vygotsky, 1978). The *zone of proximal development* can be defined as the difference between what learners can do independently in relation to what they can do when their learning is scaffolded by more knowledgeable adults or peers. One of the most important features of scaffolding is that it involves a gradual transfer of responsibility from teacher to student. Thus, by having students eventually take ownership for their own learning, they simultaneously are able to develop self-regulation.

Wood, Bruner, and Ross (1976) first used the term *scaffolded learning* to apply to the process of supporting students achieve a goal or complete a challenging task. Scaffolded instruction exemplifies this principle; it involves teachers being intentional about reaching every student's conceptual and linguistic potential. Heritage and Chang (2012) elaborate on this notion by saying that "scaffolding is the 'just right' kind of support required by students to engage in practice that helps them mature processes which are on the cusp of developing" (p. 2).

Scaffolding instruction underscores a key use of academic language—*explain*—for students should be informed of how something should be done and why; in return, they should be able to explain the *how* and *why* of their work to others. It also can entail other key uses: *recount*, by having students summarize using gestures and visuals, and *discuss*, by having pairs ask and answer provocative questions to each other. Relying on DARE, students can dive deep into content and language to negotiate meaning.

Scaffolding and differentiating are related yet distinct approaches to instruction. They share the goal of enabling all students to maximize access and achieve grade-level content through language. Additionally, both keep in mind how students can

We invite you to reimagine the usability of your instructional materials through the eyes of your students. In particular, we would like you to evaluate the effectiveness of the materials, particularly in classrooms that have students from a variety of linguistic and cultural backgrounds.

Teacher or Teacher Team: _____   Date: _____

Instructional Material: _____   Grade: _____

THE INSTRUCTIONAL MATERIAL	SELECT ONE		
	CONSISTENTLY	INCONSISTENTLY	NOT AT ALL
1. Has a broad coverage of ideas that represent multiple linguistic and cultural perspectives			X
2. Presents information in a manner that is inclusive of all your students		X	
3. Makes it easy for students to see themselves			
4. Avoids stereotyping and limits the amount of bias in the presentation of ideas		X	
5. Offers opportunities for students to interact with each other in their preferred language(s)			
6. Presents learning activities that include multicultural contexts			
7. Places equal value on college, career, community, and 21st century skills for students		X	
8. Models uses of academic language for a variety of purposes			
9. Respects students' different language and cultural influences on their learning			
10. Fully integrates language and culture into the material, rather than being tangential to it			
11. Presents academic language within meaningful and relevant contexts for students			
12. Includes illustrations and photos that depict our multilingual, multicultural world	X		

actively engage in learning without diminishing higher-order thinking, per Bloom's revised taxonomy—that is, they have opportunities to apply, evaluate, and create. Scaffolded and differentiated instruction are expressions of equity, as they address where students are and how they might be aided in getting to where they need to go.

Scaffolding requires intended learning to be broken up into manageable chunks; subsequently, a tool (e.g., a manipulative), a structure (e.g., a graphic organizer), or a resource (e.g., a digital video) is offered for each chunk to promote comprehension of concepts and the processing or production of language. When asking students to produce a historical *recount* based on a biography, for example, teachers might scaffold instruction by discussing a typical sequence of life events from students' experiences and then applying it to a timeline. From there, students could produce summaries of historical accounts of the lives of their selected person, paying attention to sequential language in their depiction of events.

For differentiating instruction, teachers would consider how different groups of students might be able to demonstrate historical *recount* conceptually and linguistically. One group, such as students with interrupted formal education (SIFE), might complete the timeline in the language of their choice, coupled with pertinent photographs, or they might compile a photojournal of major events following chronological order. Long-term English language learners (ELLs), on the other hand, might be able to create an infographic or Prezi from the information from the timeline while the remaining students would produce an oral or written summary of historical events in chronological order of their selected person's life.

Take the DARE

Sometimes, you might scaffold instruction, and other times, you might differentiate instruction in your classroom. Which tools, structures, and resources do you commonly rely on for scaffolding? Which tools, structures, and resources do you commonly rely on for differentiating instruction? How do the two approaches complement each other? How might you incorporate key uses of academic language into both?

Scaffolding instruction can boost students' academic language development, along with their achievement. Resource 4.14 provides an example of how a grade-level topic or theme can be scaffolded for each key use of academic language.

Resource 4.15 envisions scaffolding as a classroom strategy that enables teachers to potentially reach all students and gently advance their language and conceptual development.

INCLUDING METALINGUISTIC STRATEGIES

Metalinguistic strategies are geared to building an awareness of language and language learning and communicating it, often through social interaction. They encompass the dimensions of academic language—words and phrases, sentences, and discourse—and involve reflecting on the structures of language and their match with the purposes for language use. Students' development of metalinguistic strategies enhances their ability

Imagine young students creating games using different shapes. We have inserted how each key use of academic language might be incorporated into this unit of learning, along with suggested scaffolds or supports. The first example of each key use has been provided for you; there is space allotted for you to continue thinking about how to integrate DARE into scaffolding instruction.

Grade Level: _Primary_   Topic or Theme: _Applying Shapes to Playing Games_

KEY USE OF ACADEMIC LANGUAGE	IDEAS FOR SCAFFOLDING LANGUAGE INSTRUCTION	EXAMPLES OF SCAFFOLDS OR SUPPORTS
Discuss	*Discuss different games to play using <u>real-life objects</u> of varied shapes, such as throwing a <u>Frisbee</u> or flying a <u>kite</u>, with a <u>group of friends</u>*	Real-life objects (Frisbees and kites), group of friends
Discuss		
Argue	*Argue in favor of a <u>board game</u> that has shapes, display it, describe it, and give reasons for selecting it to <u>a partner</u>*	Board game, a partner
Argue		
Recount	*Recount one of the <u>games</u> you play at school or at home that involves a <u>ball</u> and give directions to <u>your class</u>*	A game with a ball, your class
Recount		
Explain	*Explain how to play a game based on rectangles, such as <u>dominoes</u>, using real objects, along with stating what to do to <u>a peer</u>*	Dominoes, a peer
Explain		

to monitor their comprehension processes. In essence, the direct and explicit teaching of metalinguistic strategies facilitates students' use of language as a tool for thinking (Lightsey & Frye, 2004).

Think-Alouds. Teacher read and think-alouds enhance students' exposure to different genres or types of text organization. With this strategy, teachers can verbalize academic language use in text, which would fall under metalinguistic awareness, or they can describe how they monitor their comprehension, which would be considered metacognitive awareness. Either way, the purpose of the think-aloud strategy is to model for students how skilled readers construct meaning from text. Equally important, student think-alouds offer opportunities for students to reflect on their academic language use. The following is an example of a think-aloud strategy, initiated by

Consider this checklist as a self-assessment of scaffolding strategies that you use as a teacher with your students. For each "yes," think about your frequency of use—some of the time (S), most the time (M), or all the time (A)—and place the appropriate letter in the column. If you do not employ a scaffolding strategy, simply mark "no."

Teacher: _____   Date: _____

AS A TEACHER, WHEN SCAFFOLDING INSTRUCTION, I . . .	YES			NO
	S	M	A	
Match the types of instructional supports to the students, the content, and the learning objectives of the lesson				
Use a variety of instructional supports, including visual, graphic, interactive, and linguistic ones		M		
Model oral and written exemplars for my students				
Allow my students to select the instructional supports that suit their learning style, language, and the task at hand				X
Am aware of my English language learners' levels of language proficiency and the needs of my students with disabilities				
Am aware of my students' conceptual understanding of the subject matter			A	
Carefully push my students to challenge and advance their academic language development together with their conceptual development				
Take cues from my students as to when they wish to be more independent and take on more responsibility for their own learning				
Give my students criterion-referenced feedback to move their learning forward	S			

teachers modeling oral reading, then pausing and asking students pertinent, thought-provoking questions along the way.

Questions associated with a think-aloud strategy that students could ask themselves about language include the following:

- What questions come to mind when I hear the title of the book (story, chapter, or article)?

- How might I say what was just read aloud in another way?

- Which words or sentences help me better understand what is happening (the information presented)?

- Do I have a picture in my head about what I just read or heard?

- What does the language of this passage tell me? How is it different from what I already know?

Take the DARE

If you have never tried a think-aloud strategy with your students, take the plunge! Make sure that you select a genre of interest to your students. Experiment by modeling some of the questions and responses about language while reading an excerpt out loud. Then, have your students try out the strategy and self-reflect based on a paragraph or so of text.

Other wonderings about language that can apply to the think-aloud strategy are specifically expressed in terms of key uses of academic language, illustrated in Resource 4.16.

RESOURCE 4.16 Applying Key Uses to Student Think-Aloud Strategies for Literature

Student: _____   Text: _____

Date: _____

As think-aloud strategies are geared to individual students, the key use *discuss* is not included, as it assumes interaction with others. As students read different types of text aloud, you might ask some pointed questions that are suggested under each key use. Tally the number of times students engage in DARE, and note what the student produces. The first example for each key use begs a metacognitive response while the second example is more metalinguistic in nature.

KEY USE OF ACADEMIC LANGUAGE	TALLY OF LANGUAGE USE	WHAT THE STUDENT SAYS
Argue What is the author thinking, and what might be an opposing point of view? What are some words, expressions, or sentences that portray an argumentative tone?	I	
Recount Can you summarize what happened in the beginning (in the middle, and at the end) of the story? What are some words and expressions that describe the main character?	LHT	"In the beginning, Ana was quiet and shy. After her 14th birthday, she changed. In high school, Ana was a leader who wasn't . . ."
Explain Why do you think that *X* occurred, or why did *Y* react in a certain way? Show me some sentences that relate how the tension in the mystery builds.		

Once students are familiar with think-aloud strategies and how to use language more intentionally, they might try thinking about their language use in conversations with peers. In considering the purpose for communicating, students are able to build their metalinguistic awareness. By gaining familiarity and experience with the pragmatics of language (gaining meaning from context) as well as story structures in both oral and written text, students will more likely be able to understand discourse. Resource 4.17 offers a set of questions that probes students' thinking about language.

<table>
<tr><td colspan="2" style="background:gray; color:white;">RESOURCE 4.17 Thinking About Language Use in Student Conversations: A Self-Assessment Checklist</td></tr>
</table>

There are a lot of purposes for using language. Check the ones that you think about when speaking with a partner.

THINKING ABOUT THE LANGUAGE I USE IN CONVERSATIONS	
My Name _____	
My Partner's Name _____	
Date _____	
Place a check (✓) next to the talk moves with your partner. In my conversation, . . .	
✓	I thought about how to ask a question about the topic (event, or character).
	I thought about how to answer a question before talking.
✓	I planned the language to use to describe my thinking.
	I asked my partner to restate what was said in a different way.
	I thought about the language to use before adding to my partner's thinking.
	I supported my partner's idea by providing evidence or additional information.
✓	I used language of respect when agreeing or disagreeing with my partner's thinking.

Source: Adapted from Assessors at Work, *Language Development Opportunities Newsletter, 23,* p. 1.

Building Metalinguistic Awareness for Multilingual Students. Multilingual students, by definition, have linguistic repertoires that encompass more than one language from which they can draw. A long research history reveals that children who are raised with two languages show advantages over monolingual peers in their metalinguistic awareness. Bialystok and Barac (2012) go further in saying that the metalinguistic performance of students in immersion settings improves with increased knowledge of the language.

In other words, there tends to be a correlation between students' language proficiency in two languages and the degree of their metalinguistic awareness.

One way to foster academic language development in multilingual students is to build their metalinguistic awareness that, in turn, will have cross-linguistic influence and facilitate their learning in two or more languages. The benefit of positive cross-linguistic influence is that multilinguals' knowledge of one language has a positive impact on their learning or use of another language.

Let's look at the key uses of academic language presented side by side in English and Spanish in Resource 4.18. It becomes readily apparent just in looking at the names of the key uses that there are similarities between the two (as they are cognates), and both teachers and students are able to make cross-language connections. The metalinguistic strategies that might accompany this chart include (1) extending students' knowledge (of key uses) from one language to the other, (2) ensuring or confirming students' understanding in one language through another one, (3) recognizing cognates as facilitators of comprehension, and (4) purposefully planning conversations for students to discover similarities and differences between languages (Escamilla et al., 2014).

RESOURCE 4.18 Visibility of Key Uses of Academic Language in English and Spanish

For those of you who work in settings where both Spanish and English are media of instruction, think about how you might cross-reference key uses of academic language within or across content areas. DARE your students to see the similarities between the features of each key use, orally and in writing, in different materials and texts.

Teacher or Teacher Team: _____   Date: _____

KEY USES OF ACADEMIC LANGUAGE	USOS CLAVE DEL LENGUAJE ACADÉMICO EN ESPAÑOL
Discuss	Discutir
Argue	Argumentar
Recount	Relatar
Explain	Explicar

REFLECT

When students come to have control over DARE, they gain confidence in communicating orally and in writing in all content areas. When students interact with each other in language-rich supportive environments, they gain a greater sense of how language works and thus increase their metalinguistic awareness. By personalizing learning through agency and participation within linguistically and culturally sustainable classrooms, students can become motivated, self-regulated, and independent learners. We feel that Figure 4.4, a vision of educational efficacy, summarizes how we collectively might move forward to enhance academic language learning and achievement for our students.

FIGURE 4.4 A Vision of Efficacy in Education

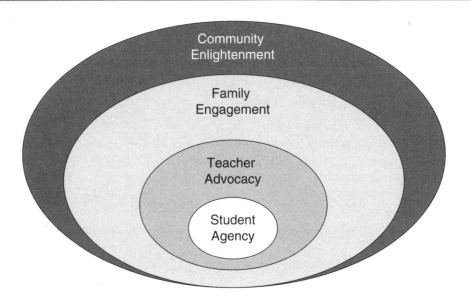

It is our conviction that in implementing key uses of academic language, students must play a substantial part in the reenvisioning of teaching and learning. Teachers must rely on their instructional expertise and make every effort to be advocates, support the active engagement of families, and rely on community resources to optimize opportunities for student success. With teachers and students working and learning together toward the same goals, equity can become a norm in all classrooms and schools.

TAKE ACTION

Instructional materials that prompt students to pursue learning through multiliteracies can serve as a call to action. When students pursue their own interests and having choices in how to learn, student agency is bound to increase. All the while, adept teachers use scaffolding techniques to enable every student to set and achieve academic content and language goals.

Here are some questions to DARE you to prompt action.

1. Where might you begin in the implementation of the key uses of academic language for your classroom, grade, and school? If you have already taken some steps, where might you go next? Think about how you and your colleagues might devise a schoolwide survey with support of school leadership

that measures the sustainability of your school's effort to highlight key uses, along with the involvement of teachers and students.

2. What ideas can you and your grade-level team suggest to highlight key uses of academic language in instructional materials? If key uses are not evident, how might you embed them within the materials? How might you encourage your team in this undertaking (e.g., tackle the task as a whole team one key use at a time or pair up, select a key use, and then jigsaw)? What new kinds of materials and resources might you then experiment with to test their linguistic sustainability and usefulness? How might you catalog students' interests and passions so that they can better connect with instructional resources?

3. What can you do to instill student agency and promote student participation in your classroom? Which strategies do you find most effective (e.g., gradual release of responsibility) in moving students toward self-regulation and independence? What do you do to set up and maintain a democratic classroom where students have a voice in determining their pathways to and demonstration of their learning?

4. What might you do to become more aware of your own academic language use and, in turn, instill metalinguistic awareness in your students and your colleagues? What might you do to promote multilingualism as an asset and build metalinguistic awareness that crosses two languages? How might metalinguistic awareness be combined with student participation to bolster confidence in students?

To what extent is student agency promoted in your classroom? Complete the rating scale as a needs assessment to determine the ways in which your students exhibit agency. Discuss your results with colleagues; then, team up, and brainstorm ideas as to how students can play a greater role in initiating and engaging in learning. Don't forget to share your findings with students for their approval.

Teacher: _____   Date: _____

AS AGENTS OF LEARNING, STUDENTS . . .	SOMETIMES	MOST TIMES	ALL THE TIME
1. Have a voice in classroom decision making			
2. Display original work all over the room			
3. Choose partners to work with			
4. Help (re)arrange the classroom			
5. Make suggestions in regard to activities and tasks			
6. Advocate the learning style that best suits them			
7. Have access to technologies (e.g., through centers) and contribute to evolving phrase/concept/learning walls and other classroom and school displays			
8. As representatives of their community, are involved in outreach and social action through classroom projects			
9. Are liaisons to families and advocates on their behalf			
10. Have time to reflect on their learning and to help set next steps			
11. Feel secure in freely participating in class			
12. Exert independence of thought and action			

Chapter 4 Resources

RESOURCE 4.2 A Checklist of Classroom Strategies That Promote Student Agency

Are these language-centered strategies present in your classroom, or would you consider implementing them? This checklist is inspired by Ferlazzo and Hull Sypnieski's (2016) ideas for promoting student agency.

Teacher(s): _____   Date: _____

STUDENT-CENTERED CLASSROOM STRATEGY	YES	NO
1. Setting Content and Language Goals: Students		
• agree on goals with teachers		
• periodically review and evaluate their goals		
• revise their goals based on evidence		
2. Heightening Awareness Through Self-Talk: Students		
• communicate *what* they are thinking (metacognitive awareness)		
• communicate *how* they use language (metalinguistic awareness)		
• communicate *what* they know about culture and how it affects the message (metacultural awareness)		
3. Teaching Others: Students		
• participate in content-related activities, become experts on an aspect of learning, and share it with others in their group (e.g., jigsaw activities)		
• tutor younger students or purposefully interact with them (e.g., story reading)		
• partner and collaborate with peers		
4. Encouraging Students' Language Development: Teachers		
• emotionally support students in their academic language development		
• offer feedback on students' academic language use to push them forward		
• model to illustrate what students are expected to do with language		

RESOURCE 4.3 Moving From Dependence on Others to Independence: A Continuum of Student Change of Classroom Roles

Based on the anchors that describe student roles, place an X along each continuum that marks the placement of students on the road to becoming agents of their own learning.

Teacher: _____   Date: _____

STUDENTS AS RESPONDERS TO LEARNING / STUDENTS AS AGENTS OF LEARNING

1. Feedback: Students

Receive feedback from teachers   Receive and give feedback to peers and others

_____

2. Assessment: Students

Take teacher-made and commercial tests   Engage in self- and peer assessment

_____

3. Activities, tasks, and projects: Students

Follow teacher directions   Choose from a menu or self-select with teacher approval

_____

4. Learning style: Students

Work alone   Collaborate and interact with peers

_____

5. Learning projects or products: Students

Produce right/wrong or constructed responses   Create original work

_____

6. Conferencing with teachers or family members: Students

Do not participate   Lead the discussion

_____

Chapter 4 Resources

Examining the four types of student engagement, use this checklist as a reflective tool to evaluate the extent to which you are maximizing students' opportunities to participate in learning.

Teacher: _____   Date: _____

TYPES OF STUDENT ENGAGEMENT AND THEIR ATTRIBUTES	PRESENT IN MY CLASSROOM	NOT AS MUCH AS I WOULD LIKE
1. Behavioral Engagement: Students . . .		
• Pay attention and are not easily distracted		
• Remain on task		
• Exert effort to learn		
• Seek assistance to carry out tasks		
2. Cognitive Engagement: Students . . .		
• Comprehend complex concepts (with or without scaffolding)		
• Are academically challenged by higher-order thinking tasks		
• Have opportunities to solve thought-provoking problems		
• Gain subject matter expertise that they apply to new situations		
3. Affective Engagement: Students . . .		
• Have interest in the academic tasks		
• Have a positive attitude toward learning		
• Are curious in seeking information and ideas		
• Feel safe and comfortable in pursuing challenges		
4. Linguistic Engagement: Students . . .		
• Have opportunities to interact with each other		
• Express themselves visually, orally, and in writing		
• Ask clarifying questions to peers and adults		
• Practice key uses of academic language in each content area		
• Rely on multiple languages as resources, when appropriate		

Discuss what you might do to be more inclusive of students participating in teacher-facilitated activities that address key uses of academic language in authentic ways throughout the teaching and learning cycle.

Unit of Instruction: _____ Grade: _____

PHASE IN THE TEACHING AND LEARNING CYCLE	IDEAS FOR LANGUAGE-CENTERED STUDENT PARTICIPATION
1. Identify applicable standards	• Guide students in translating standards into student-friendly ones • Encourage students to formulate and *recount* their content and language expectations • _____
2. Formulate learning targets	• Have students suggest which key use of academic language would best fit the standard and why • Pair students to *discuss* expectations associated with content and language targets • _____
3. Craft a final project	• Allow students to brainstorm projects they would like to pursue that fit the standards and learning targets • Ask students to take a stance (*argue*) for their choice and give reasons why • _____
4. Select instructional materials	• Let students *discuss* the pros and cons of instructional materials in small groups • Allow students to select from different categories of instructional resources • _____
5. Determine criteria for success	• Coconstruct performance criteria with students for projects based on language and content expectations • Prompt students to *argue* in favor of or against their application of criteria and the corresponding evidence in their work • _____
6. Participate in self-and peer assessment	• Direct students in applying the criteria for success to their own work and that of their classmates • Have students *explain* how the feedback they provide to their peers matches the criteria for success • _____

Chapter 4 Resources

Analyze the instructional materials for each of your units of study to identify key uses of academic language. Indicate how each key use is exemplified in text, audio, or video. Include the references in your unit plan.

Content Topic: _____   Grade: _____

DARE	DESCRIPTIONS OF KEY USES OF ACADEMIC LANGUAGE WITHIN CONTENT	INSTRUCTIONAL MATERIALS—PAGE NUMBER OR REFERENCE (E.G., URL)
Discuss		
Discuss		
Argue		
Argue		
Recount		
Recount		
Explain		
Explain		

Chapter 4 Resources

RESOURCE 4.7 Representation of the Principles of Universal Design for Learning in Instructional Materials

For each instructional material you or your team selects, either check those principles of UDL (and perhaps the page numbers or URLs for websites) that are present, or provide examples of each principle of UDL. Then, assess the extent to which UDL principles are present, and devise an action plan.

Teacher Team: _____   Grade: _____

INSTRUCTIONAL MATERIAL (TEXT, AUDIO, OR DIGITAL)	PRESENCE OF PRINCIPLES OF UNIVERSAL DESIGN FOR LEARNING		
NAME OR TYPE	1. MULTIPLE MEANS OF REPRESENTATION OF CONCEPTS	2. MULTIPLE MEANS OF ACTION AND EXPRESSION	3. MULTIPLE MEANS OF ENGAGING IN LEARNING CONCEPTS

LANGUAGE POWER

The following chart is intended to illustrates one curricular idea for each key use—DARE—as an exemplar that includes interactive, visual, and kinesthetic modes of support. Generate grade-level examples with a teacher team.

Unit: _____   Grade: _____

AUDITORY (LISTENING AND SPEAKING)	INTERACTIVE	VISUAL	KINESTHETIC
Discuss			
Argue			
Recount			
Explain			

Chapter 4 Resources

Use this rating scale to evaluate instructional materials; share it with your colleagues to determine the extent to which they agree with your judgment. You may wish to select some of the items to include in an Excel spreadsheet to maintain an ongoing inventory of instructional materials by topic or theme for yourself or for your grade-level team.

Name of instructional material: _____

Source or publisher: _____

Theme: _____

Year of publication or production: _____

Grade level(s): _____

Type of instructional material:

- ☐ Textbooks
- ☐ Articles
- ☐ Trade books
- ☐ Original-source documents
- ☐ Apps for a handheld device or computer
- ☐ Videos
- ☐ Illustrations, diagrams, or cartoons

- ☐ Other: _____
- ☐ Online resources
- ☐ Multimedia (e.g., PPTs, Prezis)
- ☐ Audio (e.g., podcasts)
- ☐ Illustrations, diagrams, or cartoons
- ☐ Other: _____

THE INSTRUCTIONAL MATERIAL	SELECT ONE		
	CONSISTENTLY	INCONSISTENTLY	NOT AT ALL
1. Addresses your instructional goals and objectives			
2. Presents information in a manner that is accessible and achievable by your students			
3. Organizes information in an intuitive manner that makes it easy for students to navigate			
4. Builds continuity in students' development of concepts and information, skills, and practices			
5. Has a balance of coverage in higher-order thinking skills			
6. Includes learning activities that are engaging, authentic, and relevant			
7. Integrates visual and graphic scaffolding related to the content into the learning activities			
8. Models use of academic language (including DARE) for a variety of purposes			
9. Includes language that is familiar and accessible when presenting complex ideas and concepts			
10. Provides opportunities for students to partake in 21st century skill development			
11. Represents ideas that are actionable			
12. Respects students' different learning styles and rates of learning by providing a variety of options for reaching the same outcome			
13. Considers the range of student performance			
14. Highlights academic language development in conjunction with conceptual development			
15. Is inviting, welcoming, and, at the same time, challenging to students			

Title of the Movie or Video: _____

The following are features of the key use *recount*. Match the features with examples from a video or movie; don't be surprised, however, if there is not an example of each feature. Share your findings with colleagues, and consider how you might replicate this exercise for your students.

Teacher or Teacher Team: _____   Date: _____

FEATURES OF THE KEY USE *RECOUNT*	EXAMPLES FROM A MOVIE OR VIDEO
State experiences	
Relate a series of facts	
Describe a sequence of events	
Summarize what happened	
Recall details related to personal events or experiences	
Reflect or comment on the experiences	

Chapter 4 Resources

Based on an informational text, how might you have students formulate an argument about the value of a metalinguistic strategy, such as digital etiquette—that is, being able to understand language? What information can they glean from the movie to use as reasons or evidence? Consider having students use both types of instructional materials to complete the chart. Carrying the topic even further, after completing the graphic organizer, students could form sides and orally debate the issue, produce a persuasive essay, or even create a rap or poem on social media.

Student or Student Team: _____   Date: _____

For each feature of *argue*, find an example or two from the text, or supply one based on your own opinion.

FEATURES OF THE KEY USE *ARGUE*	EXAMPLES FROM INFORMATIONAL TEXT
State the issue (often in the form of a question)	
Give your opinion or claim based on the issue	
Provide reasons for your opinion or claim	
Substantiate or defend your position with evidence and support	
Use a persuasive tone	
Summarize your reasoning	

Chapter 4 Resources

Teacher or Teacher Team: _____   Date: _____

For each feature of *explain* and content area, provide some suggested activities and examples of real-life objects or materials that might be useful for instruction and classroom assessment.

FEATURES OF THE KEY USE *EXPLAIN*	SUGGESTED ACTIVITIES BY CONTENT AREA	EXAMPLES OF OBJECTS OR MATERIALS
Sequence a series of steps in events, processes, or cycles		
Connect the steps in the sequence in a logical order		
Answer *why* something happens		
Answer *how* something works		
Show a cause-and-effect relationship		
Describe phenomena		

Chapter 4 Resources

RESOURCE 4.13 Revisiting Instructional Materials Through the Lens of Linguistic and Cultural Sustainability

We invite you to reimagine the usability of your instructional materials through the eyes of your students. In particular, we would like you to evaluate how effective the materials are, particularly in classrooms that have students from a variety of linguistic and cultural backgrounds.

Teacher or Teacher Team: _____ Date: _____

Instructional Material: _____ Grade: _____

THE INSTRUCTIONAL MATERIAL	SELECT ONE		
	CONSISTENTLY	INCONSISTENTLY	NOT AT ALL
1. Has a broad coverage of ideas that represent multiple linguistic and cultural perspectives			
2. Presents information in a manner that is inclusive of all your students			
3. Makes it easy for students to see themselves			
4. Avoids stereotyping and limits the amount of bias in the presentation of ideas			
5. Offers opportunities for students to interact with each other in their preferred language(s)			
6. Presents learning activities that include multicultural contexts			
7. Places equal value on college, career, community, and 21st century skills for students			
8. Models uses of academic language for a variety of purposes			
9. Respects students' different language and cultural influences on their learning			
10. Fully integrates language and culture into the material, rather than being tangential to it			
11. Presents academic language within meaningful and relevant contexts for students			
12. Includes illustrations and photos that depict our multilingual, multicultural world			

Chapter 4 Resources

We have inserted each key use of academic language; you are to supply the ideas for scaffolding instruction, along with suggested scaffolds or supports.

Grade Level: _____   Topic or Theme:_____

KEY USE OF ACADEMIC LANGUAGE	IDEAS FOR SCAFFOLDING LANGUAGE INSTRUCTION	EXAMPLES OF SCAFFOLDS OR SUPPORTS
Discuss		
Discuss		
Argue		
Argue		
Recount		
Recount		
Explain		
Explain		

Chapter 4 Resources

RESOURCE 4.15 A Checklist Rating Scale for Scaffolding Instruction and Assessment Inclusive of Language and Content

Consider this checklist as a self-assessment of scaffolding strategies that you, as a teacher, use with your students. For each "yes," think about your frequency of use—some of the time (S), most the time (M), or all the time (A)—and place the appropriate letter in the column. If you do not employ a scaffolding strategy, simply mark "no."

Teacher: _____   Date: _____

AS A TEACHER, WHEN SCAFFOLDING INSTRUCTION, I . . .	YES			NO
	S	M	A	
Match the types of instructional supports to the students, the content, and the learning objectives of the lesson				
Use a variety of instructional supports, including visual, graphic, interactive, and linguistic ones				
Model oral and written exemplars for my students				
Allow my students to select the instructional supports that suit their learning style, language, and the task at hand				
Am aware of my English language learners' levels of language proficiency and the needs of my students with disabilities				
Am aware of my students' conceptual understanding of the subject matter				
Carefully push my students to challenge and advance their academic language development together with their conceptual development				
Take cues from my students as to when they wish to be more independent and take on more responsibility for their own learning				
Give my students criterion-referenced feedback to move their learning forward				

Student: _____   Text: _____

Date: _____

As students read different types of text aloud, you might ask some pointed questions that are suggested under each key use. Tally the number of times students engage in DARE, and note what the student produces. The first example in each cell begs a metacognitive response while the second example is more metalinguistic in nature.

KEY USE OF ACADEMIC LANGUAGE	TALLY OF LANGUAGE USE	WHAT THE STUDENT SAYS
Argue What is the author thinking, and what might be an opposing point of view? What are some words, expressions, or sentences that portray an argumentative tone?		
Recount Can you summarize what happened in the beginning (in the middle, and at the end) of the story? What are some words and expressions that describe the main character?		
Explain Why do you think that *X* occurred, or why did *Y* react in a certain way? Show me some sentences that relate how the tension in the mystery builds.		

Chapter 4 Resources

There are a lot of purposes for using language. Check the ones that you think about when speaking with a partner.

THINKING ABOUT THE LANGUAGE I USE IN CONVERSATIONS	
My Name _____	
My Partner's Name _____	
Date _____	
Place a check (✓) next to the talk moves with your partner. In my conversation,	
	I thought about how to ask a question about the topic (event, or character).
	I thought about how to answer a question before talking.
	I planned the language to use to describe my thinking.
	I asked my partner to restate what was said in a different way.
	I thought about the language to use before adding to my partner's thinking.
	I supported my partner's idea by providing evidence or additional information.
	I used language of respect when agreeing or disagreeing with my partner's thinking.

Source: Adapted from Assessors at Work, *Language Development Opportunities Newsletter, 23,* p. 1.

Chapter 4 Resources

For those of you who work in settings where both Spanish and English are media of instruction, think about how you might cross-reference key uses of academic language within or across content areas. DARE your students to see the similarities between the features of each key use, orally and in writing, in different materials and texts.

Teacher or Teacher Team: _____   Date: _____

KEY USES OF ACADEMIC LANGUAGE	USOS CLAVE DEL LENGUAJE ACADÉMICO EN ESPAÑOL
Discuss	Discutir
Argue	Argumentar
Recount	Relatar
Explain	Explicar

Chapter 4 Resources

References and Further Reading

Wiggins, G., & McTighe, J. (2005). *Understanding by design* (2nd ed.). Alexandria, VA: Association for Supervision and Curriculum Development (ASCD).

Agency and Participation

Anderson, M. (2016). *Learning to choose, choosing to learn: The key to student motivation & achievement*. Alexandria, VA: ASCD.

Boykin, A. W., & Noguera, P. (2011). *Creating the opportunity to learn: Moving from research to practice to close the achievement gap*. Alexandria, VA: ASCD.

Calvert, L. (2016). *Moving from compliance to agency: What teachers need to make professional learning work*. Oxford, OH: Learning Forward and NCTAF.

Federicks, J. A., Blumenfield, P. C., & Paris, A. H. (2004). School engagement: Potential of the concept, state of the evidence. *Review of Educational Research, 74*(1), 59–109.

Ferlazzo, L., & Hull Sypnieski, K. (2016). *Navigating the Common Core with English language learners: Practical strategies to develop higher-order thinking skills*. San Francisco, CA: John Wiley & Sons.

Gottlieb, M. (2016). *Assessing English language learners: Bridges to educational equity: Connecting academic language proficiency to student achievement* (2nd ed.). Thousand Oaks, CA: Corwin.

Lave, J., & Wenger, E. (1991). *Situated learning: Legitimate peripheral participation*. Cambridge, UK: Cambridge University Press.

Rodriguez, A. J. (2002). Using sociotransformative constructivism to teach for understanding in diverse classrooms: A beginning teacher's journey. *American Educational Research Journal, 39*(4), 1017–1045.

Vander Ark, T. (2015, December 21). 10 tips for developing student agency. *Education Week*. Retrieved from http://blogs.edweek.org/edweek/on_innovation/2015/12/10_tips_for_developing_student_agency.html

Zwiers, J. (2008). *Building academic language: Essential practices for content classrooms, grades 5–12*. San Francisco, CA: Jossey-Bass.

Instructional Materials

Chingos, M. M., & Whitehurst, G. J. (2012). *Choosing blindly: Instructional materials, teacher effectiveness, and the Common Core*. Washington, DC: Brown Center on Educational Policy at Brookings.

Gottlieb, M., & Ernst-Slavit, G. (2014). *Academic language in diverse settings: Definitions and contexts*. Thousand Oaks, CA: Corwin.

National Center on Universal Design for Learning. (2014). The three principles of UDL. Retrieved from http://www.udlcenter.org/aboutudl/whatisudl/3principles

Voltz, D. L., Sims, M. J., & Nelson, B. (2010). *Connecting teachers, students, and standards: Strategies for success in diverse and inclusive classrooms*. Alexandria, VA: ASCD.

Scaffolding Instruction

Fisher, D., & Frey, N. (2010). *Guided instruction: How to develop confident and successful learners*. Alexandria, VA: ASCD.

Heritage, M. (2007). Formative assessment: What do teachers need to know and do? *Phi Delta Kappan, 89*(2), 140–145.

Heritage, M., & Chang, S. (2012, April). *Teacher use of formative assessment data for English language learners*. Paper presented at the Annual Meeting of the American Educational Research Association, Los Angeles, CA.

Vygotsky, L. S. (1978). *Mind in society: The development of higher psychological processes*. Cambridge, MA: Harvard University Press.

Wood, D., Bruner, J. S., and Ross, G. (1976). The role of tutoring in problem solving. *Journal of Child Psychology and Psychiatry, 17*(2), 89–100.

Metalinguistic Strategies

Bialystok, E., & Barac, R. (2012). Emerging bilingualism: Dissociating advantages for metalinguistic aware-ness and executive control. *Cognition, 122*(1), 67–73.

Ebbers, S. M. (2012). *Metalinguistic awareness, comprehension, and the Common Core State Standards.* Retrieved from http://www.cdl.org/articles/metalinguistic-awareness-comprehension-and-the-common-core-state-standards

Escamilla, K., Hopewell, S., Butvilofsky, S., Sparrow, W., Soltero-González, L., Ruiz-Figueroa, O., & Escamilla, M. (2014). *Biliteracy from the start: Literacy squared in action.* Philadelphia, PA: Caslon.

James, M. A. (2012). Cross-linguistic influence and the transfer of learning. In N. M. Seel (Ed.), *Encyclopedia of the sciences of learning* (pp. 858–861). Boston, MA: Springer.

Lightsey, G. E., & Frye, B. J. (2004). Teaching metalinguistic skills to enhance early reading instruction. *Reading Horizons, 45*(1), 27–37.

Collaboration and Community Outreach

Involving Stakeholders in Key Uses of Academic Language

It is time for America's young people—all of them, not just a privileged few—to take part in deeper learning. And it is time for policymakers and practitioners to create the system of teacher leadership for them to do so.

—Barnett Berry (2016)

With the dawn of the 21st century has come a change in the notion of schooling and a rethinking of the perceptions of effective leadership. Distributed leadership, where principals share the power as instructional leaders with other school leaders and teachers, has emerged as an accepted and effective evidence-based model. In it, multiple stakeholders take responsibility for the ongoing operation of school and its continuous improvement.

While we acknowledge that leadership at the top is critical to success within any educational environment, our vision is one that extends the distributed leadership model to other important stakeholders in a school system beyond that of administrators and teachers—namely, to families and students. In making school leadership more inclusive, we are able expand the educational talent pool and resources to the entire community. In order for this vision to become a new reality, we realize that school districts must convince organizational politics to allow for blurred lines between stakeholder roles (Schwartz, 2015).

How can key uses of academic language be stimuli for cementing relationships among educational stakeholders so that students can maximize their learning?

The collective expertise of multiple stakeholder groups contributing to decision making ultimately strengthens school to make it a more democratic, collegial, and equitable place. As seen in Figure 5.1, we believe that students, families, teachers, and school leaders form a powerful combination of educational stakeholders who can lead in stimulating positive change in teaching and learning practices.

FIGURE 5.1 Involving Stakeholders in Promoting Key Uses of Academic Language

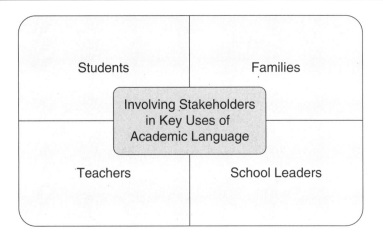

This chapter honors various stakeholder perspectives in educational decision making and illustrates how each one can have a voice in advocating sustained academic language development as part of a school's and district's mission and vision. We hope that by creating connections among stakeholders, we will help advance a unified vision across levels of implementation, from the classroom to the community and from the community to the classroom. In this chapter we ask educational stakeholders to *take the DARE* to do the following:

Discuss their respective roles (students, families, teachers, and school leaders) in advocating and implementing key uses of academic language

Argue for increased communication around key uses of academic language at school, at home, and in the community

Recount ideas for promoting teacher collaboration, strengthening school–community connections, and encouraging student interaction

Explain why they should lend their support and how they might coordinate instruction and assessment around key uses of academic language

Indeed, much coordination is necessary in moving a school system in a new direction, and key uses of academic language might serve as the impetus to prompt and maintain this collaboration of effort. From classrooms to community outreach, we advocate equity of treatment of language and content alongside equity of status of stakeholders in seeing the value and utility of key uses in any language as one of the primary vehicles for student attainment of success in school and beyond.

EXPLORE

For many years, educational success has been equated with high-stakes assessment and accountability, so much so that we have forgotten the glue that binds education: the quality of human interaction and the nurturing of relationships (Zacarian & Silverstone, 2015). Stakeholders in the educational community must join hands in unifying and enacting this relationship-based vision for 21st century teaching and learning. That includes all persons who impact the lives of children and youth, including the students we face every day.

How might all of these stakeholders have a role in shaping and reinforcing key uses of academic language within a school and throughout the community? Here are some ideas for infusing DARE for each major group.

- Students: Teachers can do the following:
  - Shower their classrooms, their schools, and their communities with displays, exhibits, original writing samples, projects, and murals that illustrate key uses of academic language within and across the content areas.
  - Show how projects centered on key uses might involve taking social action in the community and beyond.
  - Honor the use of multiple languages for different communicative purposes and audiences, and acknowledge cultural perspectives in learning.
  - Select, with students, oral and written language samples for individual collections that demonstrate growth and achievement.

- Families: Teachers can do the following:
  - Supply questions to family members (in their home languages) to ask their children about what happens in school.
  - Encourage giving children additional opportunities to develop their home language and English during everyday routines.
  - Ask family members to participate in focus groups around school issues related to language and culture.
  - Create opportunities for families to engage in professional learning to extend their understanding of language development and academic language use.
  - Solicit volunteers for school committees to help formulate language policy.

- Teachers: You can do the following:
  - Collaborate with one another—perhaps by forming content teachers, language specialists, gifted and talented, and special education teams—to intentionally and systematically integrate key uses of academic language with content.
  - Facilitate planning student-led conferences around key uses of academic language.
  - Plan common assessment for units of learning around learning targets that underscore key uses of academic language in relation to content.
- School leaders: You can do the following:
  - Create a process whereby students, teachers, family members, and the community have input in establishing the values that shape the school's culture by creating or revising the school's mission, vision, and beliefs.
  - Carve out embedded and dedicated professional learning opportunities for teachers; devote special meeting times and welcome rooms for family and community members.
  - Help make school an inviting place where student and family voices are heard and where everyone actively invests in students' academic language development.

APPLY

How might you rally students, families, teachers, and school leaders around an ongoing language-centered initiative? One suggestion that you might consider implementing is a schoolwide assessment portfolio system where every stakeholder is a proud contributor at some level. It may take multiple years to plan all of the details and see it to fruition, so begin small, with one stakeholder group or one grade level. The ideal system would ultimately consist of a school portfolio, classroom portfolios, and individual student portfolios that are organized around key uses of academic language within the content areas. Figure 5.2 gives some ideas for portfolio entries around academic language use for each stakeholder group.

Take the DARE

How might you utilize portfolios as a means of data collection, data management, assessment, or accountability? With which stakeholder group might you begin this effort? What types of entries might you collect, and how often? Which content area(s) might you highlight, which language domains (e.g., oral language or literacy), and which key uses of academic language? How might you maintain portfolios digitally through a school-based platform from semester to semester and year to year?

Having elaborated how the school community can come together and *take the DARE* through portfolios, we now apply specific strategies and ideas so that each stakeholder group can participate and take ownership of key uses of academic language.

FIGURE 5.2 Portfolios That Highlight Key Uses of Academic Language for Different Stakeholder Groups

STAKEHOLDERS AND THEIR ROLES IN DIFFERENT TYPES OF PORTFOLIOS	IDEAS FOR PORTFOLIO ENTRIES AROUND KEY USES OF ACADEMIC LANGUAGE
Students— Creators of individual portfolios	• Samples of student self-assessment and reflection of their language development and achievement • Oral language samples reflective of DARE • Written samples highlighting key uses of academic language • Samples of multimodal entries, including movies, interactive podcasts, and murals, that illustrate the key uses within content
Families— Contributors to student portfolios	• Analyses of language use in home languages and English • Student interviews with family and community members • Oral language samples of family histories and traditions (e.g., *recounts* and *explanations*) • Descriptions of artifacts representative of family languages and cultures
Teachers— Managers of classroom portfolios	• Oral and/or written logs of accomplishments highlighting students' academic language development • Social action involving key uses (e.g., *argue* against a proposed ordinance to the city council) • Projects or exhibits shared with the community or other classrooms • Criteria for success or project descriptors illustrative of key uses for interpreting student work
School Leaders— Overseers of school portfolios	• Collections of samples of DARE from each classroom • Documentation of key uses of academic language in school events or community outreach (e.g., videos) • Teacher or grade-level contributions that include key uses • Artifacts of key uses exhibited throughout the school

INVOLVING STUDENTS WITH KEY USES OF ACADEMIC LANGUAGE

Key uses of academic language—DARE—*discuss, argue, recount,* and *explain*—should be the focal point for student interaction and learning throughout the school day. Coupled with their ongoing conceptual development, students can better concentrate on not only *what* they are to learn but *how* to deepen that learning and *when* to communicate it to others. When students are given choice and voice in how and what they learn, they gain confidence, exhibit self-regulation and independence, and grow into their own identity. One way to nurture these student traits is through problem-based learning (PBL). The goal for PBL is for students to achieve standards-based content alongside 21st century skills—namely, critical thinking, problem solving, collaboration, and self-efficacy (for more on the relationship between standards and 21st century skills, see Chapter 2).

Applying key uses of academic language across the content areas—from language arts to mathematics to science, social studies, and fine arts—students can more readily connect school with their life experiences. When schooling is compatible with students' social, cultural, and language experiences, there is a greater congruence among school, home, and community. Consequently, student expectations more readily match their potential, and students are more motivated to learn.

Personal goal setting and metalinguistic reflection are two strategies that help support student agency. Other traits, including self-efficacy, self-regulated learning, persistence, and engagement, have shown to have educational advantages that lead to raising achievement for all students (Boykin & Noguera, 2011). In addition, research on collaboration among students points to its effectiveness in boosting academic performance, especially for minority students at the elementary school level. Given this strong evidence, students should definitely have a more sizable role in determining their destiny and making decisions in school.

Having input in the selection of unit projects and contributing to identifying their standards-referenced criteria for success based on personalized goals push students toward independence of thought and action. Carefully guided by teachers, students can be proactive in expressing what they know about their use of academic language and in planning what to tackle next. Figure 5.3 illustrates some language-centered classroom strategies that promote student participation in learning.

FIGURE 5.3 Supporting Students in the Classroom to Become Independent Learners

STRATEGIES THAT SUPPORT STUDENT PARTICIPATION IN THEIR OWN LEARNING	CLASSROOM EXAMPLES
Goal setting	Based on criteria for success along with peer and teacher feedback, students set realistic attainable expectations for their academic language development (based on key uses) on a monthly, quarterly, or semester basis.
Coconstructing projects	Students generate ideas for unit projects and conduct research with peers; they collaborate in producing products or performances in which key uses are embedded.
Cocrafting criteria for success	Guided by teachers and selected standards, students match features of key uses to descriptors or criteria to later evaluate the oral or written language of their projects or performances.
Personalizing learning through metalinguistic and metacognitive reflection	Students keep a log of learning strategies they experiment with that are associated with features of key uses of academic language (e.g., cognates, consistency of mood, and perspective taking).

In every chapter, we have interwoven relevant tools around key uses of academic language that can readily be incorporated into practice. We begin here with what students can do and then reach out to other stakeholders: families, teachers, and school leaders.

Students approach tasks in different ways according to their preferred learning style—some are visual learners, others are kinesthetic, and still others are auditory or tactile. Encouraging the use of multiple modalities, for both input and output, capitalizes on students' strengths by offering them opportunities to apply their learning in unique ways. By giving students options, teachers gain insight into how students can best demonstrate their learning, and at the same time, student choice is acknowledged and honored.

Instructional scaffolds, such as visual representations of concepts and graphic organizers, or strategies, such as students interacting with each other or with technology, serve as resources for supporting student learning. There is much value in instructional scaffolds, as they do the following:

- Lend meaning making for building conceptual learning

- Allow for multimodal forms of expression during learning

- Offer support for language and content learning

- Invite students to approach learning through varied venues

- Allow students to show what they have learned in a variety of ways

One effective and popular instructional support or scaffold is semantic mapping, a type of graphic organizer, as it can apply to most any content area or personal topic. As illustrated in the Figure 5.4, a semantic web can also readily be framed around key uses of academic language, in this instance, *recount*.

Transferring this semantic map onto a large poster, students could work in groups of three, where each student chooses one of the language pathways to *recount* a story. The triad then decides how to show the unfolding of their original story or one that they are familiar with. As a group, they determine the modality to make their presentation—orally, in writing, graphically, or visually—by interweaving the *who* (the characters), the *where* (the setting), and the *what* (the events).

Many narrative genres may be substituted for "stories," depending on the students' interests and their match to grade-level standards; for example, "*Recount* mysteries, fables, myths, legends, tall tales, biographies, science fiction, fantasies, romance novels, or folktales." *Recount* is also applicable for sharing information among peers, especially using a jigsaw strategy described earlier, where each student becomes an expert in one aspect of a topic before putting it all together in the form of a report or a dramatization.

After each group chooses a key use of academic language, students can then go deeper, such as in Figure 5.5, where a language function that relates one of the communicative intents of *recount*—in this instance, "*sequence* the events"—is placed in the center. Examples of the language function then branch out in a series of temporal phrases that

FIGURE 5.4 An Example of a Semantic Map for the Key Use of *Recount*

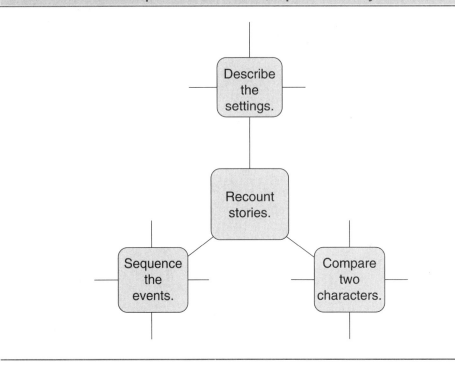

FIGURE 5.5 A Deeper Dive Into a Semantic Map for the Key Use *Recount*

Key Use of Academic Language: Recount

Language Function Related to the Key Use: Sequence events

Grammatical Forms Related to the Key Use: Temporal phrases *(in the beginning; after the first event; toward the end)*

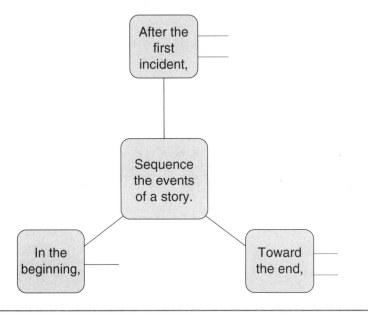

are indicative of the chronology of the narrative. Students can then build paragraphs from these starter phrases and connect them to produce or summarize a story.

These two models of semantic maps may be used as tools or serve as a jump start for students in configuring their own graphics based on narrative or informational text. Once students have practiced and have become familiar with semantic mapmaking, they can generate their own maps, either around specific content topics or the overarching purposes of academic language, as in DARE. At this point, individual or student pairs can have free reign of the design. In Resource 5.1, take a look at how BrainPOP® has highlighted semantic mapping in each of its topics as additional models for students.

RESOURCE 5.1 Students Making Their Own Semantic Maps

Scan the QR code that leads to the BrainPOP® website. "Make a Map" is a featured tool whereby students create their own concept maps for the selected topic. Manipulating a variety of shapes, colors, arrows, keywords, images, and clips from the movie, students can connect ideas for each content topic. In addition, it is suggested that students reflect on their thought processes (that enhance their metacognitive awareness) and share their maps with a teacher, a peer, or a mentor for feedback.

What other content-related ideas lend themselves to semantic mapping? How might you create semantic maps with other key uses? Think about how semantic maps could be part of previewing to introduce a topic or key use or reviewing a unit to reinforce learning. Here is a table to help organize semantic mapping.

Source: BrainPOP®, https://www.brainpop.com/english/writing/conceptmapping

CONTENT AREA TOPIC	KEY USES OF ACADEMIC LANGUAGE	INDIVIDUAL STUDENTS, PAIRS, OR SMALL GROUPS
Mathematics: Operations	Argue the best way to solve a problem	Groups of three representing three different operations

Take the DARE

What other graphic organizers do students find interesting and effective in brainstorming, planning, or illustrating their work, either independently or with others? Have students dabble with different types of organizers, and have them decide which ones they favor and why. Going even further, encourage students to invent their own graphic organizers and explain how to use them with their peers when working with DARE.

Another way in which students can become involved in monitoring their learning is by setting up a series of "I can" statements based on their individual goals or the language expectations for a unit of learning. Again, teachers should model statements that correspond to the task. From these instructional tools, students could plan to either produce scripts and perform stories in their own words, retell stories, or illustrate stories through a series of frames.

"I can" statements can be geared toward key uses of academic language. In Resource 5.2, a checklist for *recounting* folktales, fables, or stories has been set up for second graders as a self-assessment that can be used throughout a school year. It is based on both an English language arts college and career readiness standard and an English language development standard. For multilingual students who are receiving instruction in a language other than English, it would be natural to have these statements in their home language, such as "Puedo" ("I can") in Spanish, 我可以 in simplified Chinese, or 什么 in Urdu.

RESOURCE 5.2 Students Responding to "I Can" Statements Related to English Language Arts and Language Development Standards for Grade 2

Academic Content Standards:

College and Career Readiness Standards: CCSS ELA-Literacy. RL.2.2; SL 2.4

"Recount stories, including fables and folktales from diverse cultures, and determine their central message, lesson, or moral."

"Tell a story or recount an experience with appropriate facts and relevant, descriptive details, speaking audibly in coherent sentences."

Language Development Standards:

WIDA ELD Standard 2, The Language of Language Arts, Example Topic: Storytelling/Experiential recounting, Language Domain: Speaking (2012, p. 59)

Name: _____   Date: _____

My Story, Fable, or Folktale: _____

Key Use of Academic Language: (Oral) Recount the story to a partner

With a partner, take turns answering each question. Your partner circles YES or NO based on what you say. Go over the list together. See if you agree with your partner for each answer.

WHAT CAN YOU DO? RETELLING STORIES, FOLKTALES, OR NARRATIVES		
I can tell **where** the story takes place (its **setting**) to my partner.	(YES)	NO
I can tell **when** the story takes place (the **time of day or season**).	YES	(NO)
I can tell **who** the people (**characters**) are in the story.	(YES)	NO
I can tell **how** two **characters** are the same or different.	YES	(NO)
I can tell **why** the **events** in the story happened.	(YES)	NO

Source: Adapted from Gottlieb (2016, p. 148).

For older students, self-assessment or peer assessment checklists could be converted into rating scales with "I can" statements. Again, teachers should guide students in composing statements based on the language expectations for a unit of learning. Resource 5.3 is a form to get you started.

RESOURCE 5.3 Extending "I Can" Statements to a Rating Scale for Middle School

Academic Content Standards: _____

Language Proficiency/Development Standards: _____

Key Use of Academic Language: <u>Recount</u>   Topic: _____

Task or Project: _____

Based on the criteria for success for a task or a project, put an X in the box that shows how often you remember to include it. Don't forget to also put an X to show whether your assignment is one of listening and speaking, reading and writing, or a combination.

Name: _____   Date: _____

☑ WHEN LISTENING AND SPEAKING ☐ WHEN READING AND WRITING	SOME OF THE TIME	MOST OF THE TIME	ALL OF THE TIME
I can <u>describe the protagonist.</u>			X
I can <u>relate the series of events of the narrative.</u>		X	
I can <u>paraphrase the ending.</u>		X	
I can			
I can			

Another way that students can become more conscious of their language learning simultaneous with their content learning is by having them give input in the design of rubrics. Resource 5.4 is an example of an analytic scale for the key use *argue* that was part of a sixth-grade class project for a unit devoted to the virtues and dangers of shark fishing. As you see, different dimensions of arguments are captured in the four-point scale that has been constructed by students, with teacher guidance, and geared to self- and peer assessment. You are welcome to share this rubric with your students and adopt or adapt it for your own use.

When you write arguments, don't forget that you need to have claims and evidence. Read these criteria for success for persuasive pieces. Where do you see yourself? Put an X in the box that describes what you do for each aspect of written arguments (in this instance the cells are italicized).

Name: _____   Reviewer: _____

Project: _____   Date: _____

ASPECTS OF WRITTEN ARGUMENTS	ATTEMPTING	AIMING	APPROACHING	ATTAINING
Language of arguments	I use a few or I do not yet use signal words and sentence structures to show relationships.	I use some signal words and sentence structures to show relationships.	*I use signal words and sentence structures to show relationships between ideas.*	I use strong signal words and sentence structures to show relationships between ideas.
Organization of arguments	I try to organize my ideas, but I do not follow a pattern that matches the purpose.	I state the purpose, but I am not clear in some parts.	*I state the purpose, and my argument has a logical development.*	I present my claims and enhance the logical development of my argument.
Research evidence for the claims	I try to use evidence from text that is relevant to the topic.	*I use some evidence from text that is relevant to the topic to develop my argument or claims.*	I use evidence from text that is relevant to the topic to develop my argument and claims.	I use important evidence (e.g., facts instead of opinions) from texts to develop my argument and claims.
Connections between the claims and evidence	I do not yet make connections, or the connections do not match the argument or claims.	*I make connections between the argument and claims, but it is not clear.*	I make rather clear connections between the argument and claims.	I make clear connections that help readers understand the issues behind the argument and claims.

Source: Adapted from Lam, Low, and Tauiliili-Mahuk in Gottlieb (2016, p. 155).

Resource 5.5 is a skeletal analytic rubric for interpreting oral or written student samples of key uses of academic language for fifth-grade students and beyond. You are welcome to fill in descriptors or criteria in each cell, along with your students, based on the different projects or performances throughout the year.

What are your criteria for success in *discussing, arguing, recounting,* or *explaining*? You might want to decide in small groups and then reach an agreement as a whole class. After you complete this rubric and try it out, you might want to make some adjustments to reflect expectations in selected standards. Don't forget to create it in a can-do spirit.

Name: _____   Assessor: _____

Project: _____   Date: _____

ASPECTS OF (DISCUSSIONS, ARGUMENTS, RECOUNTS, EXPLANATIONS)	ATTEMPTING	AIMING	APPROACHING	ATTAINING
Language of (*Discussions*, Arguments, Recounts, Explanations)			We acknowledged multiple points of view.	
Organization of the (*Discussions*, Arguments, Recounts, Explanations)				We built on each other's ideas in a logical way.
Connections between (ideas, claims and evidence, causes and effects)		We made loose connections between our ideas.		

ENGAGING FAMILIES WITH KEY USES OF ACADEMIC LANGUAGE

Family and community engagement is increasingly seen as a powerful resource for making schools more equitable, culturally sustainable, and collaborative (Auerbach, 2009). Accordingly, families should play a substantial role in complementing a school's efforts in carrying out its mission and vision. As partners and primary stakeholders, families and school leaders should do the following:

- Take part in reciprocal learning on an ongoing basis

- Coplan, and, to the extent feasible, codeliver programs, events, or services

- Create and maintain open communication channels

- Have high expectations of each other and of students

- Respect the history, cultures, knowledge, languages, and wisdom of each other

- Acknowledge and value diversity and differences

- Evaluate the partnership annually, report the results, and, together, try to build a relationship (Kellogg Foundation, 2002)

Research indicates that family practices that are linked to learning positively impact student outcomes. Therefore, taking a learner-centered approach to family engagement should be integral to enhancing any school's instructional core (Henderson, Mapp, Johnson, & Davies, 2007). What better way to focus on enhancing family engagement than through key uses of academic language! For it is in the home environment that students accrue social and cultural experiences along with ways of thinking and communicating that are foundational to their learning in school.

Take the DARE

How might you foster greater engagement of families or greater interaction between students and family members around academic language use? How might you capitalize on the language, cultural, and experiential resources that students bring from home? Knowing that students' development, learning, and achievement are enhanced by family engagement and participation, how might you extend outreach to families by providing interesting learning opportunities inside and outside of school?

Families and community resources offer the opportunity to bring real-life connections to the learning taking place in the classroom. A visit to a local park or market, parent volunteers in the classroom, and community events are examples of community resources that can be tapped into for students to make connections between abstract concepts and everyday applications of what they learn. Planning around community resources requires not only knowing academic content standards and key uses of academic language but also knowing the community in which children live and learn. In the case of classrooms in which multilingual students learn, representing those languages and relating them to the curriculum provide opportunities for students to make stronger connections to new learning.

Important considerations when addressing key uses in community resources include the following:

- Identify and leverage the various ways in which students, families, and communities use one or more languages.

- Discuss with families the importance and role of academic language in learning and expressing academic content.

- Communicate language expectations to volunteers, guests, and other adults who visit or work regularly in the classroom.

- Plan with community leaders or staff when visiting community spaces to include a focus on language, in addition to content.

Take the DARE

Set out to learn more about your students by meeting and visiting their families and the communities in which they live. Here are some ideas:

1. Set times to meet with your students' families at the beginning of the year.

2. Schedule home visits with the families, or plan to meet them at a community center or library in the neighborhood.

3. Attend events in the community where your students live (e.g., festivals, fairs, and block parties).

4. Visit community spaces (e.g., stores and clinics) where your students and their families spend time.

5. Invite families into your classroom to share, help, or simply visit with the class.

6. Create curriculum that relates to the cultures, backgrounds, or communities of your students.

Resource 5.6 can help guide conversations between you and your students' families. It is presented here in English and translated into Spanish in the "Resource" section at the close of the chapter (Entrevista con la Familia). As the vast majority of students who speak languages other than English are Hispanic, we thought it might prove to be a helpful tool for you and your colleagues.

Resource 5.7 can be used as action research to record information about language use when you visit community spaces where your students spend time.

Given the mutual benefits of families interacting with teachers and school leaders, we have to redouble our efforts to strengthen the ties among these stakeholders. There are many different approaches to take; the following is a smattering of resources that you might find useful or that you can adjust to your setting. Some resources attempt to assure family members that school can indeed be a welcoming place while others encourage academic conversations between family members and their children.

School leaders and teachers can help empower family members by introducing them to key uses of academic language through a variety of venues and, subsequently, fortifying academic language development on an ongoing basis. Resource 5.8 suggests some ways in which families can participate in language-rich activities inside and outside of school.

Now that you have some ideas in mind, take a bit of time to think them through in Resource 5.9.

Family Engagement at Home. What better way to entice students to become absorbed in learning than through multimedia? The ready availability of technology allows students to preview, reinforce, and apply concepts, in addition to foster positive relationships between school and home. ¡Colorín Colorado! (www.colorincolorado.org)

RESOURCE 5.6 A Family Interview

Use these questions, add them to existing protocols, or modify them to learn more about the way your students use language outside of school. You may interview family members, ideally in person through home visits, or, if that is not possible, by phone.

Student's Name: _Meiying_

Date of interview: _____ Family member(s) interviewed: _Mother_

Place where interview took place: _at home_

1. How does your child use language at home? For what purposes? With whom?

   She talks a lot! She likes to tell me about school.

2. Who does your child spend a significant amount of time with? In which languages does he or she communicate?

   Grandma lives with us and only speaks Mandarin.

3. Does your child or do your family members speak languages other than English? Which languages? For what purposes?

4. How does your child communicate with others? With friends? Siblings? Family? Relatives? Others?

   She uses Mandarin with me and Mandarin and English with her little brother. Meiying often uses English with her friends.

5. What do you remember about the time when your child first learned how to speak? Read? Write?

6. What does your child enjoy talking about? With whom? When?

7. Does your child use social media? Which kinds? On which devices (i.e., cell phones, handheld devices, or computers)?

---

is a bilingual website with myriad videos and books for families and educators of multilingual students. One of its features, Learning Together at Home (see www .colorincolorado.org/article/recording-observations-capturing-and-sharing-images), offers tips to family members in English and in Spanish.

Ideas for Discussions With Young Children. Think about everyday activities where family members and children can readily participate and discuss the world around them. For example, during a nature walk with family members, including siblings and grandparents, children can explain natural phenomena and record their observations

Be an ethnographer, and use these ideas to take notes about language when you visit the community surrounding your school. Take time to listen, read, and identify how language(s) is used, for what purposes, and the messages that are transmitted.

Date: _____   Community: _____

1. Notice language around the community (e.g., signs, storefronts, billboards, and businesses). How is language used? What is being communicated?

2. Note language-rich spaces (e.g., libraries, religious spaces, and community centers). How is language used in these spaces?

3. As you navigate the community, notice language that is privileged or is most prominent and the messages that are related. Notice how language is used. What language resources are available? Which ones are utilized?

4. How are children and adults expected to use language in their community? For what purposes?

_____

with pictures, audios, or videos. As smartphones with built-in cameras and video capabilities are so accessible, family members can capture their children's voices and thoughts as they uncover and describe the world around them. Here are a couple of *why* and *how* questions that spark explanations between family members and children.

- "Why are these leaves green?"
- "Why do clouds change shape?"
- "Why do grasshoppers have six legs and pigeons have two?"
- "How does a bird build a nest?"
- "How do worms move?"
- "How do we get energy from the sun?"

Take the DARE

What are some other *why* or *how* questions that you might pose to family members and children to have them *explain* other natural phenomena, such as looking at the night sky and asking, "How do you think day turns to night?" or, "Why do stars shine?" If you are working with multilingual children and families, see if you could translate the questions ahead of time or add pictures to the questions to enhance their comprehension. Over the year, you may wish to collect additional *how* and *why* questions that families and children generate.

Here are some ideas that potentially promote family engagement around academic language use. Put a check in front of those suggestions that are most appealing or feasible for your families. Then, plan how you might implement the activities throughout the school year.

Date: _____   Class, Teacher, or School: _____

LIKE IT! ✓	LANGUAGE-CENTERED IDEAS FOR PROMOTING FAMILY ENGAGEMENT AT SCHOOL AND BEYOND
	Conduct a survey in the languages of families regarding their interests and expertise.
	Offer classes (face-to-face, hybrid, or online) that lead to paraprofessional certification or microcredentials.
✓	Design workshops or information sessions on current issues (such as technology, especially in 1:1 schools where each student has a personal device or computer).
	Plan school activities that are language centered (multicultural literacy nights, portfolio nights, and family-based multiliteracy clubs).
	Enlist family liaisons and advocates from the community who can serve as language and cultural brokers.
	Create opportunities for sharing materials, such as recipes, books, and manipulatives, to promote interaction between families (including siblings) and students.
	Generate a list of topics of interest and community speakers for classrooms and school events.
✓	Visit students' homes to become better acquainted with families and to orient them, along with the students, to grade-level language and content expectations.
	Have a dedicated space on the school's website, such as a discussion board, for families to communicate with each other in their home languages and English.
	Partner with local businesses, public libraries, or organizations to encourage families and students to participate in events or become involved through apprenticeships or internships.

In grade-level teams or professional learning committees (PLCs), contemplate the answers to these questions. Share your thoughts with school leadership, and create a plan to move forward in promoting greater family engagement.

Date: _____   Grade-Level Team or PLC: _____

Which of the ideas for family engagement that revolve around key uses of academic language in Resource 5.8 appeal to you? If none, what else might you suggest that has been effective in facilitating family engagement for your school? Our grade-level team is going to brainstorm and generate a list of at-home activities around each key use of academic language. Then, we plan to have it translated into the languages of the students. We are going to ask students and their families to select one activity per week. Students are going to keep a log of the weekly activities that they engage in with their families and reflect on their experiences.
Which of the ideas that pique your interest are most plausible in your setting? How might you consider implementing them within your classrooms with your students? How might you collaborate with other stakeholders?
How might you craft a timeline to research your ideas and get them approved? How might you get other teachers and school leaders to support your ideas?
What are some action steps you might take to make these ideas a reality?

Explanations can go hand in hand with retelling or *recounting* adventures, another key use of academic language. Upon returning home from walks, families and their children could look at the pictures or videos they have taken to recall what they saw and in what order. For example, an interchange could center on sequential language, such as, "First we looked up in the tree and saw a bird." "What did we do next?" "Then, we looked down at the ground and saw a squirrel." These academic conversations or discussions become extensions of the shared experience.

Ideas for Discussions With Older Children. Older children may require some motivation to be lured into conversation, but mealtime might be ideal for capturing their attention. Family members can elicit help from their children in measuring ingredients—using cups, tablespoons, and teaspoons—to follow a recipe. All the while, family members can ask some questions based on written recipes from the Internet or cookbooks or recipes from oral traditions. Eliciting comparative language based on the Monster Vegetable Soup recipe might include the following: "How many *more* split peas do I need than carrots?" "I need *equal amounts* of which vegetables; what does that mean?" "Why do you think that the recipe calls for the *least amount* of cayenne pepper than other ingredients?"

Take the DARE

The following ideas are intended to spark families to guide their children in conversations that involve key uses of academic language. In this case, we suggest how cooking recipes that evoke the language of mathematics and nutrition could readily involve DARE. As teachers, you may choose one and try it out, letting the class be chefs and sous chefs before suggesting this activity at home. Have students do the following:

- Match steps in the recipe to ingredients and measurement tools, retelling what to do step by step (*recount*).

- Double a recipe or halve a recipe to adjust to the number of family members; then, children can *recount* the process and *explain why* or *how* they did it.

- Create their own recipes with family members, write out the steps for the directions, and try them out! All the while, family members can ask questions that revolve around *claims* and *evidence*, chief components of arguments, such as, "Tell me *why* you chose to put in 2T of sugar instead of 6T," or, "Tell me *how* the taste changes when you put less sugar" (*argue* and *explain*).

- Decide among siblings or peers which is their favorite recipe, how they might make adjustments to it, and why (*discuss*).

Families and Students Interacting Through Discussions. Most every student enjoys videos, and what better way to learn language and content simultaneously than by watching the BrainPOP® characters, Moby and his friends, in content-rich movies. If students have computers or personal devices, there is a host of free material that corresponds to grade-level units of study. Younger students should be encouraged to watch selections with family members while older students might want to watch the movies with friends or siblings and *recount* what they see or probe deeper in animated *discussion* around a topic of interest.

MONSTER VEGETABLE SOUP

Image source: ©iStockphoto.com/macrovector

Ingredients

1 cup carrots

2 cups zucchini

1 cup quinoa

1.5 cups peas

0.5 whole onion

2 garlic cloves

8 cups vegetable broth

0.25 tsp cayenne pepper (to taste)

Directions

1. Wash and cut carrots and zucchini into large pieces.

2. Dice the onion and garlic cloves; sauté in a pan until soft.

3. Combine all ingredients (except for the quinoa), and bring to a boil.

4. Continue to simmer on medium-low heat for about 45 minutes.

5. Prepare the quinoa according to package directions, and set aside.

6. Place a scoop of quinoa in each soup bowl, and ladle soup over it.

7. Serve, and enjoy. The recipe makes about five servings. (And each serving counts as two daily vegetables!)

There is a host of possibilities for using the information from the movie experience. At the beginning of the year, teachers might ask guiding questions for each movie; as the year progresses, students might take over that responsibility and ask questions of each other. Perhaps a digital or paper bank of questions could be kept at school as a class resource. Figure 5.6 is an example of how you might want to set up an inventory around key uses of academic language.

The chart in Figure 5.6 is based on a BrainPOP Jr.® movie, *Classifying Animals* (see jr.brainpop.com/science/animals/classifyinganimals). The notion of classification, however, can apply to multiple topics in any content area, such as shapes (mathematics), land forms (social studies), instruments in an orchestra (music), or points of view (language arts), to name a few. As you see, this model highlights questions related to key uses of academic language within a science topic.

Source: BrainPOP Jr.®, https://jr.brainpop.com/science/animals/classifyinganimals

After students have watched a movie several times or have become acquainted with a topic through a variety of sources, it's time for them to think about asking pertinent questions. Teachers may wish to assist students in this task until students become adept at formulating questions on their own. Afterward, students may select questions to bring home. If possible, family members should view the movie or share the materials once more with their children; then, there can be an interchange of questions. Resource 5.10 sets up a format for generating questions for discussion.

MOVIE OR CONTENT TOPIC	KEY USE OF ACADEMIC LANGUAGE	SUGGESTED LANGUAGE-RELATED QUESTIONS FOR FAMILY MEMBERS TO ASK CHILDREN (OR "ASK ME" QUESTIONS)
Topic: "Classifying Animals"	**D**iscuss	*Which class* of animals—mammals, reptiles, or amphibians—is most interesting to you? What do you find most intriguing? *If* you were an animal, *which one* would you want to be? Give some reasons for your choice.
	Argue	Which animals do you think are stronger: vertebrates or invertebrates? Tell me your opinion and give some reasons. Which animal do you think is most intelligent, and why? Share your claim, and give some evidence.
	Recount	Can you tell me how tadpoles grow to become frogs? "*First,* they hatch from their eggs. *Then* . . ." Can you tell me how another animal grows from a baby to an adult?
	Explain	*How* are vertebrates different from invertebrates? *How* is it that amphibians can live both on land and in water? *Why* is a penguin a bird if it cannot fly?

RESOURCE 5.10 Formulating, Asking, and Answering Questions

You may use this tool as a whole-group activity with your class or perhaps with small groups of students. Begin with a review of what each key use means and perhaps a model question. Then, have students propose questions as you categorize them into key uses of academic language.

Date: _____   Class: _____

MOVIE OR CONTENT TOPIC	KEY USE OF ACADEMIC LANGUAGE	SUGGESTED LANGUAGE-RELATED QUESTIONS FOR FAMILY MEMBERS TO ASK CHILDREN (OR "ASK ME" QUESTIONS)
Topic: "Classifying Animals"	Discuss	
	Argue	Which is your favorite member of the cat family, and why?
	Recount	
	Explain	How are cats like dogs?

As shown in Resource 5.11, you may wish to have students share their conceptual understandings of a topic before, during, or after movie watching. You may even want to have the movie be a flipped assignment where students watch it ahead of time. In this instance, students would try to document, remember, and *recount* facts and concepts.

Begin with the BrainPOP Jr.® movie *Classifying Animals* and a set of questions that now have been repurposed from a language to content focus. The first row is complete with an example so that you can see the difference when language versus content is the target for learning. Write down some questions that students pose about the topic; ELLs and ELLs with disabilities should be encouraged to translate the questions for their families. Invite students and family members to convert this resource into a game format of asking and answering questions based on their movie watching. Notice that at the end of the chapter, a column has been deleted from this resource to make it easier for families. This resource may be used with endless content topics, and students could create an album, perhaps called *The Curious Classroom*, to store their inquiries throughout the year.

Name: _____

Grade: _____ Date: _____

MOVIE TOPIC	CONTENT FOCUS	CONTENT-RELATED QUESTIONS TO ASK
Classifying Animals	Life cycle of a frog	Name the steps for changing a tadpole into an adult frog.
		What are the characteristics of amphibians?

INVOLVING TEACHERS WITH KEY USES OF ACADEMIC LANGUAGE

Teacher leadership is expressed by supportive and caring administrators who allow for the sharing of power in schools. For if students are to learn deeply, the role of teachers must be transformed into one of teacher leaders or *leaders of learners* (DuFour & Marzano, 2011). Transformative teachers are able to collaborate with one another and engage in critical inquiry. As a result of teacher leadership, students come to analyze and understand the realities of their own lives and their communities so that they can take on social action (Cummins, 2000).

Teachers are mentors and language models for students where language is a medium of instruction and the primary tool for mental representation and cognitive processing. To help mediate thinking and learning, language is always surrounded by a context and a situation. The context and situation lend meaning to a message (Gibbons, 2015). Thus, in creating language-rich classrooms, teachers must be careful to create situations that involve students in listening and responding to language in contexts that are comprehensible, authentic, relevant, stimulating, and meaningful.

Effective communication in classrooms revolves around teachers' awareness of the cultural context in which information is presented and how that information is understood by students. Reflective teachers are able to articulate their thoughts to others, especially to students. Given that teachers and students are encountering increasingly higher academic language demands in standards, texts, and tests, teachers have to more effectively highlight academic language use and integrate it into their content classrooms.

Professional learning experiences are integral to teachers' personal growth. Teachers with agency are involved in emerging professional learning systems where they are constructive participants in their professional growth, acting as coplanners, designers, advisors, mentors, evaluators, and decision makers (Calvert, 2016). Opportunities for teachers to give public presentations of their learning or share their stances with other teachers, teacher leaders, or other stakeholders serve as a stimulus for reciprocal learning. Additionally, engaging in professional learning networks and other social media that address issues of academic language use and policy can be a stimulus for teacher discussion and collaboration.

Teachers increasingly need to be mindful of multimodalities and the breadth of multiliteracies, as students are able to demonstrate their understanding in meaningful ways that do not have to be text dependent. In thinking about all of the subgroups of students, in particular those who are most marginalized, such homeless students, students with disabilities, or students with interrupted formal education, here is a resource that speaks to those whose literacy may best be displayed through multimedia.

The Google Arts and Culture website (www.google.com/culturalinstitute) is a treasure trove of world wonders, offering images from over 1,000 museums and archives that are easily accessible. With wide applicability from early years through young adults (with the absence of text), students can dive into different adventures where they participate in deep academic conversations around key uses, where the context can vary from the arts and history from around the world to any of the content areas. Students should be welcome to interact in one or more languages while they explore the website and probe for answers to questions.

Figure 5.7 suggests some activities that are categorized around DARE and may be used in conjunction with the website images or similar ones that offer real-life photographs, maps, and authentic reproductions from around the world.

FIGURE 5.7 Suggested Small-Group Activities for Key Uses

KEY USE OF ACADEMIC LANGUAGE	SUGGESTIONS FOR SMALL-GROUP EXPLORATION OF ART AND ART MUSEUMS (BASED ON THE GOOGLE ARTS AND CULTURE WEBSITE)
Discuss	• Challenge ideas of peers on the quality and meaningfulness of diverse art pieces • Ask and answer questions about various virtual tours • Contrast the use of blue in periods of art (e.g., Monet vs. Picasso)
Argue	• Persuade others of your preferred art museum orally or in writing • Debate whether street art should be encouraged in your town or city • Take a position that expresses points of view regarding facial hair (see National Portrait Gallery)
Recount	• State information about art museums around the world • Relate what happened during a particular period of art • Report on biographies of artists of interest • Describe the main themes and details of paintings
Explain	• Compare different artists' approaches to the same subject matter • Trace how historical movements influenced artists • Evaluate spiritual icons in different countries and how they express the nations' cultural heritages

RESOURCE 5.12 Teacher Ideas for Student Choice

Explore the Google Arts and Culture website or another one, and choose a content area or an interdisciplinary theme where key uses of academic language can readily be interwoven. As you explore and choose some student-led activities, make sure you are also aware of the academic content standards for your grade.

Grade Level: _____   Standards: _____

Content Area: _____   Theme: _____

KEY USE OF ACADEMIC LANGUAGE	WEBSITE: WWW.GOOGLE.COM/CULTURALINSTITUTE SUGGESTIONS FOR SMALL-GROUP ACTIVITIES
Discuss	
Argue	
Recount	Which museum do you find most interesting, and why? What are the exhibits that most appeal to you?
Explain	How did the art of (Picasso) change over time?

In Resource 5.12, you may wish to apply some of the ideas in Figure 5.7 to your specific grade level, content area, or theme for a unit of learning.

We introduced graphic organizers in the section on students (see page 206). Resource 5.13 is a helpful tool for teachers and students that can serve as a preview to introduce a unit or a series of lessons. The Frayer Model (Frayer, Frederick, & Klausmeier, 1969) is a graphic organizer that lends itself to deeper understanding of a word or a concept. In this case, we present a key use of academic language coupled with a content-related task at the center and have converted each cell of the quadrant into a question.

RESOURCE 5.13 Teachers Collaborating With Other Teachers and Students: Using the Frayer Model to Promote Exploration of Key Uses of Academic Language

Use this collaborative tool for language planning around DARE between content and language teachers, teachers and instructional coaches, or teachers and students.

Grade Level: _____   Group of Teachers: _____

WHAT DOES IT MEAN TO YOU AND YOUR STUDENTS?	WHAT ARE ITS DISTINGUISHING FEATURES?
Some students may be familiar with volcanoes from around the world and can share personal experiences or those of relatives that they have heard about.	

Key Use of Academic Language + Content-Related Task

Explain how volcanoes erupt.

WHAT ARE SOME EXAMPLES?	WHAT ARE SOME NONEXAMPLES?

Once students are well versed with the format, they too might have some insightful conversations around how to apply the key use and content topic as a springboard for investigation. Figures 5.8 and 5.9 are two examples that show how you might represent the Next Generation Science Standards with this adapted Frayer model.

Figure 5.9 shows how you might set up a Grade 4 explanation. Notice that this time, instead of asking four questions that address different aspects of the key use of academic language, we present the language expectations that match up with the key use, in this case, *explain change*. You are welcome to adopt either option for modifying this graphic organizer, or create one of your own.

FIGURE 5.8 Questions Related to Scientific Argument

Grade 2 Argue, 2-PS1-4. "Construct an argument with evidence that some changes caused by heating or cooling can be reversed and some cannot."

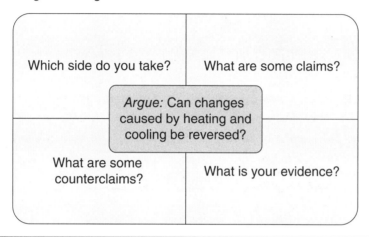

FIGURE 5.9 Statements Related to Scientific Explanation

4-ESS1-1. "Identify evidence from patterns in rock formations and fossils in rock layers to support an explanation for changes in a landscape over time."

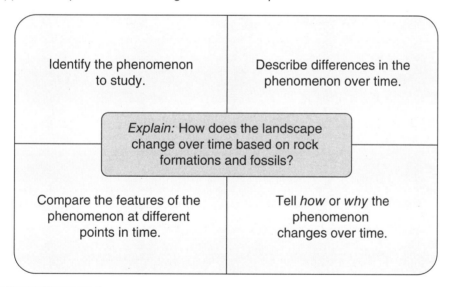

Take the DARE

Having firmly established one or more key uses of academic language for a unit of learning, how might you further collaborate with other stakeholders around interweaving representations of DARE into content instruction? What suggestions might you make for taking next steps? Think about setting up a protocol that you and your colleagues can reuse for each unit as part of the planning process, and set a schoolwide policy for incorporating this organizer into curriculum design.

INVOLVING SCHOOL LEADERS WITH KEY USES OF ACADEMIC LANGUAGE

Of all of the stakeholders, school leaders are often the exemplar and the force behind the cohesiveness in a school. Research points to the transformative nature of school leadership in being able to positively influence school culture (Horwitz et al., 2009; Marzano, McNulty, & Waters, 2005; Sebastian & Allensworth, 2012; among others). Vibrant school cultures, forged and cultivated by strong and supportive leadership, in turn, have clear connections and interdependence among students, families, and school personnel. Its leaders have a vision for the future of the school organization, can effectively communicate that vision to others, and can convey the importance of its attainment (Green, 2013).

Transformational leadership consists of charismatic heads of schools and districts who are respected role models, inspirational and motivating, intellectually stimulating, and encouraging of others to take risks and be creative. Additionally, in being transformative, these leaders take a genuine interest in everyone within their purview and help promote their personal career goals (Bass & Riggio, 2006). We suggest that transformational school leaders who are also distributive leaders in being able to *distribute* responsibility are best suited to instilling change throughout districts and schools, especially change that is language-centric.

Key uses of academic language serve as a platform for building and sustaining such change and a culture of excellence for all students and teachers. A school culture with successful academic and language outcomes provides equitable resources and offers embedded professional learning for teachers that promotes linguistic and cultural sustainability. Effective school leaders seek equitable academic expectations for all students and nurture a culture in which there is the following:

- A clear mission, with a commitment to the achievement of grade-level content and outcomes that is designed by, shared with, and transparent to all stakeholders

- A visual environment that is reflective of the student body and filled with examples of multiliteracies and multiple cultures in its hallways, exhibits, and classrooms

- Collaboration among faculty and consensus around a unified vision that has an educational philosophy that embraces students' academic language development as integral to their achievement

- Partnerships with families and the business community, as well as civic and community organizations, so that students have opportunities to participate and articulate their experiences inside and outside of school

- Ongoing professional learning of families, teachers, and school leaders to enrich a student-centered curriculum

- Recognition and appreciation of the worth and contribution of languages and cultures to the classroom, the school, and the community at large (adapted from MAEC Equity Audit)

Pedro Noguera (2003) points to the harsh reality that unless we change the culture of schools, there will be no further academic advancement; that is, whatever curriculum is introduced or organizational restructuring occurs, if the essential beliefs, norms, and relationships of a school are not transformed, nothing will change. Expanding on this idea, building a school culture must be addressed within a strategic plan and be a twin goal, alongside academic achievement (Fisher, Frey, & Pumpian, 2012). We further assert that envisioning key uses of academic language that are seen through a multicultural lens can solidify these goals and lead to schoolwide commitment and collaboration toward that end.

Take the DARE

Given the importance of both school culture and academic achievement, how might school leaders endorse key uses of academic language and support their implementation by students, family members, and teachers? How might key uses of academic language be contributors to reshaping school culture? How might a schoolwide professional learning community be a think tank for generating ideas around key uses from grade to grade? How might sustained and embedded professional learning be geared to both academic language development and achievement?

Every school has a unique personality and character that helps shape its culture. Schools that typically engage in practices associated with high performance have effective leadership, strong curriculum, professional learning opportunities, a positive school culture, and ongoing data used for school improvement (Weinstock, Yumoto, Abe, Meyers, & Wan, 2016). We have extended that base to include transparency in enacting its mission and vision, with an emphasis on academic language development.

Classrooms operate in schools, and schools are generally part of a larger educational system. The resources in this section tend to be more school based, as school leaders are educational leaders whose responsibility is to bring coherence and unity to teaching and learning across grades and departments. Resource 5.14 is a rating scale that might be useful as a self-assessment tool for principals or can be a needs assessment to inform principals and completed by teachers and school staff.

School leaders must be advocates on behalf of all the students. To do so, they must ground the mission of their schools in linguistic and cultural equity. Resource 5.15 offers a tool to measure the presence of this quality in your school and is designed for school personnel and principals.

Transformative leadership of schools may center on the principal but simultaneously be inclusive of teachers and other school personnel whose voices contribute to and support equity. The following list is a series of attributes of school leadership in which language is viewed as a pathway to academic advancement. Review it to see how you emulate a school leader; then, *take the DARE*.

Transformative educational leaders

- Stay committed to a vision of equity and excellence for all students
- Are passionate advocates of their cause and inspirational to others
- See potential in everyone and highlight positive outcomes
- Forge a pathway to success for individuals and the school as a whole
- Inspire, energize, and intellectually stimulate teachers, students, and families
- Make difficult decisions based on input from multiple stakeholders
- Adapt to a changing school demographic
- Assume an active role in the operation of the school
- Entertain ideas of others and acknowledge contributions of others
- Take risks when warranted or justifiable
- Exemplify a positive attitude that is reflected in the school culture
- Stimulate teamwork, collaboration, and sharing of information
- Display optimism and enthusiasm
- Set fair and realistic policies
- Promote democracy of education

Take the DARE

Time to be introspective. Circle the characteristics you see in yourself as a member of a school community, no matter what your position, and as an educational leader. If you could change one personal trait that would facilitate the transformational process, what would it be, and what would you do?

Next, put a star by those traits that you see in another instructional leader, such as a coach, a coordinator, a principal, or a director. Which of these characteristics epitomize transformational leadership to you? Give an example or two.

REFLECT

The future of education lies in the collective advocacy of stakeholders who are unified in working for the growth and advancement of each and every student. This chapter offers some insight into four stakeholder groups and how they might interact to promote academic language development inside and outside of school. In it are practical suggestions to take the DARE—*discuss*, *argue*, *recount*, and *explain*—either as individuals or in collaboration with others. Although each stakeholder is treated separately, in no way should that discourage their interaction. Together, students, families, teachers, and school leaders are,

RESOURCE 5.14 The Inclusion of Language Policy in the Mission and Vision of School

Based on your school's mission and vision, decide whether each of the following traits is present, absent, or under consideration in your school, and place an X in one of the three boxes. Then, answer the related questions so that you will be able to articulate how academic language use contributes to building an aligned and equitable system.

THE VISIBILITY OF OUR SCHOOL'S MISSION AND VISION

A. Our school has a clear mission statement that acknowledges academic language use as a central principle.

Yes X	Not Yet	Under Consideration

What is the school's mission? What can you do to ensure that it is one of equity?

The mission of Diego Andrés Primary School, with its multilingual, multicultural population and a tradition of quality education, is to ensure that each student achieves optimal linguistic, academic, and personal potential in a safe, nurturing, and engaging learning environment where opportunities abound in a culturally rich and cognitively challenging curriculum in more than one language that fosters partnerships with families, the community, and schools worldwide.

B. Our school's vision values and promotes multilingualism and biliteracy as a pathway to achievement for all students.

Yes X	Not Yet	Under Consideration

What is the school's vision? To what extent do you consider it inclusive of the students' languages and cultures?

Our vision is to create a K–5 school that is highly regarded for its multilingualism, multiculturalism, academic excellence, and community engagement.

C. Our stakeholders, starting with students and family members, have had input in and are familiar with the school's mission and vision.

Yes	Not Yet	Under Consideration

How have stakeholders contributed to the school's mission and vision, and how are they informed? If not, what might you suggest as community outreach?

D. Our school has a specific language policy crafted by the community, family members, staff, and leadership.

Yes X	Not Yet	Under Consideration

What is the school's language policy? If it doesn't have one, where might you begin?

At Diego Andrés Primary School, we value and are enlightened by the languages of our students, our families, and of the world; we offer ongoing opportunities for learning and enrichment for every student in multiple languages and seek community resources to enhance our worldview.

(Continued)

E. Our school has a plan of action based on its language policy, mission, and vision.

Yes	Not Yet	Under Consideration

What is the school's plan of action—how are its mission and vision carried out? If you are not aware of its plan, seek it out, and become familiar with it.

F. Our school faculty, along with school leaders, monitors the implementation of the plan of action.

Yes	Not Yet	Under Consideration

How does and how often does the school monitor its plan of action? If not, what might you do as a principal or member of a grade-level team to promote its implementation?

G. Our school exemplifies its mission and vision and carries out its policies in accordance with those statements.

Yes	Not Yet	Under Consideration
x		

What is an example of your school's coordinated effort to unify its mission, vision, and language policy? If it is not visible, what might you suggest to ensure its transparency?

H. The major components of our educational system—its curriculum, assessment, and instruction—are aligned to its mission, vision, and language policy.

Yes	Not Yet	Under Consideration
x		

In what ways does your school reflect a unified educational system? How inclusive is the system for all students—for example, gifted and talented, students with disabilities, and English language learners?

in some ways, bound by a common thread: suggesting and participating in social action that involves academic language use and permeates schools, homes, and communities.

Key uses of academic language can be leveraged to promote equity and excellence for your school, your students, and your families. Take the DARE to think outside the box, and encourage your colleagues, students, and families to be innovative, such as setting up entrepreneurships with community organizations or helping to invest in pop-up stores within existing businesses to promote school and community services. Together, with language power and collective will, we can propel our thinking and doing forward.

A positive school spirit is one where there is unequivocal respect for the students, their families, and their interaction with school personnel. Use the following criteria to rate the extent of your school's linguistic and cultural sustainability from 1 to 4: (1) traces, (2) intermittent signs, (3) noticeable presence, and (4) a celebratory spirit of students' languages, cultures, and experiences.

LINGUISTIC AND CULTURALLY SUSTAINABLE SCHOOLS	1	2	3	4
Evidence of the value of multilingualism and multiculturalism is present throughout the school, from signage to murals, displays, and conversations in the halls and in the office.				X
High expectations are set for all students, and students are encouraged to reach their personal goals in one or more languages.				X
Languages and cultures are the springboard for building classrooms, and schools are reflective of students' interests, dreams, and passions.			X	
The linguistic and cultural resources of the community, along with family members, are an extension of the school and are an acknowledged source of "funds of knowledge" and academic language use.				X
Varying perspectives and viewpoints represented in student and school identities are integrated into curriculum, instruction, and assessment.			X	
Every adult in the school is an advocate on behalf of students, and special attention is paid to the role of languages and cultures in thinking, learning, and being.			X	
The school exemplifies a can-do spirit that emphasizes each student's assets, gifts, and potential.				X
There is respect for and strength in diversity and differences, as shown by students and by personnel throughout the school.			X	

Source: Adapted from Gottlieb (2016, p. 12).

TAKE ACTION

Many stakeholder groups are vested in the education of our youth. How can we take socially, linguistically, and culturally sustainable steps to better our students' opportunities for advancement and success? The following questions are intended to provoke the stakeholder groups addressed in this chapter to take action to protect the language capital of our students, families, schools, and communities.

1. How can stakeholders—in particular, students, families, teachers, and school leaders—take a more active role in coordinating a campaign for academic language use in their homes, classrooms, schools, districts, or communities? What kinds of social action might be spurred by teachers, students, and families that would spark learning and communication of that learning in personal, significant, and sustainable ways?

2. How can families and students become more involved in planning and implementing key uses of academic language at home and in the community? What are some schoolwide projects and artifacts, such as advertisements, webpages, blogs, or newsletters, that you can initiate or support that would reinforce home–community connections through key uses of academic language?

3. How might professional learning time be devoted to collaboration around the key uses of academic language? How might schools support this effort by including paraprofessionals; physical education teachers; teachers of the arts; and specialists, such as instructional coaches, special education teachers, language teachers, and Title I teachers? How can school leaders facilitate meaningful interaction between and among stakeholders in regard to students' academic language development?

4. What is your personal plan to promote collaboration with these and other stakeholders around key uses of academic language? With which key use might you initiate conversation? Can you think of another teacher or school leader you might pair with to further students' academic language development? What would be each of your roles, and what steps might you take to coconstruct a plan?

Source: BrainPOP®, https://www.brainpop.com/english/writing/conceptmapping

Scan the QR code that leads to the BrainPOP® website. "Make a Map" is a featured tool whereby students create their own concept maps for the selected topic. Manipulating a variety of shapes, colors, arrows, keywords, images, and clips from the movie, students can connect ideas for each content topic. In addition, it is suggested that students reflect on their thought processes (that enhance their metacognitive awareness) and share their maps with a teacher, a peer, or a mentor for feedback.

What other content-related ideas lend themselves to semantic mapping? How might you create semantic maps with other key uses? Think about how semantic maps could be part of previewing to introduce a topic or key use or reviewing a unit to reinforce learning. Here is a table to help organize semantic mapmaking.

CONTENT AREA TOPIC	KEY USES OF ACADEMIC LANGUAGE	INDIVIDUAL STUDENTS, PAIRS, OR SMALL GROUPS

Chapter 5 Resources

RESOURCE 5.2 Students Responding to "I Can" Statements Related to English Language Arts Standards and Language Development Standards

Academic Content Standards: _____

_____

_____

Language Proficiency/Development Standards: _____

_____

_____

Name: _____ Date: _____

My Story, Fable, or Folktale: _____

_____

_____

_____

Key Use of Academic Language: _____

_____

_____

_____

With a partner, take turns answering each question. Your partner circles YES or NO based on what you say. Go over the list together. See if you agree with your partner for each answer.

WHAT CAN YOU DO? RETELLING STORIES, FOLKTALES, OR NARRATIVES		
I can tell **where** the story takes place (its **setting**) to my partner.	YES	NO
I can tell **when** the story takes place (the **time of day or season**).	YES	NO
I can tell **who** the people (**characters**) are in the story.	YES	NO
I can tell **how** two **characters** are the same or different.	YES	NO
I can tell **why** the **events** in the story happened.	YES	NO

Source: Adapted from Gottlieb (2016, p. 148).

Academic Content Standards: _____

Language Proficiency/Development Standards: _____

Key Use of Academic Language: _____ Topic: _____

Task or Project: _____

Based on the criteria for success for a task or a project, put an X in the box that shows how often you remember to include it. Don't forget to also put an X to show whether your assignment is one of listening and speaking, reading and writing, or a combination.

Name: _____ Date: _____

☐ WHEN LISTENING AND SPEAKING ☐ WHEN READING AND WRITING	SOME OF THE TIME	MOST OF THE TIME	ALL OF THE TIME
I can			
I can			
I can			
I can			

Chapter 5 Resources

When you write arguments, don't forget that you need to have claims and evidence. Read these criteria for success for persuasive pieces. Where do you see yourself? Put an X in the box that describes what you do for each aspect of written arguments.

Name: _____   Reviewer: _____

Project: _____   Date: _____

ASPECTS OF WRITTEN ARGUMENTS	ATTEMPTING	AIMING	APPROACHING	ATTAINING
Language of arguments	I use few or I do not yet use signal words and sentence structures to show relationships. ☐	I use some signal words and sentence structures to show relationships. ☐	I use signal words and sentence structures to show relationships between ideas. ☐	I use strong signal words and sentence structures to show relationships between ideas. ☐
Organization of arguments	I try to organize my ideas, but I do not follow a pattern that matches the purpose. ☐	I state the purpose, but I am not clear in some parts. ☐	I state the purpose, and my argument has a logical development. ☐	I present my claims and enhance the logical development of my argument. ☐
Research evidence for the claims	I try to use evidence from text that is relevant to the topic. ☐	I use some evidence from text that is relevant to the topic to develop my argument or claims. ☐	I use evidence from text that is relevant to the topic to develop my argument and claims. ☐	I use important evidence (e.g., facts instead of opinions) from texts to develop my argument and claims. ☐
Connections between the claims and evidence	I do not yet make connections or the connections do not match the argument or claims. ☐	I make connections between the argument and claims but it is not clear. ☐	I make rather clear connections between the argument and claims. ☐	I make clear connections that help readers understand the issues behind the argument and claims. ☐

Source: Adapted from Lam, Low, and Tauiliili-Mahuk in Gottlieb (2016, p. 155).

What are your criteria for success in *discussing, arguing, recounting,* or *explaining*? You might want to decide in small groups and then reach an agreement as a whole class. After you complete and try out this rubric, you might want to make some adjustments to reflect the expectations in selected standards. Don't forget to create it in a can-do spirit.

Name: _____ Assessor: _____

Project: _____ Date: _____

ASPECTS OF (DISCUSSIONS, ARGUMENTS, RECOUNTS, EXPLANATIONS)	ATTEMPTING	AIMING	APPROACHING	ATTAINING
Language of (Discussions, Arguments, Recounts, Explanations)				
Organization of the (Discussions, Arguments, Recounts, Explanations)				
Connections between (ideas, claims and evidence, causes and effects)				

Chapter 5 Resources

Use these questions, add them to existing protocols, or modify them to learn more about the way your students use language outside of school. You may interview family members, ideally in person through home visits, or, if that is not possible, by phone.

Student's Name: _____

Date of interview: _____   Family member(s) interviewed: _____

_____

Place where interview took place: _____

1. How does your child use language at home? For what purposes? With whom?

2. Who does your child spend significant amount of time with? In which languages does he or she communicate?

3. Does your child or do your family members speak languages other than English? Which languages? For what purposes?

4. How does your child communicate with others? With friends? Siblings? Family? Relatives? Others?

5. What do you remember about the time when your child first learned how to speak? Read? Write?

6. What does your child enjoy talking about? With whom? When?

7. Does your child use social media? Which kinds? On which devices (i.e., cell phones, handheld devices, or computers)?

Use these questions for Spanish-speaking families, add them to existing protocols, or modify them to learn more about the way your students use language outside of school. You may interview family members, ideally in person through home visits, or, if that is not possible, by phone.

Nombre del estudiante: _____

Fecha de la entrevista: _____ Miembro(s) de la familia entrevistada: _____

_____

Lugar donde se llevó a cabo la entrevista: _____

1. ¿Cómo usa el lenguaje su hijo(a) en casa? ¿Con qué propósitos? ¿Con quién?

2. ¿Con quién pasa tiempo significativo su hijo(a)? ¿En cuáles idiomas se comunican?

3. ¿Hablan su hijo(a) o los miembros de sus familias otros idiomas además del inglés? ¿qué idiomas? ¿con qué propósitos?

4. ¿Cómo se comunica su hijo(a) con otros? ¿con amigos? ¿con hermanos? ¿familiares? ¿otros?

5. ¿Qué recuerda de cuando su hijo(a) aprendió a hablar? ¿a leer? ¿a escribir?

6. ¿De qué le gusta hablar a su hijo(a)? ¿con quién? ¿cuándo?

7. ¿Su hijo usa medios de comunicación social? ¿qué tipos? ¿en qué dispositivos (i.e., teléfonos celulares, tabletas, computadoras)?

Chapter 5 Resources

Be an ethnographer, and use these ideas to take notes about language when you visit the community surrounding your school. Take time to listen, read, and identify how language(s) is used, for what purposes, and the messages that are transmitted.

Date: _____   Community: _____

1. Notice language around the community (e.g., signs, storefronts, billboards, and businesses). How is language used? What is being communicated?

2. Note language-rich spaces (e.g., libraries, religious spaces, and community centers). How is language used in these spaces?

3. As you navigate the community, notice language that is privileged or is most prominent and the messages that are related. Notice how language is used. What language resources are available? Which ones are utilized?

4. How are children and adults expected to use language in their community? For what purposes?

Here are some ideas that potentially promote family engagement around academic language use. Put a check in front of those suggestions that are most appealing or feasible for your families. Then, plan how you might implement the activities throughout the school year.

Date: _____   Class, Teacher, or School: _____

LIKE IT! ✓	LANGUAGE-CENTERED IDEAS FOR PROMOTING FAMILY ENGAGEMENT AT SCHOOL AND BEYOND
	Conduct a survey in the languages of families regarding their interests and expertise.
	Offer classes (face-to-face, hybrid, or online) that lead to paraprofessional certification or microcredentials.
	Design workshops or information sessions on current issues (such as technology, especially in 1:1 schools where each student has a personal device or computer).
	Plan school activities that are language centered (multicultural literacy nights, portfolio nights, and family-based multiliteracy clubs).
	Enlist family liaisons and advocates from the community who can serve as language and cultural brokers.
	Create opportunities for sharing materials, such as recipes, books, and manipulatives, to promote interaction between families (including siblings) and students.
	Generate a list of topics of interest and community speakers for classrooms and school events.
	Visit students' homes to become better acquainted with families and to orient them, along with the students, to grade-level language and content expectations.
	Have a dedicated space on the school's website, such as a discussion board, for families to communicate with each other in their home languages and English.
	Partner with local businesses, public libraries, or organizations to encourage families and students to participate in events or become involved through apprenticeships or internships.

Chapter 5 Resources

In grade-level teams or professional learning committees (PLCs), contemplate the answers to these questions. Share your thoughts with school leadership, and create a plan to move forward in promoting greater family engagement.

Date: _____   Grade-Level Team or PLC: _____

Which of the ideas for family engagement that revolve around key uses of academic language in Resource 5.8 appeal to you? If none, what else might you suggest that has been effective in facilitating family engagement for your school?
Which of the ideas that pique your interest are most plausible in your setting? How might you consider implementing them within your classrooms with your students? How might you collaborate with other stakeholders?
How might you craft a timeline to research your ideas and get them approved? How might you get other teachers and school leaders to support your ideas?
What are some action steps you might take to make these ideas a reality?

You may use this tool as a whole-group activity with your class or perhaps with small groups of students. Begin with a review of what each key use means and perhaps a model question. Then have students propose questions as you categorize them into key uses of academic language.

Date: _____   Class: _____

MOVIE OR CONTENT TOPIC	KEY USE OF ACADEMIC LANGUAGE	SUGGESTED LANGUAGE-RELATED QUESTIONS FOR FAMILY MEMBERS TO ASK CHILDREN (OR "ASK ME" QUESTIONS)
Topic:	Discuss	
	Argue	
	Recount	
	Explain	

Chapter 5 Resources

Begin with a BrainPOP Jr.® movie and questions that now have been repurposed from a language to content focus. The first row is complete with an example so that you can see the content target for learning. Invite students and family members to convert this resource into a game format of asking and answering questions based on their movie watching.

Name: _____

Grade:_____   Date:_____

MOVIE TOPIC	CONTENT FOCUS	CONTENT-RELATED QUESTIONS TO ASK
Classifying Animals	Life cycle of a frog	What are the changes from a tadpole to an adult frog?

Explore the Google Arts and Culture website or another one, and choose a content area or an inter-disciplinary theme where key uses of academic language can readily be interwoven. As you explore and choose some student-led activities, make sure you are also aware of the academic content standards for your grade.

Grade Level: _____   Standards: _____

Content Area: _____   Theme: _____

KEY USE OF ACADEMIC LANGUAGE	WEBSITE: WWW.GOOGLE.COM/CULTURALINSTITUTE SUGGESTIONS FOR SMALL-GROUP ACTIVITIES
Discuss	
Argue	
Recount	
Explain	

Chapter 5 Resources

RESOURCE 5.13 Teachers Collaborating With Other Teachers and Students: Using the Frayer Model to Promote Exploration of Key Uses of Academic Language

Use this collaborative tool for language planning around DARE between content and language teachers, teachers and instructional coaches, or teachers and students.

Grade Level: _____   Group of Teachers: _____

WHAT DOES IT MEAN TO YOU AND YOUR STUDENTS?	WHAT ARE ITS DISTINGUISHING FEATURES?

Key Use of Academic Language + Content-Related Task

WHAT ARE SOME EXAMPLES?	WHAT ARE SOME NONEXAMPLES?

Based on your school's mission and vision, decide whether each of the following traits is present, absent, or under consideration in your school, and place an X in one of the three boxes. Then, answer the related questions so that you will be able to articulate how academic language use contributes to building an aligned and equitable system.

THE VISIBILITY OF OUR SCHOOL'S MISSION AND VISION

A. Our school has a clear mission statement that acknowledges academic language use as a central principle.

Yes	Not Yet	Under Consideration

What is the school's mission? What can you do to ensure that it is one of equity?

B. Our school's vision values and promotes multilingualism and biliteracy as a pathway to achievement for all students.

Yes	Not Yet	Under Consideration

What is the school's vision? To what extent do you consider it inclusive of the students' languages and cultures?

C. Our stakeholders, starting with students and family members, have had input in and are familiar with the school's mission and vision.

Yes	Not Yet	Under Consideration

How have stakeholders contributed to the school's mission and vision, and how are they informed? If not, what might you suggest as community outreach?

D. Our school has a specific language policy crafted by the community, family members, staff, and leadership.

Yes	Not Yet	Under Consideration

What is the school's language policy? If it doesn't have one, where might you begin?

(Continued)

E. **Our school has a plan of action based on its language policy, mission, and vision.**

Yes	Not Yet	Under Consideration

What is the school's plan of action—how are its mission and vision carried out? If you are not aware of its plan, seek it out, and become familiar with it.

F. **Our school faculty, along with school leaders, monitors the implementation of the plan of action.**

Yes	Not Yet	Under Consideration

How does and how often does the school monitor its plan of action? If not, what might you do as a principal or member of a grade-level team to promote its implementation?

G. **Our school exemplifies its mission and vision and carries out its policies in accordance with those statements.**

Yes	Not Yet	Under Consideration

What is an example of your school's coordinated effort to unify its mission, vision, and language policy? If it is not visible, what might you suggest to ensure its transparency?

H. **The major components of our educational system—its curriculum, assessment, and instruction— are aligned to its mission, vision, and language policy.**

Yes	Not Yet	Under Consideration

In what ways does your school reflect a unified educational system? How inclusive is the system for all students—for example, gifted and talented, students with disabilities, and English language learners?

A positive school spirit is one where there is unequivocal respect for the students, their families, and their interaction with school personnel. Use the following criteria to rate the extent of your school's linguistic and cultural sustainability from 1 to 4: (1) traces, (2) intermittent signs, (3) noticeable presence, and (4) a celebratory spirit of students' languages, cultures, and experiences.

LINGUISTIC AND CULTURALLY SUSTAINABLE SCHOOLS	1	2	3	4
Evidence of the value of multilingualism and multiculturalism is present throughout the school, from signage to murals, displays, and conversations in the halls and in the office.				
High expectations are set for all students and students are encouraged to reach their personal goals in one or more languages.				
Languages and cultures are the springboard for building classrooms, and schools are reflective of students' interests, dreams, and passions.				
The linguistic and cultural resources of the community, along with family members, are an extension of the school and are an acknowledged source of "funds of knowledge" and academic language use.				
Varying perspectives and viewpoints represented in student and school identities are integrated into curriculum, instruction, and assessment.				
Every adult in the school is an advocate on behalf of students, and special attention is paid to the role of languages and cultures in thinking, learning, and being.				
The school exemplifies a can-do spirit that emphasizes each student's assets, gifts, and potential.				
There is respect for and strength in diversity and differences, as shown by students and by personnel throughout the school.				

Source: Adapted from Gottlieb (2016, p. 12).

Chapter 5 Resources

References and Further Reading

Schwartz, K. (2015). *When school leaders empower teachers, better ideas emerge*. Retrieved from https://ww2.kqed.org/mindshift/2015/03/03/when-school-leaders-empower-teachers-better-ideas-emerge

Students

Boykin, A. W., & Noguera, P. (2011). *Creating the opportunity to learn: Moving from research to practice to close the achievement gap*. Alexandria, VA: Association for Supervision and Curriculum Development.

Fletcher, A. (2014). *The guide to student voice* (2nd ed.). Olympia, WA: Soundout.

Gottlieb, M. (2016). *Assessing English language learners: Bridges to educational equity. Connecting academic language proficiency to student achievement*. Thousand Oaks, CA: Corwin.

Hammond, Z. L. (2015). *Culturally responsive teaching and the brain: Promoting authentic engagement and rigor among culturally and linguistically diverse students*. Thousand Oaks, CA: Corwin.

Quaglia, R. J., Corso, M. J., & Hellerstein, J. (2015). *Student voice: Turn up the volume activity book, K–8*. Thousand Oaks, CA: Corwin.

Families

Auerbach, S. (2009). Walking the walk: Portraits in leadership for family engagement in urban schools. *School Community Journal, 19*(1), 9–31.

Henderson, A., Mapp, K., Johnson, V., & Davies, D. (2007). *Beyond the bake sale: The essential guide to family–school partnerships*. New York: New York Press.

W. K. Kellogg Foundation. (2002). *Engagement in youth and education programming*. Battle Creek, MI: Author.

Zacarian, D., & Silverstone, M. (2015). *In it together: How partnerships with students, families and communities advance engagement and achievement in diverse classrooms*. Thousand Oaks, CA: Corwin.

Teachers

Berry, B. (2016). *Teacher leadership and deeper learning for all students*. Center for Teaching Quality. Retrieved from http://www.teachingquality.org/deeperlearning.

Berry, B., Byrd, A., & Wieder, A. (2013). *Teacherpreneurs: Innovative teachers who lead but don't leave*. San Francisco: Jossey Bass.

Calvert, L. (2016). *Moving from compliance to agency: What teachers need to make professional learning work*. Oxford, OH: Learning Forward and NCTAF.

Cummins, J. (2000). *Language, power and pedagogy: Bilingual children in the crossfire*. Clevedon, UK: Multilingual Matters.

DuFour, R., & Marzano, R. J. (2011). *Leaders of learning: How district, school, and classroom leaders improve student achievement*. Bloomington, IN: Solution Tree.

Frayer, D., Frederick, W. C., & Klausmeier, H. J. (1969). *A schema for testing the level of cognitive mastery*. Madison, WI: Wisconsin Center for Education Research.

Gibbons, P. (2015). *Scaffolding language, scaffolding learning: Teaching English language learners in the mainstream classroom* (2nd ed.). Portsmouth, NH: Heinemann.

School Leaders

Bass, B. M., & Riggio, R. E. (2006). *Transformative leadership* (2nd ed.). Mahwah, NY: Lawrence Erlbaum.

Fisher, D., Frey, N., & Pumpian, I. (2012). *How to create a culture of achievement in your school and classroom*. Alexandria, VA: Association for Supervision and Curriculum Development.

Green, H. L. (2013). *Transformational leadership in education: Strengths-based approach to change for administrators, teachers & guidance counselors* (2nd ed.). Dayton, TN: GlobalEd Advance Press.

Horwitz, A. R., Uro, G., Price-Baugh, R., Simon, C., Uzzell, R., Lewis, S., & Casserly, M. (2009). *Succeeding with English Language Learners: Lessons learned from urban school districts*. Washington, DC: Council of Great City Schools.

Marzano, R. J., McNulty, B. A., & Waters, T. (2005). *School leadership that works: From research to results.* Aurora, CO: Mid-continent Research for Education and Learning.

Noguera, P. A. (2003). *City schools and the American dream: Fulfilling the promise of public education.* New York: Teachers College.

Sebastian, J., & Allensworth, E. (2012). The influence of principal leadership on classroom instruction and student learning: A study of mediated pathways to learning. *Educational Administration Quarterly, 48*(4), 626–663.

Weinstock, P., Yumoto, F., Abe, Y., Meyers, C., & Wan, Y. (2016). *How to use the School Survey of Practices Associated with High Performance* (REL 2106-162). Washington, DC: U.S. Department of Education, Institute of Education Sciences, National Center for Education Evaluation and Regional Assistance, Regional Educational Laboratory Midwest. Retrieved from http://ies.ed.gov/ncee/edlabs

Glossary

21st century skills: A set of competencies that are critical for students to successfully participate in college, career, and community life, including collaboration, global interconnectedness, multiliteracies, problem solving, and creativity.

Academic achievement: Students' demonstration of concepts, skills, and knowledge associated with school-based curriculum.

Academic language: The language of school related to acquiring new and deeper understandings of content related to curriculum, communicating those understandings to others, and participating in the classroom environment.

Advocacy: Unequitable support for, recommendation, or promotion of particular causes, positions, or policies.

Agency: The bridge that connects knowledge with transformative action (Rodríguez, 2002).

Argue: To give an opinion with reasons, make a claim backed up evidence, or debate a topic with the intent of persuading others.

Assessment: The planning, collection, analysis, interpretation, and use of data from multiple sources for a specified purpose and use.

Assessment portfolios: Original student work samples, along with other data, that serve as evidence of what students can do in regard to their academic language use and achievement based on specified criteria.

Checklists: Dichotomous scales (ones with two choices) where traits, functions, skills, strategies, or behaviors are marked as present or absent.

Cognates: Words or expressions in one language that correspond, both in form and meaning, to words and expressions in another language.

Cognitive functions: Mental processes or activities used in negotiating meaning and making sense of the world, often interpreted in terms of Bloom's revised taxonomy or Webb's depth of knowledge.

College and career readiness standards: The concepts and skills descriptive of student content area expectations for each grade, K–12, as in English language arts, mathematics, and literacy in history or social studies, science, and technical subjects in Grades 6–12.

Common assessment: A multistep, standards-referenced process for designing, implementing, and interpreting data based on the same measures or tasks in multiple classrooms by educators who have mutually agreed upon their purpose and use.

Content objectives: A component of curricular design that identifies observable student behaviors or performances expected at the end of a lesson related to specific concepts or skills of a discipline.

Content targets: A component of a curricular framework or design that identifies the overall concepts, ideas, or knowledge of a topic expected of all students for a unit of study.

Criteria for success: Specific, measurable descriptors for learning, often tied to standards and related targets or objectives that are shared by teachers and students.

Cross-linguistic influences: Ways in which the different languages in the linguistic system of multilingual individuals interact and affect their language development or performance.

Curriculum: The systematic organization of meaningful and relevant learning experiences for students, generally into units of learning.

DARE: A conceptual tool that includes four key uses of academic language—*discuss*, *argue*, *recount*, and *explain*—and that teachers can use to organize language-centered content instruction and assessment.

Differentiated instruction: An approach based on the philosophy "all students can learn" that provides groups of students with different avenues to acquire content based on challenging teaching materials.

Disciplinary practices: Classroom habits of learning and routines in which students and teachers engage to construct knowledge, concepts, and skills in particular subject areas, many of which are expressed in college and career readiness standards.

Discourse: The ways in which oral and written language are connected, organized, and communicated.

Discuss: To interact with others or with content in order to negotiate meaning, cocreate new knowledge, or simply share information.

Distributed leadership: The sharing of decision-making power among stakeholders in a school (from the principal to teachers to students and family members).

Efficacy: The conviction that one can execute what is required to produce the expected result (Bandura, 1977).

English language learners (ELLs): Linguistically diverse students who are in the process of developing English as an additional language while being exposed to grade-level content.

Equity: In the educational context, being fair so that opportunity to learn is personalized for every student to succeed.

Explain: To make ideas, situations, or problems clear; to account for causes or effects; or to describe complex relationships by providing details or facts.

Genres: The socially constructed ways in which we communicate for academic purposes.

Instructional assessment: Varied measures used in classrooms, such as performance tasks, embedded in teaching that use various forms of documentation to interpret student performance; assessment occurring during instruction *for* learning.

Instructional scaffolds: Sensory (e.g., manipulatives), graphic (e.g., semantic webs), and interactive (e.g., working in pairs) resources embedded in instruction and assessment used to assist students in constructing meaning from language and content.

Key uses of academic language: The major categories that represent overarching purposes for communicating in academic settings—namely, DARE: *discuss, argue, recount,* and *explain.*

Language development standards: Expectations that are descriptive of the developmental progressions of language learning.

Language functions: Descriptions of how we use language for specific purposes within sociocultural contexts.

Language objectives: Specific, observable language outcomes designed for individual lessons.

Language targets: Overall literacy and/or oral language outcomes for a unit of study.

Levels of language proficiency: Designated stages of language development generally defined with criteria from performance definitions associated with language standards for language learners.

Linguistic and cultural sustainability: Maintaining support of students' learning by using resources from their homes and communities to relate to and build on what they already know.

Metacognitive awareness: Understanding and expressing the mental processes involved in learning.

Metacultural awareness: Understanding and expressing one's sociocultural identity that shapes the lens through which one learns and sees the world.

Metalinguistic awareness: Understanding and expressing the nuances and uses of language, including the process of reflecting on the features and forms of language.

Metalinguistic strategies: Ways to encourage thinking about and manipulating the features and forms of language to gain understanding of how language works.

Mission: The overall goal of a school, school system, or organization; a precise statement that exemplifies its purpose for being.

Multiliteracies: A 21st century approach to making meaning that relies on multimodal ways to make sense of the world in addition to print, such as digitally, visually, and through gestures.

Multimodalities: The use of visual, digital, and print materials to give students opportunities to creatively demonstrate learning.

Peer assessment: Descriptive feedback on student work based on standards-referenced criteria given by fellow students.

Performance assessment: Planning, collecting, and analyzing original student work, such as hands-on instructional tasks and curriculum-related projects, that is interpreted and reported based on specified, predetermined criteria.

Pragmatics: The social norms for using language.

Professional learning communities (PLCs): Groups of educators who meet, communicate, and collaborate to ensure that all students learn.

Reciprocal learning: An interactive approach whereby a pair of students or teachers (or other educational stakeholders) take turns coaching each other to tackle a thorny issue.

Recount: To inform, retell experiences or events, or display knowledge, information, or ideas.

Scaffolds: The use of instructional supports or strategies to allow students to work within their zones of proximal development to facilitate learning.

School culture: The beliefs, perceptions, relationships, attitudes, and policies of a school that shape how it operates.

Self-assessment: Students' application of performance criteria or descriptors to monitor and interpret their own work as a means of reflecting on their language and content learning.

Self-efficacy: Personal judgment of one's capability of organizing and carrying out a course of action required to attain a desired performance (Bandura, 1986).

Self-regulation: One's own monitoring of thoughts and actions that impact learning and behavior.

Sociocultural context: The close connection and codependence of language with culture and society that forms the basis for meaning making and interpretation within the learning space.

Student engagement: The attention, curiosity, interest, perseverance, or passion with which children approach learning.

Student voice: Listening to students, honoring what they say, and allowing them to make decisions on their own behalf.

Students with interrupted formal education: Generally older ELLs who are recent arrivals and have not have been afforded continuous opportunities for schooling.

Syntax: The rules that govern the ways words are arranged to form phrases, clauses, and sentences.

Think-alouds: A strategy whereby persons share their inner thoughts and reactions with others, usually verbalizing their opinions, feelings, or interpretation of text.

Universal Design for Learning: A framework intended to optimize teaching and learning for all students based on principles of how people learn that is applied to minimize the need to make instructional or assessment adaptations or to give specialized treatment.

Vision: A series of statements that embodies the best thinking about teaching and learning for a school, school system, or organization and includes its direction and steps toward meeting its goal.

Visual literacy: An expression of multimodality; the ability of students to express complex ideas and concepts using visualizations, such as drawings, photographs, images, film, and other media.

REFERENCES

Bandura, A. (1977). Self-efficacy: Toward a unifying theory of behavioral change. *Psychology Review*, *84*(2), 191–215.

Bandura, A. (1986). *Social foundations of thought and action: A social cognitive theory*. Englewood Cliffs, NJ: Prentice Hall.

Rodríguez, A. J. (2002). Using sociotransformative constructivism to teach for understanding in diverse classrooms: A beginning teacher's journey. *American Educational Research Journal*, *39*(4), 1017–1045.

Index

collaborative learning communities and, 200, 203, 220, 222, 223 (figure)

curriculum design and, 75, 77, 77 (figure), 83, 84, 97

disciplinary practices and, 65

discussion and, 20, 22 (figure), 27–29, 44–45

equitable classroom learning and, 150, 157, 160–161, 163, 183

explanation and, 20, 22 (figure), 38–40, 41, 53–54

guidelines for, 42

instructional scaffolds and, 168

integrated academic language uses and, 58, 60, 61, 62 (figure)

language functions and, 21, 22 (figure)

language learning, facilitation strategies for, 8–9

planning instruction and, 60, 61

reenvisioned teaching/learning and, xix, 40, 41, 42

recounting and, 20, 22 (figure), 32, 34–36, 34–35 (figures), 48–52

social studies content area and, 125–126, 126–127 (figures)

students receiving support services, language use of, 11–12

See also Academic language uses; Inquiry cycle; Integrated academic language uses

Dewey, J., 5, 59

Differentiated instruction, 169–170

curriculum design, unit-level academic language and, 77

See also Curriculum design; Instructional scaffolds; Interrupted formal education; Reciprocal learning; Universal Design for Learning framework

Disciplinary practices, 64–66, 65 (figure), 67, 87–88

Discourse, 21

Discussion, 20, 21, 22 (figure)

English language learners and, 27, 28

example tasks of, 27, 27 (figure)

monitoring language use and, 28, 44

oral language development/social interaction and, 27

promotion of, resources for, 29, 45

See also Academic language uses; DARE (discuss/argue/recount/explain) framework

Distributed leadership, 199, 226

Education stakeholders. See Collaborative learning communities

Efficacy, 176, 176 (figure)

See also Self-efficacy

ELPA 21 consortium, 64

English language learners (ELLs), 64

academic language, development of, xiii, 7, 10

arguments, development of, 31

assessment process and, 107, 108, 109, 114, 116, 122, 141

checklists for language use and, 38

communication context, interactive factors in, 25

content-related targeted language support and, xiii

cross-linguistic influence and, 175

differentiated instruction and, 77, 170

discussion/oral language development and, 27

English proficiency/English language development standards and, 64

language proficiency assessment and, 123, 124, 143

language targets and, xiii

language use, documentation of, 11–12

linguistic engagement and, 157, 158, 181

manipulatives/real-life objects, use of, 167, 189

metalinguistic awareness, facilitation of, 174–175, 195

multimodal approaches to learning and, 2–3, 32, 74, 75

See also Collaborative learning communities; Equity; Interrupted formal education; Language development standards; Linguistic/cultural sustainability; Metacultural awareness

Equity, 8–9, 10, 102, 149

agency and, 30–31, 74, 103–104, 151, 152–156, 153 (figure), 159, 178–180

agency needs assessment/planning checklists and, 153, 154–155, 178–179

agentic teaching practices and, 152–153, 153 (figure)

argument/informational text and, 165, 166, 188

backward design and, 150

cognates charting and, 175, 195

communication options, teacher facilitation of, 159

communities of practice, collaborative learning and, 154–155, 156, 180

cross-linguistic influence and, 175

DARE framework and, 150, 157, 160–161, 163, 183

differentiated instruction and, 169–170

digital etiquette recounting/discussion and, 163, 165, 187

education leaders, agency of, 152

English language learners and, 157, 167, 174–175, 189, 195

implementing academic language in classrooms and, 149–150, 150 (figure), 151

instructional goals/standards, materials selection and, 163, 164, 186

instructional materials, linguistic/cultural responsiveness and, 168, 169, 190

instructional materials, selection of, 159–168, 169, 183–190

interest-based instruction and, 151

language, intentional focus on, xiii, 7

linguistic engagement and, 157, 158, 181

manipulatives/real-life objects, use of, 167, 189

metalinguistic awareness, facilitation of, 174–175, 195

metalinguistic teaching strategies and, 151, 165, 170–175

minority backgrounds, experiences/perspectives of, 8

pragmatics of language, 174, 194
presence of argument language evaluation, 31, 33, 47
recount blog, 115, 139
recounts from original sources, 35, 48
scaffolded instruction/learning, 171–172, 191–192
school leadership self-assessment, 229–230, 247–248
school-year language use monitoring/recording, 41, 55
scientific investigation assessment checklists, 124–125, 143–144
social studies explanation chart, 129, 145
student choice in content area, 223, 245
student engagement opportunities, 158, 160, 181, 182
student language use evaluation, 31, 32, 46
student self-assessment checklists, 112–113, 136–137
think-aloud strategy application, 173, 193
21st century schools and teachers/leader needs assessment, 72–73, 91–92
21st century skills/standards in curriculum planning, 71, 90
21st century teaching needs assessment, 69, 70, 89
Rodriguez, A. J., 149, 152
Ross, G., 168
Rugen, L., 104

Scaffolds. *See* Equity; Instructional scaffolds
School culture, 226–227, 231, 249
See also Mission; Vision
School leadership. *See* Collaborative learning communities
Science content. *See* Assessment; Next Generation Science Standards (NGSS)
Secada, W. G., 118, 141
Self-assessment, 29, 104, 105 (figure), 111, 112–113, 122, 134, 136–137, 209
Self-efficacy, 204, 204 (figure)
Self-regulation, 168, 176, 203
Semantic mapping, 205–207, 206 (figure), 233
Small-group activities, 222–224, 223 (figure)
Social studies. *See* Assessment; *College, Career, and Civic Life (C3) Framework for Social Studies State Standards*
Sociocultural context, 27
academic language, development of, 7
dialogue and, 5
global interconnectedness and, 9–10
scientific explanations and, 122
social studies content, assumptions in, 125
student academic success and, 5
See also Collaborative learning communities; English language learners (ELLs);

Equity; Linguistic/cultural sustainability; Metacultural awareness
Sortify® classification game, 29
Stakeholders in education. *See* Collaborative learning communities
Standards. *See College, Career, and Civic Life (C3) Framework for Social Studies State Standards*; Common Core State Standards (CCSS); Curriculum design; Integrated academic language uses; Next Generation Science Standards (NGSS)
Student engagement, xiii, 74
academic language, role of, 19
affective engagement and, 157, 158, 181
behavioral engagement and, 157, 158, 181
classroom management/instructional strategies and, 155, 157–159, 181
cognitive engagement and, 157, 158, 181
curriculum design and, 74, 75, 77, 77 (figure)
linguistic engagement and, 157, 158, 181
multifaceted nature of, 157
new knowledge, generation of, 4
self-assessments and, 29
sociocultural context and, 5–6
student-centered assessment and, 103–104, 105 (figure)
types of, 157
See also Academic achievement; Assessment; Assessment portfolios; Collaborative learning communities; College/career readiness (CCR) standards; Criteria for success; English language learners (ELLs); Equity; Universal Design for Learning framework
Student voice, 11 (figure), 149, 151
Students with interrupted formal education (SIFE), 10, 170
Success. *See* Academic achievement; Assessment; Collaborative learning communities; College/career readiness (CCR) standards; Criteria for success; Differentiated instruction; Interrupted formal education; Student engagement

Teaching practices. *See* Assessment; Collaborative learning communities; Curriculum design; Differentiated instruction; Inquiry cycle; Instruction; Resources
Think-aloud strategy, 171–174, 193
Tuttle, C. L., 117
21st century skills, xv, 66
academic content standards and, 67, 68–69 (figure)
academic language, key uses of, 66
character qualities and, 10
collaborative instructional practice and, 67
competencies and, 9–10
curriculum design and, 69, 71, 90
foundational literacies and, 9–10, 66
game/problem-based learning and, 69

global interconnectedness and, 9–10
See also Integrated academic language uses;
Multiliteracies; Multimodalities

Universal Design for Learning framework,
162–163, 184

van Lier, L., 17
Virginia Standards of Learning, 68
Vision, 176, 176 (figure), 227, 229–230, 247–248
Visual literacy, 9, 74
Visualization, 2–3

Voice. *See* Student voice
Vygotsky, L. S., 5, 59, 168

Webb, N. L., 81
Wisconsin Center for Education Research
(WIDA), 20, 26, 31, 63, 64, 76
Wood, D., 168
Woodfin, L., 104
World Economic Forum, 9–10

Zone of proximal development, 168
Zwiers, J., 126

CORWIN

A SAGE Publishing Company

CORWIN HAS ONE MISSION: to enhance education through intentional professional learning.

We build long-term relationships with our authors, educators, clients, and associations who partner with us to develop and continuously improve the best evidence-based practices that establish and support lifelong learning.